: **LOST BODIES**

LOST BODIES

Inhabiting the Borders of Life and Death

Laura E. Tanner

Cornell University Press
Ithaca and London

Copyright © 2006 by Cornell University

All rights reserved. Except for brief quotations in a review, this book, or parts thereof, must not be reproduced in any form without permission in writing from the publisher. For information, address Cornell University Press, Sage House, 512 East State Street, Ithaca, New York 14850.

First published 2006 by Cornell University Press
First printing, Cornell Paperbacks, 2006

Printed in the United States of America

Library of Congress Cataloging-in-Publication Data

Tanner, Laura E., 1961–
   Lost bodies : inhabiting the borders of life and death / Laura E. Tanner.
     p. cm.
   Includes bibliographical references and index.
   ISBN-13: 978-0-8014-4422-7 (cloth : alk. paper)
   ISBN-10: 0-8014-4422-5 (cloth : alk. paper)
   ISBN-13: 978-0-8014-7313-5 (pbk. : alk. paper)
   ISBN-10: 0-8014-7313-6 (pbk. : alk. paper)
   1. American literature—20th century—History and criticism. 2. Art, American—20th century. 3. Death in literature. 4. Death in art. 5. Diseases in literature. 6. Diseases in art. 7. Bereavement in literature. 8. Bereavement in art. 9. Body, Human, in literature. 10. Human beings in art. I. Title.
   PS228.D43T36 2006
   809'.9335480904—dc22

                                                                       2005035781

Cornell University Press strives to use environmentally responsible suppliers and materials to the fullest extent possible in the publishing of its books. Such materials include vegetable-based, low-VOC inks and acid-free papers that are recycled, totally chlorine-free, or partly composed of nonwood fibers. For further information, visit our website at www.cornellpress.cornell.edu.

Cloth printing   10 9 8 7 6 5 4 3 2 1
Paperback printing   10 9 8 7 6 5 4 3 2 1

*For my sister, Beth,
my brothers, Christopher, Taren, Lance, and Todd,
and—always—for my mother, Nancy Clark Tanner*

Contents

List of Illustrations	ix
Acknowledgments	xi
Introduction	1

Part One: The Dying Body

1. Terminal Illness and the Gaze	19
Shifting the Gaze	20
The Death-Watch in Sharon Olds's The Father	25
Sympathetic Seeing	38
2. Haunted Images	40
Seeing AIDS	40
Billy Howard's Epitaphs for the Living	44
Nicholas Nixon's People with AIDS	53
3. The Body in the Waiting Room	64
"Empty" Spaces	64
Johnnies and Handbags	67
Literary Representations of the Medical Waiting Room	68

Part Two: The Body of Grief

4. The Contours of Grief and the Limits of the Image	83
Hands	83
Unraveling the Chiasm	87

Images of Grief in Marilynne Robinson's Housekeeping	*92*
Camera Lucida *and the Body of the Photograph*	*107*
Disembodied Spaces in the Images of Shellburne Thurber	*115*
Remembering the Body	*131*
5. TEACHING THE BODY TO TALK	*133*
The Language of Grief	*133*
Words and Flesh in Carolyn Parkhurst's The Dogs of Babel	*135*
The Ghost of the Body in Don DeLillo's The Body Artist	*152*
6. OBJECTS OF GRIEF	*176*
The Object Embrace	*176*
A Sensory Semiotics	*182*
Bodies and Objects in Mark Doty's "The Wings"	*185*
The AIDS Memorial Quilt	*201*
POSTSCRIPT: LAYING THE BODY TO REST	*211*
Bringing the Dead to Life in Popular Culture	*212*
September 11 and Beyond	*222*
NOTES	*237*
BIBLIOGRAPHY	*249*
INDEX	*259*

Illustrations

Figure 1. Billy Howard, Untitled	*47*
Figure 2. Billy Howard, Untitled	*49*
Figure 3. Billy Howard, Untitled	*51*
Figure 4. Billy Howard, Untitled	*52*
Figure 5. Nicholas Nixon, "Tom Moran, Boston, January 1988"	*56*
Figure 6. Nicholas Nixon, "Joey Brandon, Boston, April 1988"	*57*
Figure 7. Nicholas Nixon, "Tom Moran, East Braintree, Massachusetts, September 1987"	*58*
Figure 8. Nicholas Nixon, "Donald Perham, Worcester, Massachusetts, July 1988"	*59*
Figure 9. Nicholas Nixon, "George Gannett, Barrington, Rhode Island, February 1989"	*61*
Figure 10. Shellburne Thurber, "Chesson House: Corner with broken windows, view #1"	*120*
Figure 11. Shellburne Thurber, "Gholson Homeplace: Upstairs hallway with window and torn curtain"	*122*
Figure 12. Shellburne Thurber, "Chesson House: Abandoned bed with dark window"	*128*

Acknowledgments

Through this book, I hope to speak not just for mysef but for those who shared their stories with me at conferences and in conversations about dying and loss, as well as for some of those whose voices have not been heard. For those—in my family and elsewhere—who have inhabited the experiences I struggle to articulate and theorize in these pages, I offer these words not as compensation for absence but in recognition of the many complexities of embodied presence in the face of death.

The photographs of Billy Howard, Nicholas Nixon, and Shellburne Thurber are reproduced here with their permission. I am deeply grateful for the opportunity to work with their powerful images and to explore the questions about representation that they raise. I am also grateful for permission to reprint from the following sources.

Excerpts from *The Body Artist* reprinted with the permission of Scribner, an imprint of Simon & Schuster Adult Publishing Group, from *The Body Artist* by Don DeLillo. Copyright © 2001 by Don DeLillo.

Excerpt from "The Ship Pounding," from *Without: Poems by Donald Hall.* Copyright © 1998 by Donald Hall. Reprinted by permission of Houghton Mifflin Company. All rights reserved.

Excerpt from "Kill the Day," from *The Painted Bed: Poems by Donald Hall.* Copyright © 2002 by Donald Hall. Reprinted by permission of Houghton Mifflin Company. All rights reserved.

From *The Father* by Sharon Olds, copyright © 1992 by Sharon Olds. Used by permission of Alfred A. Knopf, a division of Random House, Inc.

From *The Dogs of Babel* by Carolyn Parkhurst. Copyright © 2003 by Carolyn Parkhurst. By permission of Little, Brown and Co., Inc.

Excerpt from *Housekeeping* by Marilynne Robinson. Copyright © 1981 by Marilynne Robinson. Reprinted by permission of Farrar, Straus and Giroux, LLC.

A version of chapter 1 appeared previously as "Death-Watch: Terminal Illness and the Gaze in Sharon Olds's *The Father*," in *Mosaic: A Journal for the Interdisciplinary Study of Literature* 29.1 (Spring 1996): 103–122. A version of chapter 2 was published previously as "Haunted Images: Photographic Representations of People with AIDS," in *Genre: Forms of Discourse and Culture* 29.1–2 (Spring/Summer 1997): 135–159 and is reprinted with the permission of the University of Oklahoma Press. Portions of chapter 3 appeared as "Bodies in Waiting: Representations of Medical Waiting Rooms in Contemporary American Fiction," in *American Literary History* 14.1 (Spring 2002): 115–130.

Thank you to Boston College for its generous support of this project, including the award of an undergraduate research assistant and a recent sabbatical which allowed me to finish the first draft of the book. Joseph Halli, my research assistant, not only tracked down articles and suggested possible texts but engaged with my project intellectually as well; his efforts made this finished product possible.

I am grateful to Cornell University Press for supporting this project, with special thanks to Bernie Kendler for enthusiastically shepherding the manuscript through the review process and to John Ackerman for so generously overseeing its path to publication. I am thankful, as well, for the perceptive analysis and thoughtful suggestions of the readers whose careful responses to my argument have shaped the final version of the text.

Many of my friends and colleagues have generously shared their questions and insights during the writing process. My special thanks go out to Elizabeth Graver and Alex Chasin, who shared ideas over coffee and read sections of this manuscript with great care and creativity. Thank you to Robin Lydenberg, who first introduced me to Merleau-Ponty's idea of the chiasm in a conversation that still reverberates in my work. I am grateful for Chris Wilson's continuing personal and professional support, not limited to but including his characteristic close attention to my argument about the waiting room. Olu Oguibe's perceptive response to my work on grief was vital in helping me to think about cultural differences in perceptions of loss; I thank him for his ideas and for his amazing artistic representations. Kevin Ohi's willingness to reach across theoretical borders and entertain the possibilities of my arguments has helped me to articulate my assumptions and sharpen my thoughts; I count myself very lucky to have him as a colleague. For challenging me intellectually and catching me when I fall, I owe a great debt to Anne Fleche, who continues to remind me of the joys of a life that includes the luxury of hard thinking and the pleasure of intellectual friendship. I was fortunate to share graduate school with a group of friends who, fifteen years later, continue to show me the many forms academic community can assume; thank you to each of them for sustaining me not just in our visits each summer but all year long. Finally, without reading a word of this manuscript, Mary Crane made it possible as she pushed, pulled, and prodded me toward its completion; her daily presence affirms the fact that it is possible to write books and raise boys at the same time.

Watching the lives of those boys unfold along with the chapters of this book has been the greatest pleasure of my life. To my sons, Gray Tanner and Cole Krasner, I owe my sense of perspective, my faith in the future, my life in the moment. My husband, James Krasner, is the other voice in this dialogue. To him and to the quiet passion of his embodied presence, I owe not just the thoughts I bring to this book but the world that welcomes me back from its pages.

LOST BODIES

Introduction

Although I wasn't aware of it at the time, this book began more than ten years ago, on the unseasonably warm October day that my brother was married. My father was very ill at the time of the wedding—he would die at home only two weeks later—but he attended both the wedding and the reception, propelled at various points by one or the other of his six children in a wheeled office chair from home. Although he was tired and quite weak, he was clearly himself: gentle, funny, surprisingly relaxed for someone probably in pain. In contrast, the dozens of friends and relatives who visited his table in the crowded reception hall were anything but comfortable. Many of them, having avoided the house in recent weeks, paraded by to pay their respects; forcing a smile, they mumbled apologies and escaped quickly, not wanting, they said, to tire him. His embodied presence unsettled the large room. Sitting by his side, I would catch his friends and relatives—at the next table or on the dance floor or across the room—trying to slide out of a gaze that had snagged on his familiar, unfamiliar form: the harsh angles of bony shoulders under his good jacket, the dark circles around his eyes, the gaunt hollows under his cheekbones. The unease in that crowded room circled around a body rendered so abject by the process of dying that it transformed the familiar subject into an unfamiliar object. My father's body registered his impending death; in turning away from it, they would turn away not from him but from the anticipation of his loss and their own implied mortality.

As I was neither the subject nor the object of that uncomfortable gaze, my own position in the room was less clearly marked. My chair pulled close to my father's, I lacked both the distance required to register the shock of his changed appearance and the intimacy necessary to experience his dying body as my own. In the weeks before the wedding and in those to follow, caring for my father at home immersed all of us in the sudden breakdown of his body: bleeding tumors, swollen ankles, leaking colostomy bags. A lifelong athlete, physically strong, a man who worked with his hands, my father in his last days found himself straining to perform even the simplest acts as he struggled, physically and psychically, to negotiate what he described simply as "the pressure of dying." In trying not to do for him but with him, I bent, stooped, leaned, listened, touched, asked, all the while feeling the boundary between death and life give way. When I tried, after my father's death, to unbend my body from the posture of care giving, to straighten up and reaffirm a wholeness lost through intimacy with the physical and psychical experience of dying, I found myself locked in a grief that formed itself around the lost contours of his missing body.[1] Even as the countless sympathy cards that I received propelled me through the experience of corporeal loss toward the consolations of religion, psychology, and memory, I returned again and again to the fact of embodied loss and its representational absence in cultural discourses of mourning. If the dying body makes us flinch and look away, struggling not to see what we have seen, the lost body disappears from cultural view, buried along with the sensory traces of its corporeal presence.

My book explores representations of life-threatening illness and grief to chart the way that the experience of embodiment complicates the construction of subjectivity and the formation of cultural norms. My interest lies not only in focusing on bodies lost to death or imperiled by the threat of loss but in exploring the way in which the body of illness or grief is absent from critical discourses and lost to cultural view. Even as the body's simultaneous intimacy and alterity pressure the dying subject to renegotiate the borders of the self, the threatened dissolution of boundaries between the living and the dying pushes healthy subjects to reconstitute themselves as disembodied. Artificially constructed boundaries that isolate the vulnerable body from the embodied subject also shape the experience of grief by excluding the immediate effects of corporeal absence from culturally sanctioned structures for articulating loss. In this book I chart the impact of social and representational forces that pull us out of our bodies to insist—even in the face of mortality—upon the subject's status as healthy, autonomous, and whole. In an attempt to resist dynamics of cultural displacement that reduce embodied experience to a footnote, I figure the subject in terms of the body. Following in the wake of Maurice Merleau-Ponty's philosophical revisions of the mind/body problem, I explore the tensions of embodied experience by attempting to recast the categories of mind and body as abstract manifestations of incarnate existence. In so doing, I seek not to reverse classical hierarchies of body and mind (a maneuver that would preserve their dichotomous placement in culture) but to denaturalize existing cultural assumptions about the self and explore the possibilities that result from turning dominant models of identity inside out. Contemporary American culture's insistence on isolating and disavowing the bodily dimensions of illness and grief, I argue, functions not to mitigate but to reinforce the embodied subject's experience of fragmentation in the face of a shared vulnerability to loss.

Representations of the body offer a means of interrogating the cultural assumptions and representational conventions through which illness, death, and grief are constructed and understood in contemporary America. In the attempt to situate the cultural and representational practices I explore within a shared historical framework, I have chosen a variety of texts from American literature and culture, most of which were written or produced in the last quarter century. Representations of the body in these texts reflect, reproduce, or trouble assumptions about embodiment and mortality in contemporary American culture. While I do not attempt to trace these assumptions to their larger cultural origins, the work of many recent cultural critics suggests how circulating ideas of the perfectible, plastic, nonmortal body speak to broader economic, historical, and institutional dynamics in American culture. In late capitalist consumer culture, the body, in Susan Bordo's words, "more and more has come to be understood not as a biological given which we have to learn to accept, but as a plastic potentiality to be pressed in the service of image—to be arranged, re-arranged, constructed and deconstructed as we choose" (Bordo 1997, 452). The problems of illness, aging, and death continually constitute a challenge to capitalist assertions of individual consumer agency, assertions which function by implicitly obscuring the inevitability of human deterioration to construct the body, in Mike Featherstone's terms, only as "a vehicle of pleasure and self-expression" (Featherstone 2001, 80). In a postmodern image culture, the dying body's threat to the illusion of agency perpetuated by a consumer society often rebounds on the medicalized subject. Even as the patient is objectified by the medical gaze,[2] he or she is simultaneously held accountable for a vulnerability to death which the culture would disavow. In "Medicine as an Institution of Social Control," Irving Zola describes the contradictory assumptions behind what he terms "the myth of accountability": "The issue of 'personal responsibility' seems to be reemerging within medicine itself. Regardless of the truth and insights of the concepts of stress and the perspective of psychosomatics . . .

they bring man, not bacteria, to the center of the stage and lead thereby to a reexamination of the individual's role in his own demise, disability, and even recovery" (Zola 2001, 203).

In an age where "the wondrous new machine of global exchange imprints its current expectations of total commodification and relentless performativity upon the substance and forms of the body" (Luke 2003, 99), contemporary culture's promised erasure of the body's abject or animal qualities renders the healthy subject's disavowal of the dying body especially urgent. In *Hiding from Humanity: Disgust, Shame, and the Law,* Martha Nussbaum suggests that those who bear the marks of illness and disability bear the contradictions of a culture that must police itself in order to avoid confrontation with the realities of embodiment. Arguing that the disgust triggered by specific bodies reflects the irrational aspiration to transcend the fact of having an animal body, Nussbaum traces not only the psychological dynamic in which "the discomfort people feel over the fact of having an animal body is projected outwards onto vulnerable people and groups" but the existence of specific social and legal practices that result from such a dynamic (Nussbaum 2004, 74). If, as Nussbaum contends, the "myth of the citizen as a competent independent adult" (311) demands policing the presence of those who expose the fiction of invulnerability, I would argue that definitions of mourning which disavow the embodied dynamics of grief reflect a cultural discomfort with the rupture of autonomy manifest in both the fact of embodiment and the recognition of intercorporeality. Cultural narratives highlighting the struggle to achieve psychic stability after the death of a loved one figure mourning as a motion toward the restoration of an imagined autonomy belied both by the survivor's location in a vulnerable body and the breach of boundaries rendered apparent by the impossibility of disentangling the living subject from a lost body.[3]

My aim is not to trace assumptions about the body to their origin in larger cultural dynamics or to revise cultural histories of death and dying,[4] but to explore—through a series of representations that contribute to and reflect the tensions of a contemporary American cultural imaginary—how cultural constructions of death and grief are inextricably bound with specific assumptions about the body. This book explores representations of illness, grief, and embodiment in a variety of contemporary American literary genres, including the novel, short fiction, memoir, and poetry. Although much of my analysis thus focuses on literary portrayals of illness and grief, my interest in the visual dynamics of bodily objectification also leads, in the second, fourth, and fifth chapters, to analysis of contemporary photography and its representational conventions. My interest in photography stems partly from my concern with issues of referentiality raised by the juxtaposition of literary and visual representational codes. Photography consistently returns the gaze to the body; as Roland Barthes observes, "In the Photograph, the event is never transcended for the sake of something else: the Photograph always leads the corpus I need back to the body I see; it is the absolute Particular, . . . the *This* . . ." (Barthes 1981, 4). In exploring the representational dynamics of imaging the body, this book not only probes photography's claim to render the particularity of bodily presence with representational transparency but uses the dynamics of the gaze suggested by individual photographs to locate and critique a cultural gaze that is much more difficult to apprehend. In highlighting tensions between the body and its representation, materiality and language, I also turn occasionally to other means of representation (exploring, for example, Olu Oguibe's powerful art installation about September 11 and the tactile and visual elements of the AIDS Memorial Quilt) as well as to my own experiences with illness and grief.

Lost Bodies looks at representations of the body both to analyze how they reflect contemporary attitudes toward illness and grief and to denaturalize processes of reading, imaging, and viewing shaped by the texts themselves and by the questions and assumptions which we as readers and viewers bring to them. In *The Threshold of the Visible World,* Kaja Silverman observes, "Although we cannot control what happens to a perception before we become aware of it, we can retroactively revise the value which it assumes for us at a conscious level. We can look at an object a second time, through different representational parameters, and painstakingly reverse the processes through which we have arrogated to ourselves what does not belong to us, or displaced onto another what we do not want to recognize in ourselves" (1996, 3). Silverman's paradigm of looking and relooking captures the impetus behind my juxtaposition of texts and theoretical paradigms. Much of the work of this book involves complicating cultural constructions of physical and psychical health that enforce disembodied norms of subjectivity. Introducing the lost body into the literary image, the photographic frame, the public space, often necessitates revealing the strategies through which we have attempted to relegate the body to the position of subject or object—extension of thought or mere thing—rather than recognizing the way its very existence blurs and complicates those categories.

Despite an established history of attention to the body in literary theory, philosophy, and feminist theory, acknowledgment of the body's role in the construction of subjectivity has only recently been extended to include acknowledgment of bodies that are marked by physical disability and advancing age.[5] My study of critical illness and grief can be situated alongside recent work in disability theory and studies of aging as an attempt to explore the way that cultural distinctions force bodies into simple binaries including youth and age, ability and disability, the healthy and the dying; such binaries not only collapse varied and dynamic experiences of embodiment into polarized terms but erect cultural boundaries that enforce the illusion of stability by disrupting our identification with our own bodies as well as the bodies of others. While I consistently draw upon the work of philosophers and theorists to highlight the theoretical significance of the body, I also employ cultural studies methodologies and sociological analysis at different points to emphasize the relationship between representation and the lived practices which it shapes and out of which it emerges. Underlying my readings of individual texts within the various critical and theoretical dialogues that illuminate them is the assumption that the analysis of aesthetic practices and critical discourses should complicate, enrich, and interrogate our lived practices rather than lead us away from the world as we know it. My theoretical assumptions, then, emerge out of a pragmatic bias that returns me not only to my father's body but to the kind of work he did in a world where materiality matters, where made things designed with care and built with the hands take up space, assume practical function, become beautiful as they endure.

Thinking about the body in the context of mortality shakes up our assumptions of the body's transparency in what I hope are theoretically productive yet culturally pragmatic ways. Those of us attending to the body in critical terms often find ourselves caught in a double bind. On the one hand, the body's immediacy renders its presence self-evident. What is there to say about an experience of embodiment that, by its very nature, involves sensations as well as ideas? How can critical discourse speak to corporeal practices that exist in a material realm, and wherein would the complexities of such a discourse lie? Academic projects most often emerge out of the attempt to render the unintelligible coherent. At some level, though, thinking about the body involves an opposite process, a process of startling the obvious into a discourse that exposes its complexities without obscuring its immediacy through abstraction and intellectualization. If we, as a culture, assume the body's existence, what kind of assumptions do we make, and how do they shape our understanding of ourselves, as well as our experience of embodiment? One of the greatest challenges of writing *Lost Bodies* has been the attempt to find language that speaks to a bodily epistemology of knowledge, that invokes the urgency of embodied experience even as it interrogates the categories within which we understand that experience.

Defining this project's goal in such a double-edged way reflects a desire to rescue the materiality of the body from those who would situate it entirely within the realm of discourse, to speak to those—many of them good friends with whom I laugh and hug and walk—who insist on marking the body's inaccessibility by calling into question the very idea of "touch." Dominick LaCapra's elegant critique of the seeming inevitability of relativism strikes me as especially relevant to an analysis of the role of embodiment in experience: "The idea that there are no pure facts and that all facts have narrative or interpretive dimensions does not entail the homogeneity of narrative or interpretation. In other words, one might agree that there is in some sense interpretation 'all the way down' but argue that interpretation is not homogenous all the way down. Indeed some dimension of fact may be so basic that one might argue that any plausible or even conceivable interpretation would have to accommodate it, hence that it would make little sense even to refer to this level as interpretive" (LaCapra 2000, 185). Although we cannot talk about the body outside the mediating discourses within which it is culturally constructed, we cannot, at the same time, disentangle knowledge or perception from the living-moving body through which we experience the world. Rather than implying the possibility or the desirability of accessing bodies *only* in the realm of physical experience, I attempt to reinstitute the pressure of materiality on a dialogue shaped by linguistic and cultural forms that privilege the subject over the object, pushing the body outside the margins of psychic discourse. In bringing the body to the center of analysis, recent theorists such as Elizabeth Grosz and Gail Weiss have tried to guard against reinstating the very binary opposition between subject and object, mind and body, which they would hope to erode. Calling for the development of an understanding of what she terms embodied subjectivity or psychical corporeality, Grosz observes: "The body image does not map a biological body onto a psychosocial domain, providing a kind of translation of material into conceptual terms; rather, it attests to the necessary interconstituency of each for the other, the radical inseparability of biological from psychical elements, the mutual dependence of the psychical and the biological" (Grosz 1994, 85). My work attends to the materiality and specificity of embodiment, not in order to reify "the body" as ontologically distinct, but in order to expose the way existing cultural and intellectual discourses of illness and grief often obscure what Grosz describes as "the radical inseparability of biological from psychical elements."

To recognize the impossibility of extricating the body from embodied subjectivity, then, entails not only recognizing the cultural constructedness of the concept of the body but charting the material constructedness of all forms of perception and knowledge. In addition to stepping back from the concepts and categories I employ here, I make an equal effort to step into a pragmatic epistemology of the body that acknowledges the pleasure of touch, the shock of pain, the sensations of motion. Inasmuch as we can intellectually question the knowability of "the body" or the "real" status of touch, we can—and should—also mark the significance of what Merleau-Ponty describes as "knowledge in the hands": the way that the sensory particularity of our lived existence shapes and defines our relationships to one another and our experience of the world. Denying that one exists as a thing or as a consciousness, Merleau-Ponty observes,

> The experience of our own body . . . reveals to us an ambiguous mode of existing. If I try to think of it as a cluster of third person processes—"sight," "motility," "sexuality"—I observe that these "functions" cannot be interrelated, and related to the external world, by causal connections, they are all obscurely drawn together and mutually implied in a unique drama. Therefore the body is not an object. For the same reason, my awareness of it is not a thought, that is to say, I cannot take it to pieces and reform it to make a clear idea. Its unity is always implicit and vague. It is always something other than what it is, always sexuality and at the same time freedom, rooted in nature at the very moment when it is transformed by cultural influences, never hermetically sealed and never left behind. Whether it is a question of another's body or my own, I have no means of knowing the human body other than that of living it, which means taking up on my own account the drama which is being played out in it, and losing myself in it. . . . Thus experience of one's own body runs counter to the reflective procedure which detaches subject and object from each other, and which gives us only thought about the body, or the body as an idea, and not the experience of the body or the body in reality. (Merleau-Ponty 1962, 198–199)

Recognizing the inseparability of nature and culture, the body and ideas about the body, Merleau-Ponty moves to assert not the impossibility of knowing the body outside the limits of discourse, but the necessity of moving in and through the lived body to acknowledge its multifaceted, "ambiguous" mode of existence. Although what Elaine Scarry describes as the world-destroying capacity of pain[6]—or what the guests at my brother's wedding revealed about the painfulness of looking at the dying body—exposes the inescapability of the body in times of extremity, pain and illness merely render visible an experience of embodiment that necessarily shapes not only our sensations but our perceptions, our interactions, and our ideas. Insofar as experience and culture naturalize the presence of the normative, healthy, functioning body, the failure to recognize ourselves in and as bodies contributes to a dematerialized ideology that shapes the way we understand, represent, and apprehend both ourselves and those among us—the sick, the aging, the disabled, the dying—through whose visible materiality we tend to name (and delimit) embodiment.

Thus, although my interest here lies primarily in the subjective and intersubjective construction of embodied identity, this work's implications, I would argue, are ethical, institutional, and social. Although certain groups afflicted with illness, such as people with AIDS, attain some amount of political visibility, and certain identifiable political constituencies, such as senior citizens, are marked by a greater susceptibility to illness and death, by and large the continuously shifting, heterogeneous group of individuals who constitute "the dying" escapes the confines of social definition and lacks the power of political agency, while the dead, as Sharon Patricia Holland explores in *Raising the Dead* (2000), have *no* voice. Insofar as the fact of mortality positions each one of us at least provisionally in the category of the dying, concern about the cultural consequences of our understanding of embodiment returns us to issues surrounding the individual construction of embodied subjectivity, and vice versa. As some critics have recently argued, collapsing the historical experience of trauma or the individual dynamics of mourning for a specific lost object into the ontological inevitability of loss leads to the foreclosing of an ethical response and the formation of a contemporary culture "beyond mourning."[7] In treating death and dying in insistently embodied terms, I attempt to pressure psychoanalytic theories that conceive of loss as "constitutive of existence" by continually returning them to the material fact of a specific absence irrecuperable through representation; at the same time, I believe our shared vulnerability to loss shapes not only our understanding of death and dying but the way we perceive dying bodies, the policies we enact to care for them, and the images we create to remember them. The abject body of dying and death collapses boundaries between inside and outside; abjection, in Julia Kristeva's words, "is above all a revolt of the person against an external menace from which one wants to keep oneself at a distance, but of which one has the impression that it is not only an external menace but that it may menace us from inside" (Oliver 1993, 55). In this book, my attempt to attend to the embodied experience of death as internal and external menace often propels me to supplement psychoanalytic theories of subjectivity and loss with contributions from literature, philosophy, sociology, and cultural studies that highlight the significance of the lived body's experiences of illness, pain, and grief.

Attending to the experiential as well as the theoretical significance of the body in the context of death thus remains an important goal of this work, even as that goal is consistently troubled by what Merleau-Ponty describes as the division between embodied experience and the reflective procedure that "runs counter" to it (1962, 198). Although I attempt to respond here to the cultural invisibility and unspeakability of the embodied subject's experience of death, my goal is not to provide a monolithic narrative of such experience but to open up a space for various and perhaps contesting representations. The motion of this project from dying to grief reflects the arc of my own experience of my father's death; undoubtedly, my secondhand experience of dying and firsthand experience of grief shape my articulations of those concerns in the pages that follow, in ways acknowledged and unacknowledged throughout. My project is also haunted by the impossibility of gesturing toward the urgency and specificity of lived experience without collapsing that experience into universalized categories that remain necessarily abstract. In her groundbreaking essay "Consuming Trauma; or, The Pleasures of Merely Circulating," Patricia Yaeger explores the danger of re-dressing the bodies of the dead in figurative tropes and specialized languages; in textualizing bodies, she argues, we generate academic discourses that thrive by consuming the very traumas they would expose. Citing the need to attend to the bodies that remain behind academic figurations of political violence, she observes, "I think, language is difficult, and objects never go into their concepts without leaving something behind, without leaving a remainder. But in this essay I find something more than a remainder—I find too many remains. There are too many bodies here and too little care for them.... Any theory pretending to account for the grim facticity of violence must stand both within and apart from the materiality it theorizes" (2002, 32, 41). Although the lost bodies that I attend to in this book are fictional as well as real, victims of illness and mortality rather than political violence, Yaeger's call for a "nervous" interpretation that stands both within and apart from the materiality it theorizes applies to the analysis of illness, grief, and embodiment that I undertake here. Critical attention to the construction of embodied subjectivity in illness and in grief emerges as a form of caring for the vulnerable body, of assuring that "death's circulation in academic writing" remains tied to the lived experiences of the dying, the grieving, and those who do or do not, can or cannot attend to them.

⁂

Structurally and conceptually, death lies at the center of this project. Whereas the threat of death often pulls the critically ill bodies in Part One perilously close to the healthy subject, establishing an uncomfortable proximity, the sensory inaccessibility of the body after death conspires with cultural norms that legislate a focus on the recuperation of psychic wholeness to establish a disembodied dynamic of grief that Part Two interrogates. The motion of *Lost Bodies,* then, not only traces the trajectory of loss from illness to grief, but reverses the cultural motion away from death and the body; in attending to the dying body, placing ourselves in proximity to it, we also create a space for acknowledging the import of embodied absence in cultural discourses of grief.

Part One explores representations of the critically ill body to chart the way that anxieties about mortality play themselves out not just in shared cultural assumptions about the imperiled body but in the very ways we experience our own bodies and the bodies of others. In exposing the dying body to view, literary and photographic representations uncover both the uncomfortable fact of impending death and the seemingly absolute boundaries between health and illness erected by our culture, boundaries which implicitly disavow the shared vulnerability of embodiment. The first two chapters explore the role of vision in negotiating these boundaries by analyzing the complex power dynamics that result when the gaze of the healthy subject is forced upon the body of a person with cancer or AIDS. Film theorists and other critics following in their wake have relied heavily on psychoanalytic models that constitute viewing in the realm of visual pleasure; as a result, they have not explored the theoretical implications of a gaze that necessarily involves pain or discomfort. This book opens by charting the effects of such a gaze, a gaze that responds not to the lingering appeal of the seductive fetish but to a series of unsettling encounters with bodies marked by illness or death. Turning the individual and collective gaze toward the person with terminal illness raises important questions about how the very act of seeing functions to naturalize assumptions about the embodied subject's location relative to the borders of life and death.

Chapter 1, "Terminal Illness and the Gaze," probes the dynamics of the gaze within a framework of intimacy defined not by the attempt to negotiate sexual difference but by the possibility of forging a connection between a healthy subject and a person with terminal illness. The chapter's opening section relies upon the work of theorists such as Mulvey, Kristeva, Silverman, and Foucault to explore the role the gaze plays in constructing the experience of dying, both for the onlooker whose visual apprehension of a dying body forces the watcher to confront the immediacy of death and for a dying patient who perceives the self as subject *and* object of the gaze. The dynamics of the death-watch emerge in the next section of the chapter through an analysis of *The Father,* a powerful collection of poems by

Sharon Olds that raises important theoretical questions about how the gaze functions to construct a relationship between the embodied subject and the dying body. *The Father,* I argue, presents a model for balancing the uneven distribution of power that marks the projection of the healthy gaze onto the diseased body. If looking sometimes lends the viewing subject intimate access to the object of desire, seeing the person with terminal illness may result in a form of uncomfortable intimacy that implicates the viewer in the experience of mortality. Bridging the gap between the dying and the living necessarily involves a radical and almost contradictory unsettling of power relations; only when the viewing subject sacrifices the distance and autonomy of the healthy gaze by refusing the empowerment of extrication does the look become a means of restoring rather than disrupting connection.

My discussion of photographic representations of people with AIDS in Billy Howard's *Epitaphs for the Living* (1989) and Nicholas Nixon's *People with AIDS* (1991) in chapter 2 focuses on the way the visual construction of knowledge about AIDS is always tied to cultural responses to the dying body. The epistemology of vision upon which photography relies is trapped within a material dynamic that accesses subjectivity only through the visually perceptible aspects of the body. The viewer's response to photographic representations of people with AIDS may thus exaggerate an already existing tendency to preserve the self by constructing impenetrable boundaries between life and death. As the marks of critical illness literally overwhelm the features of the person with AIDS, the gaze often locates the subject in a body that seems to announce its identity as the process of its own (communicable) destruction; we see the self rendered visible only as its impending absence. In an effort not to reinscribe the immediate association of AIDS with death, photographers like Howard erase the visible signs of illness from their photographs. Others, like Nixon, push their viewers to confront their own unspoken fears and assumptions about death by forcing the viewer's gaze upon dying bodies unveiled in all their physical immediacy. Despite the conflicting assumptions that underlie their representational strategies, the photographs of both Howard and Nixon are haunted by tensions of embodied subjectivity that emerge under the pressure of dying from AIDS. This chapter exposes the way photographs of people with AIDS construct their subjects and the illness they share through the manipulation of representational techniques and the appropriation of visual conventions that reinforce cultural assumptions about death and dying.

If these chapters trace the forced intimacy or imposed distance that results from visual proximity to the dying, chapter 3 literalizes the encounter between health and illness by locating it in the medical waiting room. The waiting room stages the healthy subject's encounter with the dying body both by providing a confined area in which that encounter is played out in space and by disrupting the conventions of normalcy that mediate the experience of embodiment to pressure even the healthy subject to "try on" the identity of the ill. Drawing upon narrative theory, disability theory, and theories of space, this chapter explores the way in which the apparently "empty" space of the medical waiting room stages many of our most important assumptions about illness and the body; the chapter combines spatial analysis of medical waiting rooms with cultural analysis of their fictional representations in works by Eudora Welty, Susan Kenney, Jane Hamilton, Lorrie Moore, and others. Although the body always structures our relationship to space, the medical waiting room serves as a place in which we are immobilized in and as our bodies. Our physical containment in the waiting room and the material threat of illness or disability that brings us to such a space are coupled with symbolic assaults on productivity and subjectivity that render us symbolically, if not physically disabled. The medical waiting room not only constrains bodily motion and signification but strips us of the strategic forms of cultural resistance that we erect to mask the vulnerability of the body. In the space of the waiting room, the opposing subject positions of embodied object and disembodied subject dissolve or commingle in a loss of wholeness from which it may be difficult to recover. Whereas chapters 1 and 2 explore the problems that emerge when a healthy subject looks at bodies shadowed by illness and mortality, this chapter examines a space that erases the physical and symbolic borders between illness and health to subject even the healthy subject to the experience of vulnerable embodiment.

Part Two of *Lost Bodies* moves from the tendency to normalize assumptions about healthy embodiment to the tendency to disembody mourning as it explores our culture's reluctance to acknowledge the role of embodiment in the grieving process. The continued dominance of Freud's influential theory of mourning demonstrates not only a cultural injunction to move through grief but a tendency to define bereavement and its consolations in symbolic terms that obscure the bodily dimensions of loss. Using literary, theoretical, material, and photographic texts, this section develops a theory of grief as bodily loss and considers how the gap between representation and materiality governs the process of memory and the experience of grief. Chapter 4 situates Freud's work on mourning and melancholia within a dialogue shaped by Kathleen Woodward's understanding of Grief-work and Merleau-Ponty's theory of intercorporeality to explore what it might mean to understand grief in terms of *bodily* loss (Woodward 1992–1993). For the protagonist of Marilynne Robinson's novel *House-*

keeping (1981), mourning shapes itself around the form of a missing body that she can imagine but never experience. Her vision lends purpose to the tortuous and repetitive process of grief by casting the work of mourning not within the trajectory of psychological recovery that Freud sketches but as a (necessarily failed) narrative of reembodiment. In *Camera Lucida* (1981), Roland Barthes also searches for an image of his mother that defies the immobility of the image and disrupts the immobility of grief to bring her lost body back to him. If photography exposes the ever-present gap between the living-moving body and the body as image, grief lives in the space of that gap as a permanent condition. Barthes's narrator posits the Winter Garden Photograph as the "essential" realization of a presence he labors theoretically to embody; his attempts to accomplish the "impossible" task of animating the image result in the most poignant and irresolvable tensions of *Camera Lucida* (71). Whereas Barthes's text tracks his unsuccessful attempts to embody the visual image, Shellburne Thurber's photographs of emptied rooms foreground the failure of representation by highlighting the tension between images and the bodies they cannot hold. Her photographs construct rather than resist the dynamics of grief as they emphasize the spaces left behind by bodies the image can neither access nor render. Whether images are invoked to establish or to counteract absence, tensions between the disembodied image and the embodied dynamics of grief point to the way existing cultural discourses assert the recuperability of loss by reducing presence to subjectivity.

Among theorists who address the psychology of mourning, Nicholas Abraham and Maria Torok are perhaps best known for a model that spatializes and concretizes the mourning process. Chapter 5 understands the spatialized and corporeal images of incorporation for which Abraham and Torok are famous as figures that are themselves haunted by the ghost of an embodied understanding of grief obscured through metaphorization. Shifting focus toward that which is excluded from poststructuralist theories of language and models of psychic loss, chapter 5 suggests that understanding the experience of grief within an epistemology of the body demands exploring language-centered notions of health and subjectivity that govern the way the embodied subject experiences and articulates loss. Carolyn Parkhurst's novel, *The Dogs of Babel* (2003), identifies and unsettles prevailing cultural assumptions about corporeal and linguistic forms of mourning. The protagonist's desperate struggle to intellectualize and control his overwhelming grief by teaching his dog to talk reflects a cultural injunction to rename and recast embodied loss within forms of language that render it symbolic. *The Dogs of Babel* situates its narrator's desperate canine linguistics experiment in the context of larger cultural forces that relegate the sensory dynamics of grief to the realm of the animal and insist on using language to recuperate the incoherence of loss. In the postmodern landscape of Don DeLillo's *The Body Artist* (2001), grief is figured as an expulsion from embodiment into hyper-consciousness that tests the limits of the imagination and translates its freedom into a form of psychical constraint. DeLillo's recently widowed protagonist finds herself suspended between the sensory immediacy of a strange little man who appears in her home, eerily reembodying her husband in his familiar gestures and inflections, and the disembodied models of psychic accommodation proffered by a culture invested in containing the parameters of loss within a narrative of mourning. If the logical extension of the constructivist universe in which we live is the textualization of the world, the shock of grief in a postmodern landscape is not the fact of loss but its resistance to the recuperation of language, image, and imagination.

Part Two concludes by exploring the possibility of holding onto lost bodies through objects and artifacts which assert a form of knowledge that is sensory, spatial, and material. Insofar as the embodied dynamics of grief complicate existing understandings of loss, chapter 6, "Objects of Grief," explores how the labor that Freud describes as the "work of mourning" might extend into the forms of the material world, allowing for a type of embodied memory that measures past chiasmic intercorporeality not in order to sustain it but in order to release its hold. This chapter reinstitutes the pressure of materiality on a dialogue shaped by linguistic and cultural forms that privilege the subject over the object, pushing the body outside the margins of psychic discourse and rendering objects mere signs of subjective presence. Whereas Baudrillard charts the existence of "a material world of use values which grounds the symbolic world of sign values in the system of objects" (Gottdiener 1995, 48), broadening our analysis of signifying function to read objects through the lens of the body requires attending to the way meaning is not only constructed through but located in material form. Merleau-Ponty's epistemology of the body encourages us not merely to push past or move through the object to its status as an expressive symbol, but to linger long enough to attend to its status as a thing worn, made, touched by an embodied subject. Mark Doty's long poem "The Wings" (1993) interrogates the memorializing function of objects and the limitations of art as its speaker confronts the anticipated bodily absence of his partner, who lies dying of AIDS. Although the language-based form of poetry makes it impossible for Doty to escape a sign-based hermeneutics, his poem gestures toward that which it cannot contain in its insistent representation of and interrogation of objects. The objects Doty accumulates representationally speak to his desire to hold onto the human body even as the poem presents a dynamic of textured rematerialization it can thematize but not enact. Chapter 6 concludes with an analysis of the way objects and artifacts incorporated into the AIDS Memorial Quilt—jewelry, possessions, clothing—work against the disembodied and private experience of grief to render in tactile as well as visual terms the materiality and specificity of absent bodies. The signifying power of individual panels is frequently disrupted by the revelation of the object's doubled status; a bearer of meaning, the object also bears the body's marks and holds the body's traces. The quilt disrupts the symbolic value of objects which, for the viewer, function neither as signs that can be decoded and narrativized nor as mere things that can be dismissed with acknowledgment of their commodity status. Intimately marked by a specific but unknown body, objects such as used towels, well-loved teddy bears, or worn shoes invoke an embodied presence that the quilt viewer cannot access. In simultaneously invoking and frustrating the viewer's access to the lost body, the panel maker withholds what he or she can no longer hold, preserving as private what could not be made public.

The book concludes with a postscript that addresses the popularity of death as a subject of contemporary American mass culture. Using examples from television, popular fiction, and the greeting card industry, I explore the depiction and mediation of the dead body through representational conventions that conspire to elide distinctions between the living and the dead, the real and the unreal. The appropriation of the dead in what Robert Pogue Harrison describes as "the order of the posthumous image" renders their embodied presence virtual and their virtual presence embodied (R. Harrison 2003, 150). In bringing the dead to life, the works of popular culture I examine speak for and to a prosthetic culture which, in revealing the constructedness of presence, may implicitly deny the legitimacy of absence. I conclude by discussing the tragic events of September 11, 2001, and the way the thousands of deaths associated with the terrorist attacks of that day disrupt American culture's tendency to gloss over the absent presence that underlies the embodied experience of grief. The inaccessibility of the bodies of the dead after September 11 not only exaggerates the difficulty of achieving closure for grieving families but functions as a means of articulating the gap at the center of many Americans' phantom grief. By exposing and attending to the significance of the lost body, newspaper articles, essays, and artworks such as Olu Oguibe's "Ashes" attempt to situate the culture in spatial and sensory relationship to the dead, marking our continuing—though necessarily failed—attempts to embody a loss many struggle to appropriate from the realm of the image into the domain of lived experience.

{1} THE DYING BODY

CHAPTER ONE

∞

Terminal Illness and the Gaze

The publication of Laura Mulvey's "Visual Pleasure and Narrative Cinema" in 1978 initiated a dialogue about the function of the "gaze" that has subsequently moved beyond the boundaries of film theory. Mulvey's discussion of scopophilic viewing in the cinema identifies a voyeuristic dynamic in which the erotic identity of the viewing subject is clearly separated from the object (usually a woman) on the screen; the viewer derives pleasure from objectifying the screen persona and subjecting that persona to the power of the controlling gaze. The success of film criticism in denaturalizing the act of looking in the cinema (exposing the ways the viewer's gaze may be constructed to enforce hidden assumptions or authorize conclusions that appear "natural") has led in turn to the need for unveiling the way that the gaze is constructed in other forums and defining the power dynamics that result from that construction.

In relying heavily upon psychoanalytic models that stress viewing as a form of visual pleasure, however, film theorists and adaptive critics following in their wake—in literary theory, gender studies, and cultural studies—have paid little attention to the consequences of a gaze that is painful or uncomfortable, a gaze that moves away from a lingering focus on the seductive fetish to a flitting confrontation with death and disease.[1] The way we as individuals and as a culture look at people with terminal illness raises questions about how the act of seeing can serve to naturalize assumptions about the dying body and the embodied subject. When the object of the gaze changes from an attractive female form that the viewer objectifies or a screen protagonist with whom the viewer identifies to the wasting body of a terminally ill patient, the structures of looking that Mulvey locates within a dynamic of visual pleasure demand to be revised. The act of looking at a person with terminal illness may perpetuate the dynamics of objectification that Mulvey associates with the fetishization of women in the cinema; it may, also, however, upset the very distinction between subject and object to allow for the possibility of a gaze that dissolves the distance between the two.

This chapter attempts to understand the intimacy of the gaze not as a means of negotiating sexual difference but as a way of establishing connection between a healthy subject and a person with terminal illness. The first section lays the theoretical groundwork for the argument that follows; using the work of theorists such as Mulvey, Foucault, and Kristeva, I explore the way that the gaze constructs the experience of dying both for the terminally ill patient who perceives the self as an object of the gaze and for the watcher who negotiates the idea of death through the visual apprehension of a dying body. The second section expands this dialogue of critical voices through an analysis of Sharon Olds's *The Father* (1992), a volume of contemporary American poetry that serves to raise important theoretical questions about how the dynamics of watching are implicated in the construction of a relationship between the dying body and the embodied subject. Focusing on the slow process of her father's death from cancer, Olds offers an unflinching exploration of what it means to turn the gaze toward the dying body. Her volume opens with a description of watching—"I would be there all day, watch him nap, / be there when he woke, sit with him / until the day ended" ("The Waiting," 26–28)—and continues by probing the way that looking and being looked at not only reflect but constitute identity. *The Father* offers a response to theories of the gaze that focus exclusively on eroticized and sadistic power dynamics; it presents not only an unflinching investigation of the gaze's dehumanizing power but a model for balancing the uneven distribution of power that marks the projection of the healthy gaze onto the diseased body.

Shifting the Gaze

Michel Foucault describes his study of modern medicine, *The Birth of the Clinic*, as a book "about the act of seeing, the gaze" (1973, ix). Foucault's volume begins to raise questions about how the gaze is constructed in medicine, about the forces that dictate what a doctor sees and does not see when he looks at a patient. In his exploration of these questions, Foucault defines a dichotomization of patient and disease that underlies much of modern medicine:

> Paradoxically, in relation to that which he is suffering from, the patient is only an external fact; the medical reading must take him into account only to place him in parenthesis. Of course, the doctor must know "the internal structure of our bodies"; but only in order to subtract it, and to free to the doctor's gaze "the nature and combination of symptoms, crises, and other circumstances that accompany diseases." It is not the pathological that functions, in relation to life, as a *counter-nature*, but the patient in relation to the disease itself. . . . Hence the strange character of the medical gaze. . . . It is directed upon that which is visible in the disease—but on the basis of the patient, who hides this visible element even as he shows it. (8–9)

In order to render disease visible, the medical gaze must factor out the person with illness; seeing the patient as an embodied subject, then, emerges as not only inconsequential but actually counterproductive. In the examining room, the person with illness becomes the white space in the picture, the absence which allows the illness to be seen. As James Dawes argues, "If the diseased cannot be seen they cannot be treated; but if they are seen, they are reduced to the *merely* treatable" (Dawes 1995, 40).[2]

Because the medical gaze sees disease only by blocking out the human subject whose body bears the mark of illness, illness becomes increasingly visible as it becomes increasingly incontestable. The person with terminal illness, then, may feel abandoned to the consequences of the medical gaze; such a gaze, as Foucault observes, sees its logical extension in the absolute obliteration of the person by the disease, in death (1973, 9). In "The Patient Examines the Doctor," an eloquent essay describing his experience with an untreatable cancer, Anatole Broyard charts the effect of such a gaze on its object: "There is the way a doctor looks at you. One doctor I saw had a trick way of almost crossing his eyes, so he seemed to be peering warmly, humanistically, into my eyes, but he wasn't seeing me at all. He was looking without looking" (1992, 49). Broyard's desire to be "seen" by his doctor emerges as more than a plea for "humanistic" intention or psychological affirmation; it also suggests a struggle to sustain life in the face of death. Broyard seeks a physician willing to look hard enough at him to reclaim him from the critical illness that threatens to obscure his subjective presence: "If he could gaze directly at the patient, the doctor's work would be more gratifying. Why bother with sick people, why try to save them, if they're not worth acknowledging? When a doctor refuses to acknowledge a patient, he is, in effect, abandoning him to his illness" (50). The "direct" gaze, in this scenario, becomes a means of reversing the process of the disease, of enacting the turn through which the person overwhelms the disease within and not vice versa.

Vision always accesses the subject through the body visible to the eye, and the destructive dynamics of the gaze often result from a look that reduces an embodied presence to an objectified body. When a body bears the visible marks of illness—the lesions that often accompany AIDS, the uncontrollable muscle spasms of Parkinson's disease, the gaunt, hollowed face of a person dying from cancer—its function as a multiple sign system is often ignored in favor of an interpretation that renders itself as concrete vision. As the marks of critical illness literally overwhelm the features of the person with disease, the gaze often locates the subject in a body that seems to announce its identity as the process of its own destruction. The medical gaze, then, merely extends and exaggerates a dynamics of looking that forces the person with terminal illness to see the self rendered visible only as its impending absence.

While Foucault's and Broyard's discussions focus on the relationship between doctor and patient, the "medical gaze" as a broader cultural phenomenon also influences the visual dynamics operating between the terminally ill and their friends and family members. For the subject of the healthy gaze as well as its object, the dynamics of looking are exaggerated and problematized by a visual confrontation with the dying body. If the distant gaze perpetuates objectification, the intimacy of emotional attachment often makes identifying the dying body with/as the beloved even more disturbing. While Anatole Broyard eloquently describes the yearning of terminally ill patients for a "direct" gaze, the memoir of his wife, Sandy Broyard, portrays with equal eloquence the painful visual dynamics experienced by caregivers attempting to direct their unflinching gaze at a dying loved one whose body seems to signify not the presence of the self but the process of its dissolution:

> Thinking of Fran, the right side of her face fallen, deflated, already dead because of the pressure of the tumor on her brain. Remembering Anatole, his thinness, the swollen legs and feet. How a body distorts and deflates in these random ways. The internal rhythms, balance, and homeostasis disordered by cancer cause the body to unmold, literally lose the familiar shape, so that by which we recognize one's personhood becomes an image of horror. The misshapenness is the dying made visible. (Broyard 2005, 153)

Sandy Broyard dwells on the body's formal outline as a signifier for subjectivity. As disease "deflates" or "unmolds" that shape, the body becomes not simply unrecognizable, but a signifier of the subject's undoing, "an image of horror." Claire Levine offers a similar description of her husband's body first losing its form and then taking on a different countenance, which she describes as "the look of death": "What I really struggle with is trying to come to terms with Robert's physical deterioration. I've never ever experienced someone so physically ill, his body being out of control. Every part of his body did not work. And then he got that death look. Going from being a beautiful man to a look of death—I don't think I'll ever come to terms with that" (Levine 1999, 31). Both Sandy Broyard and Claire Levine describe a two-part process in which the cherished body loses its familiar form to take on a new and horrible aspect. What disturbs them is not simply that the beloved becomes unformed, or identity-less, but that he takes on a new identity—"And then he got that death look"—which is eerily familiar; not simply faceless, the beloved wears the face of death.

The threat that such a body poses to the gaze can be framed, in Julia Kristeva's terms, as the threat of the abject, of "death infecting life" (Kristeva 1982, 4). Materiality and corporeality emerge in Kristeva's work as necessary conditions of subjectivity which the subject must nonetheless disavow in order to preserve the illusion of stability, unity, wholeness. Although Kristeva defines the corpse as "the utmost of abjection" (4), the body of the person with terminal illness may function as even more of a threat; such a person often exhibits the bodily signs of impending death while yet resisting the inanimate coldness that helps us to classify the corpse as Other.

Mainstream film, as Mulvey claims, attempts to allay the fear of castration by portraying "a hermetically sealed world which unwinds magically, indifferent to the presence of the audience, producing for them a sense of separation and playing on their voyeuristic phantasy" (Mulvey 1978, 9). Looking at a person with terminal illness—even through the frame of literary or visual representation—often challenges such a sense of separation. The terminally ill body assaults the healthy gaze by threatening to unveil without fetishistic mediation the viewing subject's vulnerability, a vulnerability that stems from mortality itself.

The "healthy" gaze, in order to maintain what Mulvey describes as "a sense of separation" or what Sander Gilman describes in *Disease and Representation* (1988) as the need for distance from the ill, may attempt to move itself outside the expanding parameters of the sick body by establishing a way of viewing that destroys the link between viewer and viewed. Louise Harmon points out that seeking distance from the physical presence of the terminally ill is common, even among caregivers in hospitals:

> Studies in healthcare settings show that doctors and nurses are also guilty of fleeing from a dying patient.... They distance themselves; they express anger at the patient; they limit conversations; they avoid contact altogether.... The effect on the dying person can be devastating. The abject

loneliness of the situation, the depersonalization, and the denial of any kind of significant social role are forms of social death. (Harmon 1988, 125–126)

Harmon's use of the term "abject loneliness" suggests how the patient takes on an apprehension of the self as abject, as no longer the self but a polluting body—"death infecting life." Whereas the fear of castration can be manipulated by covering a visual absence that suggests sexual difference, the person with terminal illness resists such easy manipulation, and indeed seems to move over his or her boundaries into the viewer's own. Because the object of the gaze announces not only difference but sameness, the subject's recognition of a shared mortality lends power to the very threat that the healthy gaze would dispel. Defining abjection as "a desire for separation," Kristeva describes it as a reaction to a menace both external *and* internal, a threat to autonomy heightened by the subject's failure to locate it clearly outside the boundaries of the self (Oliver 1993, 55). The diseased body frequently refuses to maintain the distance that marks separation between subjects; when the body is overwhelmed by illness, it begins to swell, ooze, sweat, and bleed until it intrudes upon public space. The healthy gaze that risks intimacy with the person with disease thus sacrifices the seeming mastery of distance.

Within Kristeva's theory of the abject, erotic pleasure emerges as a symbolic response to the uncontainable threat of mortality. Defining the erotic not merely as a response to the threat of castration but as an attempt to sustain life itself in the face of death, Kristeva defines the eroticization of abjection as "an attempt at stopping the hemorrhage: a threshold before death, a halt or a respite" (Oliver 1993, 55). Kristeva's formulation of the relationship between the erotic and the abject lays the groundwork for an interrogation of the gaze that reverses the tendency in feminist film criticism to privilege the sexual aspect of looking. Although critics like Mulvey may cite the fear of castration as the source of the look, for example, they shy away from issues of mortality to focus primarily on the erotic dynamics of the gaze.

In *Over Her Dead Body: Death, Femininity, and the Aesthetic*, Elisabeth Bronfen addresses the limitations of such gendered notions of castration:

What is put under erasure by the gendered concept of castration is the other, so often non-read theme of death, forbidden maybe because far less conducive to efforts of stable self-fashioning than notions of sexual difference. To see the phallus as secondary to the scar of the navel means acknowledging that notions of domination and inferiority based on gender difference are also secondary to a more global and non-individuated disempowerment before death. (1992, 35)

Although Bronfen's discussion of "a notion of anxiety not based on sexual difference" (34) is not formulated in terms of the gaze, her Freudian revisions suggest new ways of thinking about the dynamics of looking at a person close to death. Focusing on Olds's *The Father,* I will explore the way that the subject/object dynamics of the gaze are complicated by the act of looking at a person with terminal illness. I wish to use the concept of the gaze to discuss the process through which looking becomes a means of negotiating identity in the face of death. Rather than attempting to refute or replace gendered notions of the gaze based on theories of sexual difference, my argument attempts to switch the reader's frame of vision in a way that makes it possible not only to recognize the theme of death which Bronfren describes as under erasure but also to see what is at stake in the act of seeing that constitutes the death-watch.

The Death-Watch in Sharon Olds's *The Father*

Calvin Bedient opens his review essay of *The Father* with words that express genuine shock:

> Sharon Olds's fourth book of poems, *The Father,* is easily one of the oddest ever published—even, one of the most outrageous. Consider: a sequence of fifty-one poems on the poet's ghoulish, erotic death-watch of her father, who was hospitalized for cancer, and the grieving aftermath. His dying both steps up and makes safe (unrealizable) her lust to be him and to have him: she is Electra, a babe who will suck from his "primary tumor." (Bedient 1993, 169)

Bedient's response to what he describes as Olds's "eroticization of a devastating illness" leads him on a critical quest to "account for the astonishing peculiarity of the book" (171). That quest is framed in psychoanalytic terms; he locates the source of the poems' "strong appetite for the ugly, the gruesome" in what he sees as the underlying issue in the collection: Olds's final acknowledgment of "her egregious idealization of the father she also hated and feared" (170, 171). Invoking Jessica Benjamin's *The Bonds of Love,* Bedient usefully unveils some of the complex psychological dynamics that underlie the speaker's relationship with her father in this sequence of poems. Yet in tracing the poet's "eroticization" of her father's illness back to Olds's desire for individuation and sexual agency, Bedient relegates that illness to symptom and masks its urgent presence in the poems he discusses.

The Father's revelation of the diseased and dying body—perhaps as much as any metaphorical eroticization of the relationship between father and daughter—constitutes a violation of the cultural codes through which contemporary Western civilization renders the terminally ill body visible.[3] If one method of containing the threat of the abject is to eroticize it, Bedient's manipulation of Olds's poetry can be understood in just that way. Concentrating on Olds's "outrageous" eroticism, he obliterates the embodied presence of Olds's father in the poems to embrace the symbolic function that the father serves in the daughter's construction of sexual identity. As Olds's speaker watches her father's body deteriorate from cancer and witnesses his death, the material urgency of his embodied presence erupts again and again in the text; in glossing over the volume's representation of that bodily eruption and the poet's attempt to come to terms with her own role as spectator of it, Bedient ignores the truly radical representations of disease and dying in *The Father.*

In Olds's poetry, erotic metaphors serve not as "a respite" from the threat of death but as acknowledgment of the intimate consequences of looking upon her father's dying. "My Father's Eyes" compares the exchange of looks between Olds and her father to "the sudden flash / of sex that jumps between two people" (ll. 22–23). If Freud is correct in aligning sexuality with the life force and against death, this volume of poems represents Olds's attempt to use the gaze as a means of dissolving boundaries rather than maintaining distance, as a way of claiming her father's embodied presence rather than reducing him to an objectified absence. In the process of the death-watch that she both enacts and critiques in these poems, Olds finds herself pulled across the border of her father's dying body, "turning . . . / around his death" ("The Glass," ll. 36–37). The awkward and sometimes forced intimacy reflected in the erotic overtones of Olds's poems, then, emerges at least in part from the dynamics of a deathwatch that blurs the distinction between seer and seen, subject and object, eye and body.

Olds opens her collection with "The Waiting," a poem that testifies to the objectifying power of the look. When she descends from the guest room in her father's house each morning, the speaker (whom I will take the license of referring to throughout my argument simply as "Olds") is confronted with the motionless body of her father:

> By then, he knew he was dying,
> he seemed to approach it as a job to be done
> which he knew how to do. He got up early
> for the graveyard shift. When he heard me coming down the
> hall he would not turn—he had
> a way of holding still to be looked at,

> as if a piece of sculpture could sense
> the gaze which was running over it—
> he would wait with that burnished, looked-at look until
> the hem of my nightgown came into view,
> then slew his eyes up at me, without
> moving his head, and wait, the kiss
> came to him, he did not go to it. (ll. 9–21)

In this rendering, Olds's father displays himself for the gaze that he is incapable of resisting; she images him as an artifact that absorbs the look but does not return it. Indeed, the "job" of dying that the father undertakes seems to involve a kind of collapse into matter, an abdication of agency that allows only the negative expression of subjectivity.

Unlike the sculpture to which he is compared, however, Olds's father can sense the gaze that runs over him, can *know* the look that renders him material. This knowledge of his own objectification emerges as one of the few signs of the father's subjective presence; the look as gaze is rewritten as the "burnished, looked-at look" not emanating from but inscribed on the father's body. Denied both the agency of the gaze and the inviolability of the object, Olds's father is caught between the definition of himself as subject and as diseased body.

Critical illness exaggerates the vexed dynamics of subjective embodiment by subjecting the person with disease to the absolute tyranny of a body at the very moment when that body seems least the subject's own. In *The Body in Pain,* Elaine Scarry unveils the way extreme pain pins the suffering subject to a body that overwhelms the outer world and the inner self until that "increasingly palpable" body appears to subsume all else (1985, 30). When disease acts on the human body, it assaults not only organs and tissue but the subject's very notion of agency. Living with a body that may shrink, swell, bleed, and ooze but that necessarily moves toward self-destruction, the person with terminal illness may be forced to renegotiate the construction of the self in a manner that accounts both for the body's absolute identification with the subject—its essential and undeniable connection to the suffering self—and for the subject's absolute alienation from a diseased body that may be as unfamiliar as the body of a stranger.

This alienation emerges in the form of the father's seeming complicity in his own objectification. While Olds becomes the real subject of the poem, her father emerges only as the "something someone has made" (l. 6). As his daughter's look reduces him to the material status of a body that moves steadily toward death, the father's own gaze begins to collapse into the material. Rather than registering subjective presence, the father's sidelong look—he "slew his eyes up at me, without / moving his head" (ll. 19–20)—registers the dissolution of subjectivity and its replacement with a fully conscious yet objectified self.

As Olds's father seems to embrace the motion toward his own death, the poem's final lines explore the connection between the material dynamics of vision and the subjective empowerment of the gaze:

> . . . Not until the next
> dawn would he be alone again, night-
> watchman of matter, sitting, facing
> the water—the earth without form, and void,
> darkness upon the face of it, as if
> waiting for his daughter. (ll. 29–34)

In this parody of Genesis 1:1, the omnipotent father is rendered powerless, his gaze an unfocused "facing" of the "face" of darkness. He becomes the watcher instead of the watched only when his daughter—whose presence as subject of the poem is emphasized by its conclusion with her name—is sleeping; he watches a formless matter that his gaze is unable to objectify or clarify. The father's status as "night-watchman of matter" reflects the way in which his illness traps him between the worlds of subject and object and prefigures his eventual collapse into sightlessness on his death bed: "They said he was probably not seeing anything, / the material sphere of his eye simply / open to the stuff of the world" ("My Father's Eyes," ll. 11–31).

This collapse of vision into vacant material presence denies Olds's father the power of the gaze; her look confirms—rather than resists—the process of his objectification. In beginning *The Father* with this poem, Olds not only calls attention to the significance of the gaze as a force in constructing the person with terminal illness, but also suggests how her status as artist as well as observer exaggerates her role in turning subject into artifact, human into matter. In the poems that follow, Olds attempts to negotiate a way of looking at her father that is not also a perpetuation of the objectifying dynamics of the gaze.

Instead of redirecting the look away from her father's body, Olds attempts to unsettle the strict definition of subject and object within the dynamics of vision. Although she continues to look upon her father's dying body, in later poems of the volume her gaze comes to serve as an extension rather than a refutation of his subjective presence. As such, it begins to realize the kind of healing gaze that Broyard defines in "The Patient Examines the Doctor": "My ideal doctor would resemble Oliver Sacks. I can imagine Dr. Sacks *entering* my condition, looking around at it from inside like a kind landlord, with a tenant, trying to see how he could make the premises more livable. He would look around, holding me by the hand, and he would figure out what it feels like to be me" (1992, 42–43). The healing gaze, as Broyard images it here, is a double-edged one, a look that violates the perceived boundaries between subject and object to locate itself variously; Broyard imagines Sacks moving outside the corporeal confines of his own gaze to enter the sick body, "looking around at it from *inside*" (emphasis mine).

Broyard's metaphorical revisioning of the gaze reveals the extent to which vision remains, despite its limitations, "the core component of the epistemophilic project" (Brooks 1993, 100).[4] The look as a way of knowing seems to offer a grounded, almost scientific form of accessing the "truth" of a situation that, in the case of terminal illness, is defined by a fundamental confusion about the very way in which the self can be known. Although the person with terminal illness lives *in* the dying body, experiencing disease not only in its visible manifestations on the body's surface but in its invisible assault on the nerves, that person often has no clearer sense of cause and effect than the observer who looks on from without. Indeed, part of the horror of critical illness can be located in its invisibility; because the gradual weakening of arteries to the heart or the slow spread of cancer from one organ to another often occurs invisibly, the person with terminal illness may "know" the disease within the body only by constructing it in the mind. The unpredictability of illness may emerge in the subject's experience of disease as a foreign agent within the self; frequently, that agency seems more powerful and more incontestable precisely because it refuses to make itself known directly. Broyard invites his doctor "inside" his condition so that he might "figure out what it feels like to be me"; in the process of imaging the other's entrance into the body, however, Broyard lends Dr. Sacks the power of a gaze the absence of which defines his own experience of illness.

The disjunction between these two experiences of the diseased body emerges in the imagistic fracturing of Broyard's self. Rather than portraying Sacks looking "at me" from the inside, Broyard portrays him looking "at it," something distinct from Broyard himself. Indeed, Broyard imagines himself embodied within his body, holding Sacks's hand, both of them staring wonderingly at the strange structure around them. To say that the healthy subject does not experience itself as embodied is less true than to say that the healthy subject often naturalizes a particular, familiar body as a material extension of the self. As that body is denaturalized in the course of a critical illness, its object status is exaggerated not only for others but for the embodied subject who experiences him/herself through and in it.[5] Because illness fractures the symbolic unity between the self and the body, the sick person experiences the physical self as a stranger in the mirror, while the sense of the "true" embodied self remains as an ineradicable sense memory. It is this ghostly physical self of Broyard (me in my body as I know it) that holds hands with Sacks, and helps him understand the diseased body in which he lives. In figuring out "what it feels like to be me," Sacks must relate to the embodied self within yet separate from the self's body; he must understand the fragmentation of embodied identity fundamental to the experience of illness.

Because the unity or coherence of embodied identity is always to some degree illusory, the healthy subject's temporary experience of fragmentation constitutes a very real threat to its sustaining illusion of stability; the healing gaze that Broyard images unsettles subject and object oppositions in part by exposing the terminal aspect of every human life. In her discussion of the abject, Kristeva comments on the threat posed by the collapsing of boundaries between death and life, illness and health, the dying body and its apparently healthy counterpart: "No, as in true theater, without makeup or masks, refuse and corpses *show me* what I permanently thrust aside in order to live. These body fluids, this defilement, this shit are what life withstands, hardly and with difficulty, on the part of death. There, I am at the border of my condition as a living being. My body extricates itself, as being alive, from that border" (Kristeva 1982, 3). Throughout this volume of poetry, Olds's eroticized language charts the difficulty of first connecting with and then extricating her body from her father's, of "thrusting aside" not only the visible signs of illness but the very experience of her own mortality. The problematic construction of identity that Bedient describes is thus embodied in the dynamics of disease that bring to a crisis the poet's connection with and separation from her father. The uneven distribution of power that marks the projection of the healthy gaze onto the diseased body can be repaired only by an imaginative merging that refuses—however temporarily—the empowerment of extrication. The "eroticization of abjection" (Oliver 1993, 55) that Kristeva describes as a means of holding off the Other within the self can also, as Olds reveals, be turned to its opposite: Olds's use of a sexual vocabulary describes the intimacy of moments in which the subject not only projects the gaze onto an object but intermingles with it.

"The Lifting" traces Olds's reaction when her father attempts to direct the gaze that renders him object in "The Waiting." When he exposes his naked body before his daughter's eyes, he not only receives but commands her look:

> Suddenly my father lifted up his nightie, I
> turned my head away but he cried out
> *Shar!,* my nickname, so I turned and looked.
> He was sitting in the high cranked-up bed with the
> gown up, around his neck,
> to show me the weight he had lost. I looked
> where his solid ruddy stomach had been
> and I saw the skin fallen into loose
> soft hairy rippled folds
> lying in a pool of folds
> down at the base of his abdomen,
> the gaunt torso of a big man
> who will die soon. (ll. 1–13)

Sitting high above his daughter on the "cranked-up bed" with his gown around his neck, Olds's father renders himself completely exposed to the look. Not only inviting but commanding his daughter's gaze, the speaker's father thrusts his dying body in the line of her vision; as he does so, he upsets both the sexual dynamics of looking and the distribution of power conventionally associated with the gaze.

The healthy gaze that would distance and separate itself from the abject is here forced to focus upon the corporeal immediacy of a body revealed in all its material excess. Although Olds's desire to turn away from her father's nakedness seems to issue from a sense of sexual decorum, the marks of disease overwhelm the signs of sexuality written on her father's body. As Olds's vision is drawn toward the naked body from which she would have turned away, her gaze moves first not to the penis but to the signs of disease written on her father's sagging belly. Whereas the "solid ruddy stomach" of a healthy man reflects the gaze of desire, the gathered folds of abdominal skin that confront Olds mark the visible motion of her father's body toward death. Looking at his naked body, she is confronted not with the difference of his sex but with a transforming, almost androgynous body; even as the signs of emaciation on her father's body draw Olds's eye away from the penis, the "loose / soft hairy rippled folds" of skin on her father's stomach evoke the presence of female rather than male genitalia.

Despite the radical assertion of agency that distinguishes the presence of Olds's father in this poem from his purely material manifestation in the opening poem of the volume, he continues to exist here as an object of the gaze. Offering himself up to his daughter's vision even as he commands her look, Olds's father reveals that he can no longer construct himself as subject without apprehending himself as object. His desire to look at himself and to be looked at is a mark of both the separation that he feels from his material being and his desire to know himself in that being. No longer able to present his body as a sign of his subjectivity, his health, his fitness, Olds's father loses control of both the visible surfaces that would announce his embodied presence and the interpretive system that allows others to read him through his body.

In directing his daughter's look, Olds's father appropriates her vision to reclaim his status as subject of the gaze as well as its object. Forced in "The Waiting" to know himself as the object of a gaze that rendered him as artifact, Olds's father here attempts to direct and participate in the look that he cannot avoid. As he pushes his wasting torso into the line of his daughter's gaze, the father violates the conventions of decorum to implicate himself in his body; his "rueful smile" and "cast-up eyes" signify the bemused uneasiness with which he reveals the unfamiliar object that his body has become. In inviting his daughter's "interested" gaze, Olds's father asks her to share in his own fascinated and uneasy response to a body that is both his and not his; his distance from a body transformed by illness allows him, along with his daughter, to marvel at its presence even as his discomfort registers "the lifting" as an act of exposure.

In commanding his daughter's gaze, Olds's father cultivates the distance of her look as a means of negotiating the gap that he experiences between his presence as body and as embodied subject. If the experience of the person with terminal illness is defined by the ever-present body, the epistemology of sight is trapped within a material dynamic that accesses subjectivity only through the visible aspects of that body. As long as the gaze sees as its object a diseased body but not the diseased person's experience of embodiment, the look only perpetuates the dislocation experienced by the person with terminal illness. In cultivating his daughter's look, Olds's father asks her not to reverse the process of the medical gaze that Foucault describes but to redefine its dynamics. He asks her not to see him in spite of his illness—abstracting the illness out of the subject in the way that the medical gaze might abstract the patient out of the body—but rather to locate him in his unfamiliar body without reducing him to it.

The experience of illness denaturalizes the body that had come to signify Olds's father's identity, rendering that body unfamiliar and disconnected at the very moment that it asserts its presence as absolute. The person with terminal illness experiences the fissure that opens up between the body and the embodied subject as a gap that may blur distinctions not only between subject and body but between one subject and another, between one body and another. Entrapped within a changing body which he can no longer recognize as an essential manifestation of his subjective presence, Olds's father looks along with her at a body that both may claim but which necessarily belongs to neither. As his tumors grow larger and more visible and his body grows gaunter and more unfamiliar, Olds's father finds himself absolutely connected to a body that seems as alien to him as the body of a distant relative, an old woman, a friend.

If illness exposes the contingency of the subject's relationship to the body, it also renders malleable the problematic subject/object dynamics of the gaze. Like the patient in Broyard's essay who holds the hand of his doctor as both look at the diseased body, Olds's father serves as both subject and object of his own look. In recognizing that his connection to the dying material body is inessential but absolutely determining, Olds's father gives up the claim to agency that often accompanies the assertion of subjectivity. At the same time, however, the father's admission that his body fails to speak for, signify, and enact his will as subject leads to a new flexibility that also allows him to defy the status of pure object.

In this poem, the power dynamics of looking that depend upon the distance between subject and object begin to dissolve, along with the perceived essential connection between subjects and bodies, opening up the possibility of using the gaze as a means of forging new connections rather than asserting difference.[6] As he draws her look onto his wasting torso, Olds's father becomes the subject of the look as well as its object; as she confronts his starkly naked form, she finds herself written there as well:

> Right away
> I saw how much his hips are like mine,
> the long, white angles, and then
> how much his pelvis is shaped like my daughter's,
> a chambered whelk-shell hollowed out,
> I saw the folds of skin like something
> poured, a thick batter, I saw
> the rueful smile, the cast-up eyes as he
> shows me his old body, he knows
> I will be interested, he knows I will find him
> appealing. If anyone had ever told me
> I would sit by him and he would pull up his nightie
> and I would look at him, at his naked body,
> at the thick bud of his penis in all that
> dark hair, look at him
> in affection and uneasy wonder
> I would not have believed it. (ll. 13–29)

If the power of the viewing subject depends upon pleasure in looking and mastery over the object of the gaze, the speaker in Olds's poem finds herself disempowered; when her father commands the look and directs it onto his dying body, Olds sees her mortality rather than her desire mirrored in the object of the gaze. Caught unaware, Olds is the subject of a look that is not preformulated, distanced, or empowered; in a flash of recognition, she sees her father stripped down almost to his bones and finds those bones shockingly familiar. As illness wears away at her father's flesh, what remains is not the stark sign of essential sexual difference but the long angles of hips that the speaker compares to her own and the shared curve of a pelvis "shaped like my daughter's, / a chambered whelk-shell hollowed out."

Gaylyn Studlar's *In the Realm of Pleasure* (1988), her study of the masochistic aesthetic in film, explores the way that an object can function as a subject; she traces the disruption of a mastering vision to the presence of characters in film who return the look of the audience, who become subjects of the gaze themselves. In *The Father*, the subject of the gaze identifies herself with its object; as Olds recognizes the continuity between her body and her father's, her sympathetic look undermines the distance that underlies the process of objectification. In finding herself in her father's emaciated body, Olds claims that body for him; embracing his bones, she locates herself in this almost-skeleton, resignifying the materiality that threatens to erupt from within as a mark of the link between father and daughter and a sign of shared mortality. Olds's gaze penetrates the changing surfaces of her father's body to unearth a sameness, a continuity invisible even to him; in acknowledging connection rather than maintaining separation, her form of visual essentialism locates identity in a body that seems to speak difference to the very person who experiences his world through and in it.

This poem, then, offers a version of the look that Mary Ann Doane has defined in another context as "the female gaze." In "The Clinical Eye: Medical Discourses in the 'Woman's Film' of the 1940s," Doane describes a form of "female spectatorship" that aligns women's way of looking with an apparent excess of emotion, sentiment, and empathy:

> From this perspective, the female gaze exhibits, in contrast to male distance, a proximity to the image which is the mark of over-identification and hence, of a heightened sympathy. But the concept of sympathy is a physiological one as well, of particular interest to the female subject. The meaning of "sympathy" in physiology and pathology is, the Oxford English Dictionary tells us, "a relation between two bodily organs or parts (or between two persons) such

that disorder, or any condition, of the one induces a corresponding condition in the other." Sympathy connotes a process of contagion within the body, or between bodies, an instantaneous communication and affinity. . . . Unable to negotiate the distance which is a prerequisite to desire and its displacements, the female spectator is always, in some sense, constituted as a hysteric. (1985, 172)

The medical films that Doane addresses encourage the female spectator to reject a sympathetic, "feminine" way of looking in favor of a "masculine" clinical gaze; the woman who fails to do so is diagnosed with "the paradigmatic female disease" of hysteria, a disease characterized, in Doane's formulation, by a body so completely in sympathy with a psyche that there is no differentiation between them.

If the medical films that Doane describes are constructed to contain the female spectator's "over-identification" and "heightened sympathy" with the object of the gaze, in "The Lifting" Olds expresses the radical consequences of the sympathetic look. In this poem, the "process of contagion . . . between bodies" manifests itself in the dissolution of distance between the healthy subject and her diseased counterpart, the female looker and the male object of the gaze. Because Olds's look claims a connection with her father's emaciated body, she is able to gaze with "uneasy wonder" not only at her father's naked form but "at the thick bud of his penis in all that / dark hair" (26). Although Olds transgresses cultural norms that would prohibit a grown daughter from looking at her father's genitalia, her identification with her father's dying body emerges as a much more dangerous consequence of the act of looking than any incestuous desire. Having exposed herself to the contagion of mortality, Olds, like Doane's female spectator, finds herself moved out of a cycle of desire and displacement predicated upon the distance of the gaze. If the danger of female looking is contained, as Doane argues, in the diagnosis of hysteria, a disease in which there is no differentiation between body and psyche, the radical potential of sympathetic looking is realized here in a gaze that intertwines bodies and psyches so thoroughly that the subject/object dynamics of looking are undermined. Although critics like Bedient read Olds's sympathy as a form of sexual hysteria culminating in her "ghoulish, erotic death-watch of her father" (Bedient 1993, 169), what emerges as truly radical is the motion of this poem away from the erotic power dynamics of the gaze and into a form of looking as subjective intermingling.

In "The Last Day," Olds finds herself confronted once again with the sight of her father's naked, wasting body. This time, however, her father's motion toward the purely material is exaggerated by his lapse into unconsciousness. Literally unable to present or obscure himself before the look, Olds's father becomes the object not only of the medical gaze but of his daughter's penetrating stare. As Olds gazes unchecked into her father's open mouth, the reader registers with forceful immediacy the intimacy of looking:

> The daylight was shining into his mouth,
> I could see a flake, upright, a limbless
> figure, on his tongue, shudder with each
> breath. The sides of his tongue were dotted with
> ovals of mucus like discs of soft ivory,
> I sat and gazed into his mouth. (ll. 25–30)

Having lost all power to control or direct the look, Olds's father collapses into a body violable in its slackness. The powerful light that shines into his mouth, rendering every oval of mucus and drop of spittle visible to the eye, highlights the extent to which he is unable to arrange himself before the look. The potential horror of such exposure emerges in Olds's image of the limbless figure perched upright on her father's tongue, denied any language but an inarticulate shudder.

In looking at her father, Olds carries on his wish to look at himself. She turns to the gaze in an attempt to place her father, to locate him in the unfamiliar matter of his dying body: "I sat and gazed into his mouth, I had / never understood and I did not / understand it now, the body and the spirit" (ll. 30–32). Unwilling to discard the body before her as a mere shell of a spirit soon to be liberated, Olds keeps her vigil by turning into her father's body, penetrating past its surfaces into mucous and saliva. Matter issuing from the orifices of the body, in Mary's Douglas's words, emerges as "marginal stuff of the most obvious kind. Spittle, blood, milk, urine, faeces or tears by simply issuing forth have traversed the boundary of the body" (1969, 121). As her father's unconscious form challenges Olds's sympathetic gaze, her look forces past the boundaries of her father's body, moving closer and closer to the "physiological" concept of sympathy that Doane describes as "a process of contagion . . . between bodies" (172). Although Olds perceives her father's body at its most abject and encroaching, she allows her gaze to be pulled in and, in Doane's terms, infected by his embodied mortality.[7]

In the final moments of her father's dying, then, Olds's gaze emerges as increasingly embodied. Having given up the strict separation of subject and object that would allow her to declare her difference and her distance from her father's dying body—to "extricate" herself, in Kristeva's terms—

Olds "stay[s] bent" before him, varying her posture and repositioning her own body to accommodate the object of her gaze. Although she does not inhabit the ailing body that frames her father's every breath, her identification with him emerges when the source of her gaze is unveiled; whereas in "The Waiting" the father "would wait with that burnished, looked-at look" for his daughter's gaze, here it is Olds who "wait[s] and wait[s] for the next breath," her own vision trapped in the material origin of a cramped body. Having seen herself in her father's dying body, Olds sacrifices a gaze that objectifies and masters for an embodied look that is no more omniscient than she is immortal.

Olds responds to the nurse's silent announcement of her father's death by literally abolishing the distance between her body and his: "I put my head on the bed beside him / and breathed and he did not breathe, I breathed and / breathed and he darkened and lay there, / my father" (ll. 63–66). Despite her physical proximity to her father, Olds is thrust further and further away from him; the gap between her living body and his silent form expands with each of her breaths. When her imaginative merging with her father collapses under the force of his silent breathlessness, Olds is thrust back into her own pulsing body; for the first time, Olds's father emerges as the object that he has figuratively threatened to become throughout the volume.

If her gaze contributed to her father's objectification in the opening poem of the volume, the concluding lines of the poem recounting his death show Olds turning to the gaze as a means of locating her father in the inanimate form before her. When she turns to her father's lifeless body, Olds's look is less a distanced, detached gaze than a touch, a caress:

> I laid my hand on his chest
> and I looked at him, at his eyelashes
> and the pores of his skin, cracks in his lips,
> dark rose-red inside the mouth,
> springing hair deep in his nose, I
> moved his head to set it straight on the pillow,
> it moved so easily, and his ear,
> gently crushed for the last hour,
> unfolded in the air. (ll. 66–74)

In a reversal of the conventional dynamics of the gaze, Olds uses the act of looking to negotiate the distance that physical closeness has exaggerated. Vision approaches tangible form as her gaze fills the gaps and sutures the wounds of the body's surface. In an earlier poem, "Last Acts," Olds describes her desire to wash her father's face before he dies, to enter along with the cloth she holds the dips and valleys of his pores as a way of pushing past the boundaries between them. This poem recasts that act of touching as a look; in doing so, it challenges assumptions about the dynamics of looking articulated by Irigaray in her argument about the gaze: "[The gaze] sets at a distance, maintains the distance. In our culture, the predominance of the look over smell, taste, touch, hearing, has brought about an impoverishment of bodily relations" (Stam 1989, 159). Olds never eschews the gaze's focus on the body's surface to find another epistemological entry into her father's being; instead, her own gaze risks the intimacy of embodiment to overcome the "impoverishment of bodily relations" that Irigaray connects with the distance of the look. As Olds's penetrating gaze enters the cracks in her father's lips and the pores of his skin, she responds to the margins of his body not as contaminating surfaces but as points of material and emotional interface. Physical proximity yields distance whereas the kind of intimacy that Olds renders elsewhere in erotic terms surfaces here in the gaze.

As Olds looks at her father's lifeless body, the manipulative dynamics of the gaze are literalized in her ability to arrange and rearrange the pliant form before her. The gaze that in "The Waiting" reduces the speaker's living father to an artifact of her creation, however, here accesses the father's inanimate body through the frame of his absent agency. If seeing is always a form of creating, Olds's creation in this poem garners its authority not from her desire but from her father's. His body has literally become an object that she manipulates, but she has earned the right to do so; as she moves his head to set it straight on the pillow, she images her act as restoration rather than creation: "his ear, / gently crushed for the last hour, / unfolded in the air" (ll. 72–74). The body that Olds rearranges as text is one that she owns exactly because she has owned up to it, one in which she can locate her father because she has located herself in it.

Sympathetic Seeing

In an excerpt from his journal, Anatole Broyard observes, "What a critically ill person needs above all is to be understood. Dying is a misunderstanding you have to get straightened out before you go. And you can't be understood, your situation can't be appreciated, until your family and friends, staring at you with an embarrassed love, know—with an intimate, absolute knowledge—what your illness is like" (1992, 67). Broyard's formulation of the sympathetic gaze as an "embarrassed" stare reflects the way that the death-watch both invokes and unsettles the dynamics of looking. Olds's discomfort as her father thrusts his naked body before her eyes reveals the consequences of the kind of look that Broyard invites here; the viewing subject experiences such a look as intrusive rather than distancing, as disturbing rather than empowering. If the erotic gaze sometimes lends the viewing subject intimate access to the object of desire, seeing the person with terminal illness may result in a form of uncomfortable intimacy that implicates the viewer in the experience of mortality. Broyard's description of the "embarrassed" look acknowledges the inherent difficulties of such sympathetic seeing but calls for a viewer who "stares" through such embarrassment with an unflinching, directed gaze. Such an "embarrassed" stare expresses both power and powerlessness, interest and fear, discomfort and affection. Bridging the gap between the dying and the living must involve such a radical and almost contradictory unsettling of power relations; if the look is to become a means of restoring rather than disrupting connection, the viewing subject must sacrifice the distance and autonomy of the healthy gaze by refusing the empowerment of extrication. As the death-watch becomes a means of locating the presence of the embodied subject in the dying body it dissolves the subject/object dynamics of the gaze until the healthy subject is forced to acknowledge its own mortality and the watcher becomes the watched.

CHAPTER TWO

☙

Haunted Images

Seeing AIDS

The enormous controversy generated by photographs of people with AIDS is largely due to the weighty burden of signification that such photographs carry. In addressing photographs of people with AIDS not only as individual portraits but as representations, cultural critics have begun to analyze the way such pictures reflect the conditions of their construction and create specific social effects even as they figure individual subjects.[1] Although medical advances continue to extend the life expectancy of HIV and AIDS patients, the cultural horror that AIDS has generated remains tied to its status as a terminal illness from which none of us can be guaranteed protection. The communicable threat of AIDS stems not merely from the physiological possibilities of contagion but from its construction as a gay illness and its status as an exaggerated and sometimes threateningly visible marker of shared mortality. In exploring photographs of people with AIDS in the context of a discussion of unveiling the dying body, I hope not to obscure the specific manifestations of this illness and the politics of sexual identity that necessarily accompany it,[2] but to think about the way representations of people with AIDS render visible codes of health and illness which often mediate our perceptions of embodiment in the context of death.

The vexed dynamics of signification that always underlie the camera's construction of subjectivity through visual codes and material objects including the human body are exaggerated when that body must be depicted as marked or unmarked by the signs of impending death. In the years immediately following widespread awareness of the existence of AIDS as an identifiable medical condition, the fight to develop a cure for the virus was accompanied almost immediately by a struggle over questions of how best to represent its impact in human terms. Almost all of the intellectual discourse surrounding AIDS for the first decade of the epidemic, Thomas Yingling argues, focused on one goal: "to secure a subjectivity for the person with AIDS that was not simply an erasure of his or her previous subjectivity, that did not simply read the illness as the end of meaning" (Yingling 1997, 22). In photography, Billy Howard's *Epitaphs for the Living: Words and Images in the Time of AIDS* (1989) and Nicholas Nixon's *People with AIDS* (1991) constitute two of the earliest and most influential responses to that representational dilemma.[3] In their often opposing responses to the question of how to picture people with AIDS, these two works function to initiate a continuing dialogue about representation's role in exposing the tensions of embodied subjectivity at the borders of life and death without contributing to the distorting and disempowering dynamics of disease.

If representations of the dying body reduce people with AIDS to powerlessness and obscure the potential for *living* with AIDS, photographs that consistently depict people with AIDS as untouched by illness may represent a qualified affirmation that celebrates subjective presence only by erasing signs of bodily vulnerability. Photographers like Howard resist the implications of cultural constructions of AIDS that reduce people with AIDS to anonymous markers of their own impending death. While Howard thus consciously erases the visible signs of AIDS-related illness from his subjects's portraits, Nixon unveils the dying bodies of his subjects in intimate detail. If the subjects of Howard's collection emerge as "normal-looking people who happen to be dying of AIDS" (Howard 1989, xii), Nixon's photographs capture subjects unavoidably marked by the process of physical degeneration. In forcibly directing the viewer's gaze onto the dying body, Nixon would push viewers to acknowledge and confront their own discomfort in the face of mortality. The collections of both photographers authorize their representational choices by obscuring the artifice of their method and approach to exempt themselves from the charge of manipulation. Howard's introduction describes his work as "forgoing manipulative images of horrific suffering" (xii), whereas Nixon's attempt to present his images as capturing the "baldest of truths" (viii) is accepted by critics who describe his photographs as "translucent . . . largely without any obvious stylistic inflections that would divert our attention from the subject to the photograph itself" (Grundberg 1990, 209). Although their representations reflect opposing assumptions, the images of both Howard and Nixon remain haunted by the tensions of embodied subjectivity that accompany the experience of living with and dying from AIDS. In this chapter, I aim not to offer a prescription for successful representation but to expose the way the photographs of Howard and Nixon construct their subjects by invoking a series of representational codes and viewing conventions that naturalize unspoken conclusions about cultural norms of health and disease.[4]

The bodies depicted in photographs of people with AIDS are often already the material sites on which contested subjectivity is negotiated and renegotiated. In *The Body in Pain,* Elaine Scarry defines the dynamics through which extreme pain pins the suffering subject to a body that overwhelms the outer world and the inner self until that "increasingly palpable" body appears to subsume all else (1985, 30). For the person with end-stage AIDS, the physical form that once seemed to function as a material extension of subjective presence is often recast as a prison that limits and restricts the expression of desire. In such circumstances, negotiating the experience of embodiment also involves renegotiating the relationship between body and subjectivity. As I explore in chapter 1, terminal illness disrupts the healthy subject's experience of a familiar body as the material incarnation of identity. As illness denaturalizes the subject's experience of embodiment and self-identification, it exaggerates the object status of the ailing body not only for onlookers who may reduce the person with AIDS to the visible signs of impending death but for the embodied subject, a subject whose physical form emerges as increasingly inescapable even as it becomes progressively unfamiliar.

For the person with AIDS, then, the attempt to define subjectivity often emerges as a delicate negotiation between two conflicting and simultaneous experiences of the body. As the body's transformation by disease renders it alien to the very subject whose presence it would seem to signify, it constantly and painfully asserts its undeniable connection to the suffering self. James Dawes echoes Scarry's analysis of pain's effects in his descriptions of the embodied subject's experience of AIDS: "As corporeality is increasingly foregrounded during the course of the disease (feel my sweat, look at my fingers), one's sphere of consciousness shrinks (feel my sweat, look at my fingers) until the ultimate preoccupation with the body (feel my sweat, look at my fingers) traps the self within the confines of one's own skin" (Dawes 1995, 33). The subject that would know itself in—and in spite of—such a physical form can neither deny the presence of the diseased body nor affirm its essential signifying power; as illness reduces subjectivity to the experience of embodiment that Scarry describes, it simultaneously disrupts the essentialized relationship between body and self naturalized by culture and experience.

Insofar as it poses a threat to the healthy subject's sustained illusion of stability, terminal illness is always communicable. Contact with the dying forces us to acknowledge shared mortality and threatens to collapse boundaries between death and life, illness and health, the dying body and its apparently healthy counterpart.[5] In her discussion of the abject, Julia Kristeva theorizes that living is predicated upon a subject's ability to "permanently thrust aside" the ever encroaching markers of a death that menaces the self not only from without but from within (Kristeva 1982, 3). Describing the way that the abject encroaches on the psychic border that separates life from death, Kristeva concludes, "My body extricates itself, as being alive, from that border" (Kristeva 1982, 3). The physiological possibility of transmitting AIDS lends form and justification to what Kristeva exposes as the infectious threat of all mortality. Representations that unveil the suffering bodies of people with AIDS may force the viewer into contact with a communicable horror that must be controlled and contained if the viewing subject is to forestall acknowledgment of a threat that may undermine the construction of his or her own embodied identity.

The limitations of visual epistemology that shape the viewer's response to photographic representations of people with AIDS thus exaggerate an already existing tendency to preserve the self by constructing impenetrable boundaries between life and death. The epistemology of vision upon which photography relies is trapped within a material dynamic that accesses subjectivity only through the visible aspects of the body. In rendering the embodied subject object of the gaze, photography may collaborate with the effects of a cultural and medical gaze that reduces the person with AIDS to his or her illness. "The cultural logic of AIDS," in the words of James Dawes, "transforms the body into a sign. Identity is flattened out, reduced to an exposed surface" (36). Insofar as photography renders the subject as its surface, it ignores the body's function as a multiple sign system to produce an interpretive construction disguised as concrete vision. When a body bears the visible signs of AIDS, the image may contribute to a cultural imaginary which reduces the subject's identity to the fact of its impending and communicable mortality. Roland Barthes describes the referential operation of all photography in terms that expose its potential to exaggerate representationally the destructive dynamics of a cultural logic that equates people with AIDS with their suffering bodies: "It is as if the Photograph always carries its referent with itself, both affected by the same amorous or funereal immobility, at the very heart of the moving world: they are glued together, limb by limb, like the condemned man and the corpse in certain tortures . . ." (Barthes 1981, 59–60). If the body with AIDS often delimits the embodied subject's experience of the world, photographic representations of people with AIDS may perpetuate that violence by "gluing" the subject they represent to the corpse-like figure the photograph images. Barthes's metaphor points to the way the visual epistemology of photography seems to limit its potential to resist both the experiential dynamics of the disease and the kind of cultural assumptions that reduce people with AIDS to objectified Others. In *The Threshold of the Visible World*, Kaja Silverman posits an alternative model for understanding the representational politics of visual culture, a model that relies upon the metaphor of bodily representation as a removable cloak: "We need visual texts which activate in us the capacity to idealize bodies which diverge as widely as possible both from ourselves and from the cultural norm. Those representations should also be ones which do not at the same time work to naturalize the end result of that psychic activity in a way that might be ultimately productive simply of new, reified ideals. The bodily representations which I am imagining here are ones that would not so much incarnate ideality as wear it, like a removable cloak" (Silverman 1996, 37). In the context of extreme illness and pain, neither Silverman's metaphor of body as removable cloak nor Barthes's formulation of a visible body "glued" to a subject would seem to speak adequately to the complexities of representing people with AIDS. In the pages that follow, I explore how photographic representations of people with AIDS struggle to negotiate the vexed relationship between physical form and embodied subject through a visual dynamic that accesses and constructs knowledge through images of the body.

Billy Howard's *Epitaphs for the Living*

Billy Howard's *Epitaphs for the Living* responds to photography's tendency to reduce the subject to its visual (and therefore bodily) image by constructing the bodies that it "reveals" as markers of health and subjectivity. Reprinted beneath Howard's portrait of each subject is a facsimile of a hand-written text authored by the person with AIDS in each photograph;[6] one such commentary, by David Brewster, points the reader/viewer toward the absences in the visual text that it glosses:

> Thank you, Billy, for a beautiful photograph. It's how I want to be remembered; happy, attractive, self satisfied and content with life. But in many ways the photo doesn't look like me. * It doesn't show the K.S. lesions growing on my face and body. * It doesn't show that I am half blind * It doesn't show the fact that I've had 3 bouts of Pneumocystis pneumonia in the past year and a

half * It doesn't show the fear I've have [*sic*] of what may happen to my health either tomorrow or 6 months down the road. * It doesn't show the sadness. . . . (22)

David Brewster begins by enumerating the visual marks of illness that are touched up or covered over in Howard's photograph; his cataloging of the physical effects of AIDS, however, collapses into an unveiling of the emotions connected with his experience of the disease. Brewster's written gloss of the photograph reveals that its visual construction of him as a healthy person carries with it a series of assumptions which relegate his experience as an embodied subject (as well as the visual signs of AIDS) off-frame.[7] The literal act of veiling that this photograph performs exposes the necessarily manipulative techniques that make camera work a form of cultural work and the photographic frame a space in which reality is constructed beneath the viewer's gaze.[8]

Because Howard "spares us the clinical details of cadaverous bodies and diseased skin, of medical paraphernalia and fouled bed linens often associated with end-stage AIDS" (Howard 1985, xii), his photographs resist collapsing the identity of all people with AIDS into a single representation of a skeletal, lesioned Other (in contemporary photographs, Grundberg claims, "emaciation has become emblematic of AIDS" [1990, 208]). The individuals in Howard's photographs assert their subjective presence in the context of postures, backgrounds, and compositional strategies as diverse as they are. The cost of liberating all people with AIDS from a visual frame that signifies disease, however, may be unacceptably high. In visually disavowing the objectification of the person with AIDS—his or her reduction to a suffering body marked only by the physical signs that have emerged as emblematic of AIDS—Howard risks affirming subjectivity only insofar as it is disembodied. The experience of living with—and dying from—AIDS, as David Brewster's comments affirm, is an experience that involves the continuous renegotiation of embodied subjectivity.

The difficulty of such renegotiation stems in part from the way critical illness heightens the tensions of embodied subjectivity by defamiliarizing and denaturalizing a body that overwhelmingly asserts its presence. If, as Elaine Scarry argues, intense pain destroys the world and confuses the very distinction of inside and outside,[9] patients with end-stage AIDS may struggle to reconcile the inescapable intimacy and alterity of the body. The tension between identification with and alienation from a familiar, unfamiliar body defines the construction of embodied subjectivity in the face of terminal illness not as a theoretical endeavor but as a series of postural, sensory, and psychic accommodations. Such accommodations are made even more difficult by the cultural coding of the visual signs of AIDS.[10] Although the erasure of Brewster's K.S. lesions in his portrait assists him in relocating his old, familiar body, it does so at the expense of acknowledging his personal and public experience of the disease. The photographic return to a body, a visual text that refers to his existence as subject without signifying the presence of AIDS, represents not only a contingent affirmation of Brewster's subjectivity but—in some important ways—reference to a different subject altogether.

Although Howard's photographs succeed in avoiding the reduction of subject to object or person to body, they accomplish that goal not by re-signifying the material signs of AIDS within the context of embodied subjectivity but by pushing them out of the photographic frame entirely. Brewster's written text represents one attempt to restore what is marginalized in these pictures, to construct a more radical claim of subjective presence in the context of an embodiment not wholly "beautiful." The tensions that his comments point to also emerge in several of the photographs themselves, as what is glossed over, pushed off-frame, asserts its presence to haunt Howard's life-affirming images.

Because the reality that haunts Howard's photographs is nothing less than death itself, the photographs function in much the same way that Freud's fetish functions;[11] they emerge as the presence that draws our attention away from absence, an absence that Freud described as the fear of castration but that I would also associate with the fear of death itself. In formulating "a notion of anxiety not based on sexual difference," Elisabeth Bronfen reworks Freudian theories to focus on the threat of mortality, which she describes as "a more global and non-individuated disempowerment before death" (Bronfen 1992, 35). In shifting away from a critical framework that highlights the operation of sexual difference, Bronfen exposes the possibility that the loss the fetish protects against is not only symbolic castration but death. In his discussion of photography, death, and the fetish, Christian Metz calls attention to the way the photograph functions, like the fetish, as an object that "always combines a double and contradictory function" (1985, 86); it occupies the place of a terrifying absence even as it is haunted by the displaced threat it would obscure. The off-frame space of the photograph exists only as it is invented, imagined, or in Metz's term "hallucinated" by a viewer for whom it remains "an irreversible absence" (87):

> The spectator has no empirical knowledge of the contents of the off-frame, but at the same time cannot help imagining some off-frame, hallucinating

FIGURE 1

it, dreaming the shape of this emptiness. It is a projective off-frame . . . with no remaining print. Yet nevertheless present, striking, properly fascinating (or hypnotic)—insisting on its status *as excluded* by the force of its absence *inside* the rectangle of paper, which reminds us of the feeling of lack in the Freudian theory of the fetish. . . . the photograph, inexhaustible reserve of strength and anxiety, shares, as we see, many properties of the fetish. (87)

If Howard's images exaggerate the fetishistic potential of still photography by glossing over the visual signs of dying written on the body of the person with AIDS, his photographs remain haunted by the very realities which they exclude.

Howard's portrait of an anonymous subject (Figure 1) functions, like many of his pictures, to exaggerate the motionless quality of the still photograph. Elegantly dressed yet caught in what seems a deliberately casual pose—sleeves rolled up to reveal a gold watchband, elbow leaning casually against a couch—the subject of Howard's photo partakes not only of a conventional pose but of the dreamy good looks of an American actor or model. Placed at the edge of the frame in a shot that centers on a pristine white couch, the man's formalized good looks render him almost invisible to a viewer/consumer used to "seeing" his or her desires reflected through the mediation of catalog models whose conventional handsomeness marks a type of capitalist transparency. This man's blond hair, clear complexion, straight nose, and square jaw signify a physical type that is naturalized by (white middle-class male) conventions of beauty that may also be read by the viewer as conventions of health.[12] As an object of the gaze, the "model" in Howard's photograph makes the viewing experience comfortable; his familiar looks, carefully pressed clothing, and relaxed pose help to construct an aesthetically and compositionally neat picture the subject of which is granted a kind of visual anonymity that extends to the absence of any signs of AIDS. "Marked" only by his placement in a collection of photographs of people with AIDS, the subject of this photograph is accessed visually through his status as a signifier of cultural norms of attractiveness. The photograph's refusal to disrupt visual convention in favor of a motion toward specificity is exaggerated by its construction of the viewer's gaze; the gaze of the photographic subject intersects the line of the viewing field and thus prohibits even the most basic "exchange" of looks with the viewer. This subject's anonymous presence reflects the extent to which visual conventions return the gaze to the viewer unchallenged, while the violation of such conventions forces attention upon the disruptive Other with threatening specificity.

If "the clinical details and diseased skin" (Howard 1989, xii) that Howard seeks to spare the viewer are pushed clearly off-frame in this photograph, the spectator's hallucination of absent horror[13] is granted a rare form of visual presence in the smaller photograph (positioned "off-frame" on the opposite page) that "haunts" the primary image of this subject (Figure 2). Whereas the vast majority of portraits in the collection stand solitary, opposite a blank page, a few are glossed by smaller photographs that serve almost as footnotes to the primary image. In this case, the marginalized image both enacts and portrays the way in which the photograph, the subject, the fetish, are "undermined and haunted" (Metz 1985, 87) by the approach of death.

In this smaller photographic gloss, Howard's subject reappears wearing the same clothing and accessories, his hair carefully styled, his gaze directed forward although still away from the viewer's. This time, however, he is encircled by another figure who embraces him from behind, leaning into his body and resting his head on the blond man's shoulder. The second figure is marked by both his similarity and his utter difference. Although his attire clearly echoes that of his companion (down to the details of his rolled-up shirt sleeves and expensive-looking watch), this man's body disrupts both "the look" that his attire would seem to imply and the gaze

Haunted Images

FIGURE 2

that the viewer directs upon him. Marked by a gaunt face, a chin obscured by an untrimmed growth of beard, and eyes sunken and ringed with dark circles, this shadowy figure seems as much a fabrication of the viewer's hallucinatory vision as a concrete presence; although his hollowed-out eyes stare directly at the viewer, forcing him or her to confront the presence of death, the man whom he embraces seems utterly unaware of his presence. Maintaining a dreamy look and model-like pose, the first man fails to respond to or acknowledge the touch of the other; instead, his relaxed posture directs our gaze down the length of his arms and out of the frame to the point where his own hands would meet to clasp one another. If the model-like figure is formalized—sculpted so successfully to the pattern of cultural codes of visual attractiveness that he almost disappears as an individual body—the skeletal grip of his lover enforces a material, bodily claim that can be read in the context of AIDS as both sexuality and death. Whereas the stylized form of the first subject emerges initially as pristine—reflecting but in no real way intermingling with the viewer's gaze—the shadowy figure that embraces him forces its way into the frame to "contaminate" our earlier vision.

In the introduction to *Death and Representation*, Sarah Goodwin and Elisabeth Bronfen extend Baudrillard's argument that social survival depends on a prohibition against death: "People . . . accrue power and control by manipulating and legislating death: by breaking any unity between life and death, disrupting any exchange between the two, and imposing a taboo on the dead" (1993, 17). The sexually communicable nature of AIDS renders it disruptive not only to the fetishistic qualities of the photograph but to any attempt to establish solid borders between life and death. The attempt to disavow anxiety about death by positioning it off-frame is frustrated by the way the threat of AIDS creeps into the shadows of Howard's photographs, blurring the introduction's visual distinctions between "the clinical details of cadaverous bodies and diseased skin" and "normal-looking people who happen to be dying of AIDS" (Howard 1989, xii).[14] The dialogue between these two images testifies to the way in which the "place of presence and fullness" (Metz 1985, 87) that constitutes the photographic in-frame fails ultimately to maintain immunity against the absence that haunts it.

In one of the few photographs of the collection that does reveal an individual marked by the visible signs of illness, the dying body once again shares a frame with an apparently healthy physical form. Howard's portrait of "Danny" (Figure 3) is shot looking into a hospital room. As in Figure 1, the eye is drawn across the picture toward the light of two windows revealing a distant natural scene; this time, however, in order to access that way out of the frame, the viewer's gaze must literally traverse the bent, pajamaed legs of the photograph's subject, whose body and hospital bed cut horizontally across the photograph. In this picture, unlike most in this collection, the person with AIDS does not conspire with the photographer to arrange himself before the camera. Instead, he stares with half-closed lids at the wall opposite, his eyes directed not toward the single object—a cross—that hangs there, but well below it, focused (if at all) on a bare wall and blank space. His arm encircled by a hospital bracelet rather than a gold watch, his hand covered with the tape that attaches his IV tubing, Danny disrupts not only the viewer's access to the natural world outside his window, but any illusions of pleasure that accompany conventions of viewing generated in a culture that almost always positions death off-frame.

For viewers steeped in a culture of visual commodification, Danny's mottled face and disheveled hair reflect an unsettling refusal—or inability—to arrange himself before the camera. In this photograph, Danny's body is marked in a way that disrupts the formalized language of portraiture convention and forces acknowledgment of a vulnerability to death that the viewer shares with the object of the gaze. As Danny huddles in the hospi-

Haunted Images 51

FIGURE 3

tal bed, his knees drawn up and his shoulders propped by pillows, his posture contrasts sharply with the formalized pose of many of Howard's subjects; the viewer's gaze collapses onto the breaks of form marked by the gaping exposure of Danny's pale stomach and the expanse of ankle and thin calf revealed by the hike in his pants.

When the still photograph traps the threat of mortality in its frame, the boundaries of the picture cease to offer protection against loss and function instead to imprison the viewer in an uncomfortable space. Howard's photograph not only makes the viewer's gaze uncomfortable but reflects upon the dynamics that render it so. Even as it invokes the viewer's anxiety, the photograph inscribes that anxiety within its frame through the presence of a second figure that embodies the viewer's presence in the scene. Positioned before the window, the second man directs his gaze not at the visibly ill body in the hospital bed but out the window onto the distant, hazy landscape. Although we can assume some measure of sympathy or connection through the very presence of this visitor in the hospital room, the photograph captures him looking out and away; for the viewer, whose only means of negotiating the photograph is through the gaze, the look of this man projects a desire to move away from the sick body on the

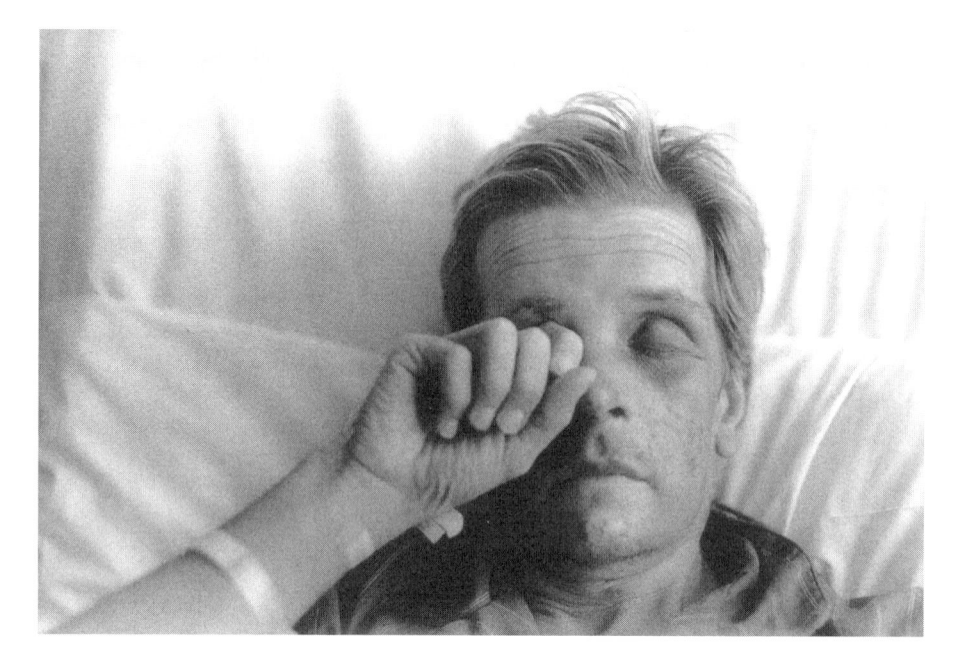

FIGURE 4

bed, outside the hospital room and—indeed—out of the frame of the photograph itself. The second figure thus inscribes within the frame the viewer's sense of being "trapped" by the person with AIDS; the horizontal positioning of the bed that forces the viewer's gaze across the diseased body even on its way "out" the window literally blocks the exit of Danny's visitor from the room.

The smaller photograph that glosses this visual text (Figure 4) functions to expose even the consolations that Howard's primary "portrait" of Danny offers. The photographic gloss disrupts the mediating effects of the larger photograph through a close-up shot that forces the viewer's gaze onto Danny's face. Unlike the larger photograph, this close-up fails to offer the gaze a way through or past death; the window that in the earlier picture points to an escape route disappears in this shrunken frame. The visual complexity of the central photograph—the composition of which offers the viewer a number of focusing options—is reduced here both by the diminishment of the frame and by the stark white pillows that provide the only backdrop for Danny's body. As the larger world that invites the gaze outside the hospital room is erased, the viewer's look is forced into an uncomfortable photographic space. In this place of "presence and fullness," the vague mottling of Danny's skin assumes the more distinct form of lesions on his face; while he rubs one eye with a hand trailing bandage adhesive, the other closed eye looms large before us, sunken into Danny's face and ringed by black, its lid heavy and swollen.

Although the majority of Howard's photographs function to push the threat of death off-frame, the intrusion of the visibly ill human body into the photographs I have discussed raises questions about the way the gaze "reads" certain postures, facial features, and poses as signifiers not only of physical attractiveness but of health. If visual coding renders the desirable body present only as convention, its form a reflective surface that returns the desire of the viewer, those same codes lend a degree of invisibility to the body unmarked by visual signs of illness. The conventions of viewing that Howard appropriates perpetuate a norm of "healthiness" that is exposed through the presence of the visibly ill bodies that rarely surface in the collection but that haunt all of its photographs. In presenting us with "normal-looking people who happen to be dying of AIDS," Howard's collection strives to celebrate the lives of its subjects; in sparing the viewer "the clinical details of cadaverous bodies and diseased skin," however, the collection renders its affirmations contingent, at least tacitly contributing to the reinscription of visual codes and conventions that enforce norms of health at the expense of acknowledging the subjective presence of those who are critically ill or dying.

Nicholas Nixon's *People with AIDS*

Nicholas Nixon's *People with AIDS* self-consciously restores the physical marks of dying that Howard's collection pushes off-frame. Whereas Howard's book offers one or at the most two photographs of each of his healthy-looking subjects, Nixon's pictures chronicle the process of dying, tracing his subjects from an appearance of apparent health to their last days of life. The narrative organization of Nixon's photographs—which are arranged chronologically and marked by date—functions to counteract the very qualities of photography that Metz describes as fetishistic. "The archive," Alan Trachtenberg observes in his discussion of another collection of images, "empowers the image, but specifically by depriving it of its traditional powers as picture, as a unique formal event occurring within an enframed space" (Trachtenberg 1989, 5). As Nixon's portrait series extends the frame of his individual photographs to take us into time, it also motions toward acknowledging the disruptive presence of death through its focus on bodies marked increasingly by the visual signs of end-stage AIDS.

If Howard's collection works to make the gaze comfortable, Nixon's strips away almost all the pleasures of viewing. His photographs are constructed to violate the visual codes that help to constitute conventions of health and "normalcy"; as he directs the viewer's gaze onto the gaunt, lesioned body of a person hospitalized with AIDS or looks down from the camera at the cloudy (once expressive) eyes of a man gone blind from the disease, Nixon forces the viewer to acknowledge the impossibility of seeing the person with AIDS without recognizing the physical consequences of the disease. Speaking of the collection's subjects, Bebe Nixon states, "These 15 people embraced us. They allowed two strangers into their lives who wanted to see and hear the baldest of truths, and who wanted to do this not once, but repeatedly" (Nixon 1991, viii). Nixon clearly views his enterprise as a kind of visual unveiling that will force the viewer—by showing what AIDS "can do to those who have it"—to "see why it is the most devastating social and medical issue of our time" (vii).

One early response to Nixon's work locates its radical innovation in its ability to push past the formalized, posed portraits that occupy much of Howard's collection. Nixon's pictures, according to Andy Grundberg, "chronicle both the visible signs of the progress of the disease and the inner torment it creates. The result is overwhelming, since one sees not only the wasting away of the flesh . . . but also the gradual dimming of the subjects' ability to compose themselves for the camera. What in each series begins as a conventional effort to pose for a picture ends in a kind of abandon" (Grundberg 1990, 208). The collapse of the subjects' ability to pose for others leads eventually to their inability to "compose themselves"; the physical pressures of dying from AIDS make it increasingly difficult for Nixon's subjects to construct a coherent image of themselves through the medium of their bodies.

Insofar as Nixon's photographs document both "the wasting away of the flesh" and the "gradual dimming of the subjects' ability to compose themselves for the camera," they capture the increasing restrictions of embodiment that often define the experience of dying from AIDS. In *Camera Lucida*, Barthes describes the pose as a means of projecting an alternative body for the camera: "I constitute myself in the process of 'posing,' I instantaneously make another body for myself" (1981, 10). The freedom that Barthes alludes to in the pose (a freedom that he introduces as a weapon to counteract the reductive referentiality of the photograph) is a freedom that is stripped away from Nixon's subjects before the viewer's eyes. At the very moment when their bodies are most present, most uncomfortable, and least familiar to them, the flexibility to reconstitute themselves and their images by presenting "other bodies" to the camera disappears. Nixon's subjects are imaged as absolutely implicated in their bodies even as—indeed, because—those bodies cease to enact the demands of agency. In losing the ability to pose, the person dying of AIDS sacrifices not only the ability to rearrange limbs and adopt changing expressions but the very ability to manipulate the interpretive codes that control the body's signifying functions.

With a single exception, each group of portraits in *People with AIDS* is structured by a master narrative that begins with a "healthy" portrait of Nixon's subject and ends with reference to his or her death. The initial portrait reflects the individuality of its subject in various ways; Tom Moran smiles straight into the camera, exposing his crooked teeth unself-consciously; Bob Sappenfield, a Ph.D. candidate at Harvard, pauses in front of an academic building, his thick glasses slipping down his nose; Paul Fowler gazes pensively into the distance, one side of his body bathed in sunlight. As viewers, we tend to read the bodies in these photographs for their hints of subjective presence. As each visual narrative unfolds, however, the body's referential system operates primarily in negative terms; the bodies of people with AIDS become, in the words of James Dawes, "the involuntary narratives of the illness within" (Dawes 1995, 36). When the visual signs that we were encouraged to read as marks of individuality are stripped away and replaced with signs of impending death, the photographs document their subjects' collapse into a kind of horrific anonymity.

Certainly to some extent the viewer's inability to effect visual differentiation is explained by what emerges in contemporary American culture as a strikingly unfamiliar sight; having seen so few people in the final days of terminal illness, many viewers may find their naive vision overwhelmed by a shared Otherness constituted in reaction to the assumed visual conventions of health. Physiological factors captured by the camera lens also contribute to the blurring of distinctions among these portraits of the dying; unlike many illnesses, AIDS is associated with symptoms that often register its presence on the body's surface. As the K.S. lesions that cover many of Nixon's subjects literally obscure their faces, individual features are often reshaped and replaced by an emaciated profile that emphasizes structural similarity rather than individual difference. Part of Nixon's challenge as a photographer, then, is to find a way to represent bodies marked by AIDS such that they signify not just impending bodily absence but the presence of embodied subjectivity.

Although Nixon accomplishes this in some photographs, his collection may also invite the viewer's gaze to settle almost too easily on the dying body; Nixon's photographs are sometimes paralyzed by what Barthes describes as the "funereal immobility" that glues the photographic subject to

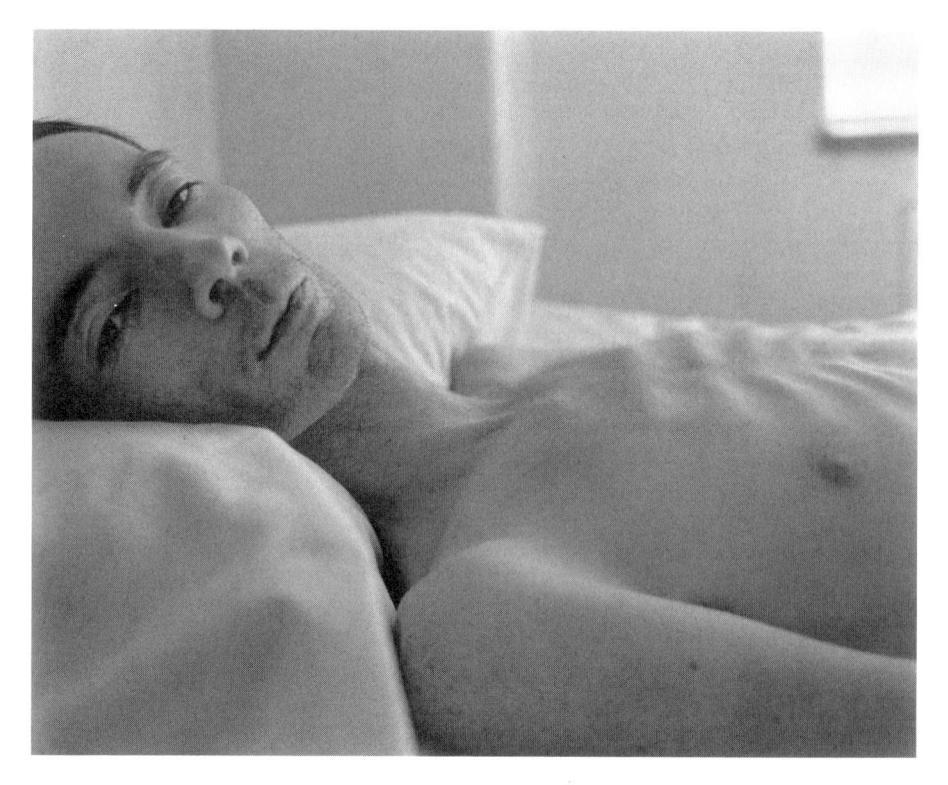

FIGURE 5

its visual image. If *People with AIDS* successfully disrupts the fetishistic dynamics of the photograph, it also contributes to the perpetuation of a series of visual conventions that render the experience of dying from AIDS disturbingly knowable. Separate photographs of Tom Moran and Joey Brandon taken in the last month of their lives, for example, capture each emaciated young man dying of AIDS in a hospital setting (Figures 5 and 6). Shared illness, gender, and age contribute only partially to the similarities of Nixon's images of these men; his photographs frame the dying subject through a series of shared techniques that not only reflect but create the perception of sameness.[15] Taken from a camera close to body level, these shots are horizontal rather than vertical; they echo the convention of the head and torso portrait even as they manipulate it by showing bodies stretched out on hospital beds and naked from the waist up. If Nixon's subjects lose the ability to arrange themselves for the camera in this final stage of life, their stiff arrangement in these pictures reflects a pose not

Haunted Images

FIGURE 6

entirely of their own choosing. The heads of both men are propped up and turned toward the viewer's gaze; the arrangement of pillows and body parts elongates their necks to further stretch out their emaciated frames.[16] The top of both men's skulls, in a technique characteristic of Nixon's work, are cut off by the shots, while their naked arms and chests exaggerate the bones that press through their flesh. If Nixon's photographs work to unveil the visual codes of healthy bodies that our culture has helped to naturalize, the way in which photographs such as these construct the viewer's gaze may contribute to the perpetuation of visual conventions of dying.

As layers of fat and muscle wear away before the viewer's eyes, the dying bodies that emerge before Nixon's camera lens often collapse into one another. A photograph of Tom Moran bears striking similarity to a photograph of Donald Perham (Figures 7 and 8), not only because of the visual characteristics the men share but because of the formal composition of the two frames. In both shots, the photographer approaches his subject from

58   *The Dying Body*

FIGURE 7

behind to capture the strong curve of a protruding spine. Both subjects are positioned in the center of the frame; their spines occupy almost the whole length of the photograph as they angle to the viewer's left. Perham's hunched, emaciated form is shockingly skeletal; Moran's emaciation is less obvious but the photographer exaggerates it as he captures the bony outline of the hand that Moran holds in front of a sunlit window. The photograph, in both cases, bears an eerie resemblance to the X-ray.[17]

As in the earlier shots, a large part of this resemblance may be due to the leveling effects of a disease that reduces humans to mere outlines of their former physical selves. What Michael Shapiro describes as photography's tendency to "naturalize social practices" suggests, however, that the elisions of difference in Nixon's work are not solely the result of the collapse of physical distinctions among people dying of AIDS: "The rhetoric of the camera, which represents persons on the basis of their appearance, has the effect of tying human classificatory practices to something physi-

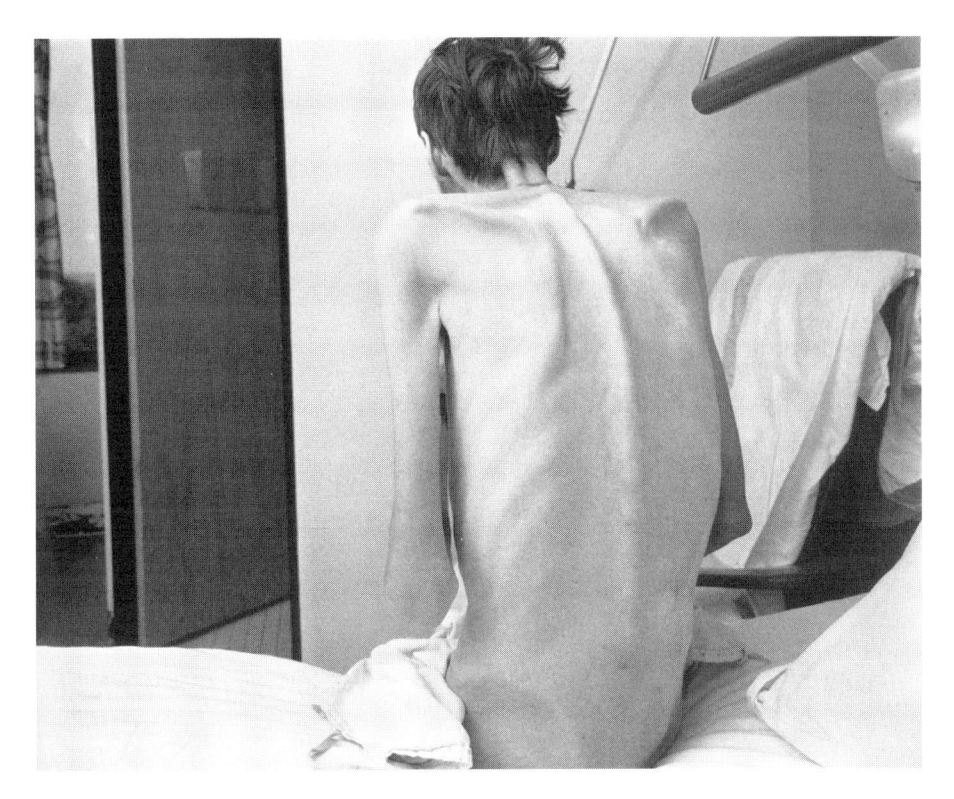

FIGURE 8

cally based and visually obvious. The systematic aspects of the camera work—angle of vision, degree of close-up, pose, and facial expressions—produce the impression that the subjects themselves are responsible for all of the appearance of sameness within classifications" (Shapiro 1988, 153). If Nixon's attempts to penetrate past the visual conventions of health are radical, the tendency of some of his photographs to collapse individual difference in favor of a formalized image of those dying from AIDS simply reinscribes cultural assumptions of Otherness in a different forum. The photographer's choice of frames, camera angles, and positioning of subjects contributes to "the appearance of sameness" among individuals dying from AIDS even as his photographs seem to authorize such categorization through the "visually obvious" similarities of dying bodies.[18] The narrative structuring of each portrait series contributes to the elision of individual difference; although the initial portraits that Nixon offers of his subjects signify their subjective presence, those portraits also function as landmarks against which the erosion of that presence can be measured and through which the subject can be held "responsible" for his or her sudden inability to signify anything but impending absence.[19]

In many of Nixon's revealing photographs of people dying from AIDS, the reality bracketed out by images that seem to reveal all is not a covered body part waiting to be unveiled but a reference to the *experience* of embodied subjectivity. As long as the gaze sees as its object a diseased body but not the diseased person's experience of embodiment, the look only perpetuates the experience of dislocation. If the material body is to render "visible" the subjective presence of the person with AIDS, it must be marked not only with the signs of a disease that often obscures the body's most familiar landmarks but with the marks of each individual's attempt to negotiate the construction of subjectivity under the increasing pressures of embodiment. Without at least some reference to these tensions, photographs of people with AIDS cannot help but construct a "knowledge" of the disease that collapses into a series of visual conventions and cultural stereotypes more dangerous than any admission of ignorance. In his description of entering the AIDS ward of Shattuck Chronic Care Hospital, a state-run long-term care facility, Mark Doty explores the enforced anonymity of a space that constructs the identity of its inhabitants only in terms of the illness they share. The men who emerge as objects of the visitor's gaze "have in common the absence of context: no personal effects, no clothes, pictures, no flowers, nothing that says, *This is who I was*. I use the past tense deliberately, since these men are already far along in the process of being erased. . . . It's the ultimate disconnection; our things, our family, our friends, our attachments to life are what expose and externalize identity. Without them, we become these narrowed and diminished faces. How small the body looks like this, with nothing to extend its limits, stripped of intimacy" (Doty 1996, 86). Insofar as Nixon's photographic techniques increase the viewer's proximity to the dying body without establishing the viewer's intimacy with the embodied subject, his photographs, like the institutional spaces in which they are often set, risk perpetuating a dynamics of erasure that enforces a symbolic distance. Photographic representations of AIDS thus render more immediate questions about visual culture's ability to overcome the limits of a visual epistemology, questions articulated usefully by Kaja Silverman in *The Threshold of the Visible World*: "The issue, then, is not merely how we might be textually encouraged to confer ideality upon the face and lineaments of another, but how, through discursively 'implanted' memories, we might be given the psychic wherewithal to participate in the desires, struggles, and sufferings

Haunted Images 61

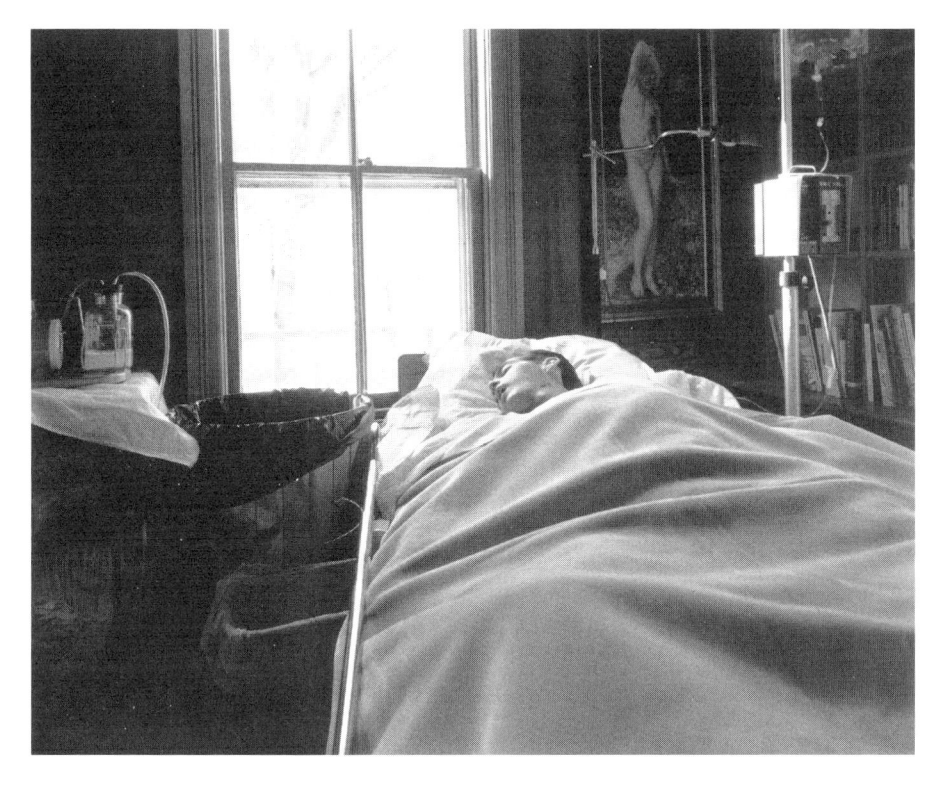

FIGURE 9

of the other, and to do so in a way which redounds to his or her, rather than to our own, 'credit'" (1996, 185).

Nixon's final photograph of George Gannett (Figure 9) points toward one possible means of "discursively 'implant[ing]' memories" or "animating" photographs in which the dying subject's body is completely overwhelmed by the presence of disease. This picture, taken from the foot of George Gannett's bed in the final days of his life, clearly signifies the imminence of his death. The raised metal bar on the bed in which Gannett lies sleeping or unconscious, his mouth gaping open, testifies to his lack of agency, as do the pieces of medical apparatus on either side of the frame (an IV pole, a bottle of liquid attached to plastic tubing that could be a catheter) and the garbage receptacles (one kitchen-sized trash basket next to an industrial-sized garbage can filled with a large plastic liner) placed anomalously close to Gannett's face.

The objects that surround Gannett and literally bracket the viewer's perception of him, however, exist in tension with other objects in the room that extend his subjective presence in material terms. The IV pole to the right of the bed stands in front of a wooden bookshelf filled with books, many of them leather-bound. As the long line of Gannett's bed leads the gaze up the length of his blanketed body toward his face, another body extends the vertical plane that draws the viewer into the picture; a rectangular frame positioned behind the bed directs the gaze past Gannett to focus on a naked figure that poses playfully before our look. The tension between the two bodies in this photograph—the painted figure we assume that Gannett purchased and displayed versus the covered form that he "owns" in a more immediate sense—brings us back to Barthes's understanding of the pose. If as "I constitute myself in the process of 'posing,' I instantaneously make another body for myself," Gannett's literal inability to control the signifying function of his diseased body in this photograph is mitigated to some extent by the visual presence of the "body" that he has chosen to display. In permitting death access into its frame, this Nixon photograph nonetheless gestures toward an animating subjectivity that emerges through what Silverman describes as "discursively 'implanted' memories." In this image, Nixon combats the "funereal immobility" which Barthes describes as gluing the photographic image to its referent by lending the photographic subject an "incarnate identity" worn, in Silverman's phrase, "like a removable cloak." Using in-frame space to motion toward all that is excluded, this photograph triggers the viewer's imagination to push past the limitations of a strictly visual epistemology.

The complexity of this photograph results from the aesthetic context that Nixon creates for his subject as well as the literal context in which the photographer finds him. In this image, Nixon alters the techniques and camera angles familiar from so many of his close-up, head-cropped shots of the dying to readjust his focus on a body now some distance from the camera. Because it sacrifices visual proximity, the image risks erasing the immediacy of the dying body. The photographer compensates for that shift by illuminating—using the light from the window and the bold white pillow—the sight of Gannett's gaping mouth and scarred neck. Although Gannett's closed eyes are turned away from the viewer and the rest of his body is obscured by a blanket pulled tight on every side, the viewer's eye reaches the image's focal point only by traveling the length of the body. As the eye moves along the constricted lines of Gannett's covered body—a body literally trapped by the taut linens pulled tight against its contours and tucked under the rail of his sickbed—the creases and uneven mounds formed by the body's press against blankets disrupt the eye's smooth traversal of the covered form. The bed covers may prevent us from gazing on

Gannett's wasted body, but they do not hide its uneven, unavoidable materiality, pushing up and out beneath them. Indeed, the covers uncover for us Gannett's experience of being bound by his body, his inability to move past it (or with it) into the extended space that figures his subjectivity. By suspending the dying body in the space of the embodied subject, the image reveals the self's "diminishment" in the face of illness even as it works representationally to "extend [the body's] limits" (Doty 1996, 86); it gestures toward the existence of a larger world now relegated—by the composition of the image and the experience of illness—to shadowy presence.

In the narrow space between Gannett's head and the painting on the wall stands an ultramodern lamp with a metal-topped pole that intersects at a right angle with a metal arm. Visually parallel to the IV pole positioned in front of it (even down to the cord that echoes the IV tubing and a short metal appendage at the top of the pole), at first glance this lamp seems like another piece of medical apparatus. Turned off and turned away from both Gannett's face and the painting on the wall, the function of this object (is it a physician's examining lamp? a display light meant to illuminate the painting behind it?) remains ambiguous. Insofar as the light could pivot in several directions, it marks the very different yet ultimately connected focuses of a photograph that potentially illuminates both a body that Gannett has chosen to display and a form that defines him in his illness. Because the subject that suffers from the devastating effects of AIDS exists both in the dying body and in spite of it, photographic representations of such subjects must continually invent ways of subverting visual conventions—not only those that code the unmarked body as "healthy," but those which would transcend the embodied dynamics of subjectivity or reduce the representational subject to an unfamiliar object the subject would choose to disavow.

CHAPTER THREE

☙

The Body in the Waiting Room

"Empty" Spaces

Although recent cultural criticism explores the stresses and fissures created when an embodied subject negotiates economic, political, and geographical landscapes,[1] the normative body such criticism posits is most often a body that is healthy, functional, and stable. In interrogating the assumptions associated with the "normal" body, critics working in the relatively new field of disability studies have begun to problematize conceptions of the body that construct it as a seamless whole, an unfragmented entity that mirrors and guarantees individual autonomy.[2] The need to regulate, control, and contain the disabled body, Lennard Davis argues in *Enforcing Normalcy*, results in a tendency to divide bodies into "two immutable categories: whole and incomplete, abled and disabled, normal and abnormal, functional and dysfunctional" (1995, 129).

The medical waiting room, I will argue, serves as a space in which the cultural categories Davis describes as "immutable" are fraught, contested, or blurred. In "The Ghost of Embodiment," Edward Casey observes, "Of course, material conditions and cultural formations meet in many places: buildings, works of art, technology. But only in the meeting-place of the living-moving body do they undergo such dynamic interaction" (1997, 214). What Casey describes as the "living-moving" status of the body is simultaneously endangered and revealed in the medical waiting room, a space that threatens mobility and mortality by assigning its inhabitants a body that is symbolically—and often biologically—impaired. If our culture functions in part by defining the body as a malleable extension of subjectivity and policing the public presentation of bodies to obscure signs of potential difference, the medical waiting room represents a rare space in which the otherwise private fact of illness or imminent death is put on public display.

In exposing the body to view in the context of its imperilment by mortality, the waiting room also "exposes" its inhabitants to what Julia Kristeva describes as the threat of the abject, of "death infecting life" (Kristeva 1982, 4). The medical waiting room uncovers the body's vulnerability to illness and injury along a continuum that ranges from the physical—the amputated leg of a diabetic or the visible tremors of a patient's hand in the neurologist's office—to the symbolic—the threat of serious illness that shadows even the most routine mammogram or colonoscopy. My interest in the medical waiting room, then, results in part from its tendency to collapse the physical and symbolic boundaries between death and life, illness and health, the infected body and its apparently healthy counterpart. As it thrusts into view that which the subject "permanently thrust[s] aside in order to live" (Kristeva 1982, 3), the waiting room both enforces and unveils cultural assumptions about subjectivity, productivity, and health that govern our understanding of our own embodiment.

Critical analyses of the waiting room are, not surprisingly, almost nonexistent. Katharine Young's recent study, *Presence in the Flesh: The Body in Medicine,* touches briefly on the significance of the waiting room in its spatial inventory of the transformations subjects undergo as they gradually move from the identity of "person" to that of "patient." Young locates the transformations she describes in the examining room, on the operating table, and even written on the scars that track the surgeon's passage across a patient's body. The medical waiting room, however, is largely exempt from her scrutiny; she describes it only as the place in which "persons *await* realm-shift, and *await,* too, the cues that tell them when to shift realms" (1997, 17; emphases mine). In moving through the waiting room with great speed, Young's book seems implicitly to reinscribe the purely formal function of a space that resists analysis because it seems to lack content.

Young's willingness to move hurriedly through the waiting room in the course of her otherwise comprehensive analysis of medical spaces may reflect the invisible force with which this liminal space simultaneously asserts its marginality and enforces its symbolic practices. A waiting room, by definition, functions as a place we pass through on the way to somewhere else, a temporary stop rather than a destination. By and large, time spent in a waiting room represents time wasted; the shorter the wait, the more successful our stay. Because it is a place in which, it would seem, nothing important happens, the waiting room holds us only briefly before it sends us on to spaces more visibly marked by content.

As I will argue here, however, the apparently "empty" space of the medical waiting room serves as a cultural stage on which many of our most important assumptions about illness and the body are rendered visible. Although the body always structures our relationship to space, the medical waiting room serves as a place where we are immobilized in and as our bodies. Our physical containment in the waiting room and the material threat of illness or disability that brings us to such a space are coupled with symbolic assaults on productivity and subjectivity that render us symbolically if not physically disabled. The body's capacity to move through space is crucial to the illusion of autonomy and self-determination that, in Rosemarie Thomson's words, "underpins the fantasy of absolute able-bodiedness" that our culture constructs and perpetuates (Thomson 1997, 46). As it immobilizes our bodies, suspends the narrative movement of time, and appropriates the motion of looking to implicate the viewer as object of a self-reflexive gaze, the medical waiting room not only constrains bodily motion and signification but strips us of the strategic forms of cultural resistance that we have erected to keep the vulnerability of the body at bay. In the space of the waiting room, what Thomson describes as "the opposing subject positions of the intensely embodied, reified, and silenced object and the abstract, unmarked, disembodied normate" (136) dissolve or commingle in a loss of wholeness from which—physical health aside—it may be difficult to recover.

Contemporary American fiction offers us fleeting glimpses into the medical waiting room, often positioning the reader in the holding pattern of that liminal space for only a paragraph or two before returning him or her to an unfolding plot. Insofar as literary representations of the medical waiting room collectively assume a limited amount of narrative space, they might appear to echo and reinforce the waiting room's status as a place with no content or substance. Instead, I will argue, these necessarily brief forays into the waiting room testify to the impossibility of "living" in a space that—in literal and symbolic terms—inhibits motion, productivity, and narrative progression. Because it demands that its inhabitants temporarily suspend their participation in lived experience, the medical waiting room functions as a space apart in both experiential and critical terms. As it denaturalizes cultural constructions of health, productivity, and narrative, this space allows us to glimpse assumptions about embodiment and normality that define our understanding of ourselves inside and outside the waiting room.

This chapter begins with a brief narrative of my experience of a specific medical waiting room and moves out to address a series of contemporary literary representations of similar spaces. The literary excerpts that I discuss here—taken from fiction by Eudora Welty, Susan Kenney, Jane Hamilton, Lorrie Moore, Mary Morris, and others—were chosen because they creatively and often succinctly raise critical issues that might, I hope, be applied to medical waiting rooms and their representations in other cultural spaces and literary texts. In moving so easily between "real" space and its representational counterpart, I aim not to deny important distinctions between the two, but to turn to literary representation as a means of accessing shared cultural anxieties about space and embodiment that are no less "real" because they are expressed in literary form.

Johnnies and Handbags

My own interest in medical waiting rooms began a few years ago when I found myself, while a patient at a Boston area Breast Center, moved from a tastefully furnished outer waiting area into another waiting room. Inhabited almost entirely by women in hospital johnnies waiting for mammograms, ultrasounds, or biopsies, that "inner" waiting room with its bare-bones decor of chairs, women's bodies, and magazines threw into relief dynamics less visible in the softly lit public space of an outer waiting room furnished with antique reproductions. In this room, neither public nor private space but a strange conflation of the two, strangers sat stiffly beside one another in rows, clutching the tops of gowns that threatened constantly to open. Handbags—large and small, leather, vinyl, scuffed, shiny—perched on laps. In the corner, one gowned woman cried silently, while another stared straight ahead as a friend in street clothes traced circles on the same endless path across her back. A thin woman with very short hair shuffled through a bulging briefcase in search of a missing paper. In the row across from me, a middle-aged woman knitted something blue. Occasionally, someone broke the silence with a general comment or nervous laughter. In the intervals between speech, the muffled voices of children playing at a daycare center filtered through the closed windows.

The sound of nurses' clogs on the Formica floor preceded each announcement of a patient's name. As she was called, each woman rose, one hand for her purse, one to hold the gown, and scurried to keep up. The contrast between tops and bottoms would have been funny in a different place. The patterned hospital johnny clashed wildly with one woman's tailored houndstooth trousers, became an ill-fitting housedress at odds with the sleek, black stockinged legs and high heels of another. In the conclusion of her study on the body in medicine, Katharine Young reformulates the traditional mind/body problem, claiming, "The proper contrast is not mind/body but 'body-as-self'/'body-as-object'" (136). If, as Young argues, we must denaturalize the concept of body-as-object that medicine promotes by recognizing it as a specialized inflection imparted to the body by a specific discourse, this waiting room points to the subject's difficulty negotiating a position from the location of a body that continues to signify the self even as it is signified as object. The striking contrast between tops and bottoms here renders visible the tensions of embodied subjectivity that emerge with the threat of objectification in all medical waiting rooms. The women who clutched gowns with one hand and purses with another could no longer choose how to hold themselves; as they twisted and hunched to defend their privacy and their possessions, their bodies seemed fragmented and disorganized, objects they owned but could not quite control.

The medical waiting room is marked by literal and symbolic assaults on autonomy; the individual's ability to control the body's signification is threatened both by awareness of the body's status as the real or potential location of illness and by the stripping away of the subject's ability to direct the body's action and presentation. This waiting room disallowed any successful attempt to establish personal territory through the kind of purposeful posture and motion that occurs so easily even in crowded locker rooms or transit waiting areas. Trapped in this space together, our bodies were awkwardly, uncomfortably, nervously limited by the waiting room's place in medical protocol, and by the waiting room itself. The necessarily faulty fit of the hospital johnny (designed not to assume the shape of the individual body it covers but to facilitate the exposure of the body to medical scrutiny) and the rigid organization of the chairs combined with a communal vulnerability to the threat of illness to enforce an odd mix of intimacy and discomfort. As the cramped lines of narrow rows facing one another made it hard not to look, women buried their heads in magazines or stared blankly at walls to avoid directing their gaze at the awkwardly wrapped bodies of others. New codes of body language had to be improvised to effect even the illusion of privacy or self-containment in such an absurdly atypical public space. Unlike the inhabitants of a home or public building, or even any waiting room in an airport or bank, we had been *placed*—physically fixed by a room that effectively immobilized us in and as our bodies.

Literary Representations of the Medical Waiting Room

Michel de Certeau's *The Practice of Everyday Life* suggests that the theoretical "message" of any space can be modified, resisted, or appropriated by the individual who inhabits or experiences it. De Certeau's theory of resistance is based on the distinction he draws between "place" and "space." Whereas the concept of "place" implies a stable configuration of positions,

> a *space* exists when one takes into consideration vectors of direction, velocities, and time variables. Thus space is composed of intersections of mobile elements. It is in a sense accentuated by the ensemble of movements deployed within it. Space occurs as the effect produced by the operations that orient it, situate it, temporalize it, and make it function in a polyvalent unity of conflictual programs or contractual proximities. On this view, in relation to place, space is like the word when it is spoken, that is, when it is caught in the ambiguity of an actualization. . . . In short, *space is a practiced place.* (1984, 117)

If, as de Certeau argues, the "ensemble of movements" deployed by individuals negotiating a certain area undermines the theoretical stability associated with "place," the configurations of the waiting room cannot completely dictate an individual's experience of that room. If the "message" of the medical waiting room is one of bodily objectification and spatial entrapment, de Certeau's model would seem to imply the possibility of resisting the force of its spatial organization. Although such resistance is certainly possible, I will argue that the medical waiting room operates not only by constructing its inhabitants' experience of embodiment and space, but by appropriating, through its very structure and function, the potential resistance of its occupants.

In de Certeau's text, walking in the city serves as the primary example of resisting spatial organization. "The act of walking," he claims, "is to the urban system what the speech act is to language or to the statements uttered" (97). Defining walking as "a space of enunciation," he claims, "The long poem of walking manipulates spatial organizations, no matter how panoptic they may be: it is neither foreign to them (It can take place only within them) nor in conformity with them (It does not receive its identity from them). It creates shadows and ambiguities within them. It inserts multitudinous references and citations into them (social models, cultural mores, personal factors). Within them it is itself the effect of successive encounters and occasions that constantly alter it and make it the other's blazon" (101). In de Certeau's example, the motion of walking becomes a metaphor for and the literal means of negotiating a place; in walking through the city, we appropriate, individualize, and resist even the most panoptic spatial organizations. Choosing our own path through the immobile set up of buildings, roadways, and landmarks, we make the place of the city into a space that is at least partially our own.

If walking exemplifies an individual's ability to transform place into space, the literal difficulties of walking in the waiting room point to the way its spatial and functional construction seem to co-opt the individual's theoretical ability to unsettle the stability of place. Although it is by no means impossible to walk around or through a waiting room, the space itself is constructed specifically to inhibit movement, to hold the patient in place until such time as he or she is summoned into motion. In *Body, Memory, and Architecture,* Kent Bloomer and Charles Moore argue: "All architecture functions as a potential stimulus for movement, real or imagined. A building is an incitement to action, a stage for movement and interaction. It is one partner in dialogue with the body" (1977, 59). As the body waiting to be surveyed medically assumes an exaggerated and objectified presence, the waiting room functions less as a "stage for movement and interaction" than as a space of literal and symbolic containment. The experience of the body in the medical waiting room might be classified, in Bloomer and Moore's terms, as a "tight fit"; whereas a "loose fit" is defined by the fact that "the body has many places and options within the space" of a structure (71), the typical medical waiting room diminishes those options not only by holding the body in inactivity but by constructing the embodied subject as unproductive.

In Eudora Welty's *The Optimist's Daughter,* the literal difficulty of negotiating the obstacles of the medical waiting room—both objects and bodies imaged in object terms—largely dictates the path of the novel's protagonist as she walks around and around the room: "Laurel began walking, past this group and the others who were sprawled or sleeping in chairs and on couches, past the television screen where a pale-blue group of Westerners silently shot it out with one another, and as far as the door into the hall, where she stood for a minute looking at the clock in the wall above the elevators, then walked her circle again" (1972, 35–36). In this representation, distance traveled is not equivalent to progress made. Laurel's expulsion from the narrative world into the suspended space of waiting is figured not only in her circular path but in her frequent need to check the clock stationed just *outside* the room in which she paces, a clock that tenuously connects her to a world of temporal and narrative motion toward which her pacing wearily gestures.

Almost all medical waiting rooms limit the bodily configurations of their occupants, despite variations in furnishings and decor. Typically, rows of seats arranged back to back or in a large square firmly situate the bodies that occupy them in legislated spaces, discouraging motion. Although the waiting room is designed to move patients in an orderly fashion from one place to another, movement *within* its boundaries is almost always awkward. In *Sailing,* her novel about one man's attempt to negotiate life in the face of a diagnosis of terminal illness, Susan Kenney figures her protagonist's struggle for autonomy and self-determination as a struggle for mobility most visible in the contrast between the motion of sailing and the immobilization of waiting. Her representation of one tiny medical waiting room visited by the novel's protagonist, for example, points to the effect of the waiting room's "tight fit" on those who inhabit it: "The rest of the small space is waiting room with rows of seats bolted to the floor along the wall. Phil stands in front of the counter; a slight, white-haired woman presses her knees sideways against her seat to give him room" (1989, 99). The "bare-bones" construction of this room exposes the way the spatial organization of bodies determines the symbolic practices of waiting. In this space, patients must press against and past each other, their bodies meeting resistance as they settle into the harsh contours of the all-too-firmly bolted chairs. From every angle, this waiting room asserts the subject's containment in a body. As she twists her legs, pulling into herself, the "slight" woman attempts to retract her body from this space; neither her physical act nor the symbolic attempt at resistance it implies, however, deliver her successfully from a condition of vulnerable objectification.

The patient's heightened self-consciousness of her body in the medical waiting room reflects the literal and symbolic force of a place that contains bodies immobilized in anticipation of the medical scrutiny to come. In the Breast Center where I was a patient, the difficult transition from immobility to graceful motion was figured in the clumsy attempts of patients to keep up with the medical personnel who called them from their seats in the waiting room and briskly turned away; fumbling for belongings, rising on legs made stiff from sitting and clutching their hospital gowns to keep them from slipping open, women in johnnies and high heels stumbled toward procedures and examining rooms. In *The Fate of Place*, a work that uses Husserl's analysis of walking to describe how place is animated and rendered dynamic by human motion, Edward S. Casey observes, "I cannot walk at all if I am utterly disjoint; to walk is to draw my body together, at least provisionally; and to do so is to constitute myself as one coherent organism" (1997, 224). Casey's observation about the need to "draw [the] body together" in order to walk is borne out in the jarring disjunction between the tops and bottoms of women whose attempts to negotiate between constructions of "body-as-object" and "body-as-self" in the waiting room emerge as strikingly awkward. The kinesthetic feelings associated with the movements of the body as it walks, Casey argues, supply a sense of unity and coherence that contributes to an individual's experience of his or her own lived body: "My body, then, is *a body*—a sheerly physical entity—as well as a source of intentionality and projects, correlations and orientations" (227). In contrast to this definition of the "lived body," medicine's specialized inflection of the human form focuses attention on an object body that constantly threatens to disrupt the subject's experience of the self as "one coherent organism."

Thus, although the literal act of waiting—sitting quietly in one place—might seem to imply a form of physical stability, that stability is frequently experienced as a collapse into the powerlessness of pure object status. In Jane Hamilton's novel *A Map of the World*, the narrator waits for days in a hospital as the critically injured child of a friend hovers between life and death. Although she herself is not sick or injured, that period of waiting transforms her experience of her own body and her relationship to the object world around her:

> We sat in the lounge for two more nights and two more days.... We closed our eyes at night, leaning against each other, listening to the world move up and down the hall on wheels. The laundry baskets were on wheels, the scales, the I.V. poles, the respirators, the meal trays, the beds, the chairs, the dressers, the bedside tables. Nothing was rooted to the floor. The nurses seemed weightless, like birds, flying down the hall, their cushioned shoes barely touching the ground. (1994, 37–38)

In the medical space that Hamilton describes, both patients and those who wait for them are locked into immobility while the world around them is unsettled into motion. The architectural potential for inciting action and movement in individuals (Bloomer and Moore 1977) is turned upside down here as the whole *building* moves in order to keep the patient still. This representation points to the institutional means through which medicine takes apart a patient's life and sets the fragments in motion around his or her body. If walking represents the possibility of gathering an embodied self and negotiating space, the disjunction of that self is figured in the wheeled furniture, food, and medical equipment that can be detached and circulated endlessly between and around seemingly interchangeable patients.[3]

Although the patient's experience of waiting room and hospital room is clearly distinct from that of the healthy individuals who wait for and with their loved ones, Hamilton's representation of her narrator's rootedness in contrast to the mobile world flying by the lounge emphasizes the way the space of waiting successfully casts even its healthy occupants outside the world of time and reference. If, as Bloomer and Moore, Casey, and other critics have argued, the body functions as the means through which we enter into and negotiate space, the fact of the body's impairment would seem to define the experience of waiting for the person with injury or illness. Merleau-Ponty's work on the negotiation of space through bodies, however, offers one explanation for the parallels between patient and healthy companion that this representation offers. In Merleau-Ponty's analysis of space, the consciousness of one's own body dictates the construction of space, but with one crucial qualification: "What counts for the orientation of the spectacle is not my body as it in fact is, as a thing in objective space, but as a system of possible actions, a virtual body with its 'place' defined by its task and situation. My body is wherever there is something to be done" (Merleau-Ponty 1962, 249–250). Just as the patient's expulsion from the domestic world in Hamilton's text is marked by the inability to determine the body's path through kitchen, living room, and bath, the narrator's enforced inactivity in the waiting room thrusts her outside the world of motion, action, and lived possibility into a place that resists animation and a "virtual body" that is symbolically impaired.

More important than the literal difficulty of walking in the waiting room, then, is its frustration of our desire for action, accomplishment, and control. In *Illness and Self in Society*, Claudine Herzlich and Janine Pierret argue that illness in today's society is defined by the sick body's inability to move, perform, or act: "Impairment of motor and functional capacities, . . . reduced ability or incapacity to 'perform,' and the resulting enforced inactivity have today become the essential perceptions of the sick body. . . . In a society in which we define ourselves as producers, illness and inactivity have become equivalents" (1987, 85). In temporarily limiting the healthy body's ability to produce itself—to announce itself in a series of actions as productive—the waiting room symbolically "impairs" even its healthy occupants. Whether the threat of sickness is immediately located on one's own body or on the body of a loved one, the virtual body the medical waiting room assigns to all its inhabitants conspires with the debilitating powers of illness. In a room where, by definition, there is *nothing* to be done, even the healthy body can be experienced as painfully immobilized.[4]

Not surprisingly, then, the narrator of Hamilton's novel depicts the waiting room as a place that not only traps her in space—she is isolated from the experiential world by windowless and carpeted walls—but denies her access to the control and productivity she associates with work:

> In the hospital, in the lounge that had no windows, there was no signal to distinguish day from night. . . . Now and then, with the need to mark time, I listened for a change in the steady hum of the fluorescent lights. . . . When there was no fluctuation, I put my ear to the carpeted wall, straining for the

sound of crickets. . . . Time and seasons were for others, for bankers and bus drivers, teachers and storekeepers. We would wait. We would wait, hour after hour in the subzero maroon-and-blue enclosure, with a rubber plant for oxygen. (23)

In a series of acts that caricature the bodily engagement of the bus drivers and storekeepers outside, the narrator pushes her ear against the carpeted wall and strains to penetrate the monotonous hum of the fluorescent lights. Her forced attempt to place herself in the experiential world, however, emerges as no more successful than her effort to breathe from the rubber plant beside her. Like the women in the Breast Center waiting room who struggle to identify the muffled sounds of children playing just outside the windows of the room that holds them, Hamilton's narrator attempts to reclaim a connection with the referential world severed not only by the physical isolation of the waiting room but by its ability to reduce the "lived body" of a subject that works and plays to "a sheerly physical entity" (Casey 1997, 227).

Hamilton's representation of the waiting room also points to the way its inhabitants' experience of physical and symbolic immobilization often extends to an experience of suspension in time. Although time, by its nature, never stands still, our experience of its progression is tied to assumptions about how we "occupy" our time, whether it be in work, leisure, or even sleep. In this passage, time belongs to those who produce—"bankers and bus drivers, teachers and storekeepers"—while the narrator (like the character in Welty's novel who constantly leaves the waiting room to check the clock outside) tries and fails to "mark" its passage. The protagonist of Lorrie Moore's short story "People Like That Are the Only People Here: Canonical Babbling in Peed Onk" engages in a similar struggle to assume ownership of time in the hospital after her infant son is diagnosed with cancer. Surrounded by mothers clad in the same anonymous and functional sweatclothes, she resists the collapse of productivity, subjectivity, and narrative temporality that the loss of her "street clothes" would imply: "This is what the sweatpants are for. . . . In case the difference between day and night starts to dissolve, and there is no difference at all, so why pretend?" (1998, 231). If the narrative of a life is structured around a series of dialogues, experiences, and activities that make up everyday existence, waiting represents the consumption of time without the creation of plot. In the waiting room, the force of time not only structures but to some extent constitutes experience, so that the temporal form of existence temporarily becomes its content.

In her novel *The Waiting Room*, Mary Morris captures the sense of being defined by time while simultaneously being suspended from participation in lived experience through the image of the magazines her protagonist encounters in a hospital waiting room: "The magazines were tattered and worn and old. No surprises. No shockeroos. Just old news. What you already know. What you expected. Zoe picked up an old *Time*—circa Nixon's resignation—and pretended to be interested" (1989, 34). Although these magazines seem to promise a bridge to the narrative world outside the waiting room—a world in which individual, social, and political plots are captured as they unfold in the latest news updates—the "tattered and worn" publications ultimately emphasize the reader's exclusion from that world; as *Time* in the waiting room is emptied of its "news" function, "reading for the plot" loses much of its pleasure. Although the reader may feign interest in old stories, the act of thumbing through tattered magazines marks exclusion from a world in which new narratives are constructed and consumed.[5]

If plot functions, in Peter Brooks's terms, as "the organizing line, demarcating and diagramming that which was previously undifferentiated" (Brooks 1985, 12), the waiting room continually returns its inhabitants to an experience of undifferentiated time that resists being remade as plot. In Morris's narrative, the "activity" of waiting reduces all experience to the act of marking time: "A young man stared out the window, tapping a finger against the pane. A woman flipped the pages of a magazine at evenly spaced intervals of about one a second, so that Zoe knew the woman couldn't be reading, or perhaps even seeing, the page" (34). Zoe's analysis not only questions whether the woman she observes could possibly be processing the narrative content of the magazine she "reads," but also recasts what would otherwise be considered an activity of the imagination as the simple, metronomic experience of marking time. In this waiting room, plot collapses into an experience of time so forceful and immediate that it resists organization into narrative structures.

In framing sickness in terms of symbolic as well as literal productivity, Herzlich and Pierret point to cultural norms that legislate the construction of identity based on maintaining the seamless integrity of the embodied subject. In representation after representation, however, the waiting room emerges as a place in which "the knowing body" fragments into a series of connected but ineffectual pieces. If the literal difficulty of walking represents the body's inability to draw itself together and "constitute [the self] as one coherent organism" (Casey 1997, 224), the inability to read in the medical waiting room may be said to result from the mind's fraught connection to a body that continually disrupts the illusion of a coherent self. Despite the fact that waiting rooms are literally filled with reading material, the activity of reading in such spaces becomes oddly difficult: "Zoe decided to look occupied. She looked through the magazines piled on the end table near the sofa. *Time, Newsweek,* some home-decorating magazines, fashion magazines. Nothing to really sink your teeth into. Literature for those with a short wait. Or with little power of concentration" (Morris 1989, 34). The act of reading involves leaving the body behind to participate imaginatively in a text that constructs its reader as an intellectual subject; that freedom, however, is often least available to those who need it most. The "power of concentration" to which Morris refers is often measured by the ability to subsume the physical demands of the body; caught up in a good book, we read on past bedtime to emerge from our chair hungry and stiff. In the medical waiting room, however, even a short magazine article becomes difficult to concentrate on, distracted as we are by the tick tock of our own uncomfortable embodiment. Although the urge to "look occupied" that Morris describes emerges in part from a desire to recontextualize the objectified body through activity, the structure of the waiting room resists this strategy as efficiently as the structure of a gym or health club promotes it. Like the small woman in the Breast Center waiting room rummaging nervously through a huge briefcase in search of a missing document, we attempt to clutch onto our identities as "producers" even as they are symbolically misplaced in/by the waiting room.

Stripped of its ability to signify productivity or identity in the Breast Center waiting room, my "object" body assumed an unwieldy status exaggerated by the sharp angles of the room's stiffly arranged furniture. Neither the soft music nor the upholstered couches of the plushest medical waiting rooms, however, can successfully cushion the embodied self's collapse into a series of material parts uncomfortably and often self-consciously arranged in anticipation of their scrutiny by the medical gaze. In *The Birth of the Clinic* (1973), Foucault locates medicine's objectifying powers in a visual dynamic; by identifying the forces that dictate what a doctor does and does not see when looking at a patient, Foucault's volume explores the way in which the gaze is constructed in modern medicine. Contemporary disability theory also focuses on the disabled subject's involuntary status as object of the gaze.[6] As Rosemarie Thomson argues, "The disabled body is the object of the stare. If the male gaze makes the normative female a sexual spectacle, then the stare sculpts the disabled subject into a grotesque spectacle" (1997, 26). Defining disability as "a specular moment," Lennard Davis's *Enforcing Normalcy* demonstrates the influence of Foucault's work on contemporary disability theory as it examines "the power of the gaze to control, limit, and patrol the disabled person" (12).

In the same way that the space of the medical waiting room tests and exposes assumptions about the construction of embodied identity through motion, productivity, and narrative time, the waiting room also functions as a space in which visual dynamics that insist on objectifying and containing the disabled body are necessarily disrupted. In *Discipline and Punish,* Foucault describes the Panopticon as "a machine for dissociating the see/being seen dyad: in the peripheric ring, one is totally seen, without ever seeing; in the central tower, one sees everything without ever being seen" (1977, 201–202). The medical waiting room, however, destabilizes such panoptic models of the gaze by unsettling distinctions between seer and seen, subject and object, normal and abnormal. As it symbolically impairs all of its inhabitants, the waiting room disrupts the illusion of empowerment that the subject often experiences with the motion of the gaze.

In the space of waiting, the patient emerges as both subject and object of the gaze. The looking that occurs in the waiting room often assumes a diagnostic quality in which the bodies of others may become symptoms of what Casey refers to as the subject's "disjointed" self. The protagonist of R. S. Jones's novel *Walking on Air* cannot help but see the deteriorating bodies as well as the familiar faces of other AIDS patients that surround him in each return visit to his doctor's waiting room. As the "five or six patients who had been coming on the same day for more than a year" greeted each other, "their eyes would lock just long enough for a quick study of each slip and fall before they turned away" (1995, 59). In this space, the quickly averted gaze signals not only the looker's hesitancy about invading another's privacy, but his uncomfortable recognition that the bearer of the gaze can easily "slip and fall" into the object position: "William wondered if they, too, saw in each uneasy smile a reflection of their own disintegration, as if each human face had become a small, round mirror" (59). If the Panopticon enforces the "constant division between the normal and the abnormal" (Foucault 1977, 199) by dividing subjects into those who see and those who are seen, the waiting room mends that division through a process of seeing that turns the gaze into a mirror and collapses the distinction between the subject and the object of the look.

Surrounded by bodies marked by the visible assault of illness, William projects the experience of entrapment within his own diseased body onto the space around him, a space imaged as increasingly restrictive and even suffocating:

> Today almost everyone in the office looked pale with imminent death. The room was so crowded that William had to squeeze into an empty space beside the magazine rack.... Sometimes when he was alone, he grew tearful with gratitude for the community he shared with the other patients, but of-

> ten when he was there he felt entombed by their contagion, as if their every twitch and tremble made him vulnerable to another disease. (60)

In the waiting room, the embodied subject the reader has come to know as the novel's protagonist is nearly squeezed out by diseased bodies that prefigure William's eventual collapse into the final stages of terminal illness. Although the theoretical possibility of "community" with other AIDS patients exists, the waiting room thrusts William into a spectatorial relationship to the bodies of others;[7] the uneasy tension between his identification with and objectification of those around him leads to a kind of "looking" that implicates rather than empowers the spectator. Kristeva describes abjection as a revolt against a force that threatens from within as well as from without; the desire to distance the self from the abject is complicated by "the impression that it is not only an external menace but that it may menace us from inside" (Oliver 1993, 55). In the medical waiting room, the gaze that lingers on the abject bodies of others engages in a form of surveillance that is ultimately self-surveillance. Although Foucault stresses that the inmates of the Panopticon are "caught up in a power situation of which they are themselves the bearers" (Foucault 1977, 201), self-surveillance in the waiting room functions quite differently; the waiting room lends its inhabitants the "power" of seeing only to unsettle the subject/object split and disrupt the stability of their identity as viewing subjects. As the stability of a single coherent subject position is threatened by a body that is both self and object, internal and external menace, the seer is no longer exempted from the objectifying power dynamics of the gaze.

Although the experience of patients in a waiting room for the terminally ill offers perhaps the clearest example of self-reflexive looking, one of the most radical functions of the medical waiting room lies in its ability to disrupt the motion of even the healthy subject's gaze by turning it back onto the self. As the waiting room reveals, the lines that separate the whole body from its fragmented, disabled, or terminally ill counterpart are tenuous and erasable. If "the disabled body is always the reminder of the whole body about to come apart at the seams" (Davis 1995, 132), the medical waiting room functions as a space in which the "hallucination" of wholeness that we fight so desperately to construct cannot be maintained. Waiting in an airport or a theater lobby is seldom an intimate experience, no matter how crowded such spaces become, because these waiting areas support our public identities. We can comfortably speculate about the travel plans or romantic entanglements of the people seated next to us or jostling us in line because, like the film we are about to see, they are comfortably distant despite their physical proximity. In parallel fashion, the gaze of others also glides off us because we come to such spaces appareled in our own motility and productivity, comfortable in our wholeness. Although physically cramped, we fit loosely—to borrow Bloomer and Moore's terms—into these visual arenas.

In the intimate public space of the Breast Center waiting room, on the other hand, women held their heads at odd angles and fixed their gazes on distant points in a largely unsuccessful attempt to avoid seeing—and knowing—too much about those who waited with them. Patients returned from their mammograms and waited either to be released or to be re-scrutinized and diagnosed; as they waited, still in their hospital johnnies, their private stories became an unwelcome form of public property. An older woman with a persistently fixed smile and a shock of white hair was called back by nurses for the third time; as she rose stiffly from her chair, the rest of us found ourselves watching, exercising the "power" of a look that offered no pleasure. Although the flimsily tied hospital gown marked the site of the white-haired woman's vulnerability to the scrutiny of a public gaze that threatened to expose the contours of her body, the repeated visual marker of that distinctively patterned gown also signaled a collective susceptibility to illness and death not located on an individual body but diffused and projected throughout the waiting room.

The waiting room, then, complicates a dynamic of interpersonal looking that defines the bearer of the gaze as the potential violator of another individual's privacy by introducing the threat of a diagnostic gaze that reflects back on the seer. Immobilized by/in the waiting room and stripped of my ability to effect action or control bodily signification, I found myself forced into a kind of looking in which the women around me became targets of speculation as well as objects of the gaze. Just as "to wait" derives from "to watch," to "speculate" derives from "to spy"; the waiting room forces its inhabitants not just to look at one another but imaginatively to pry into the medical narratives of other bodies on display. Far from offering voyeuristic pleasure, such "spying" tantalizes the looker with a narrative of pain that she replays again and again as she waits, surrounded by bodies covered in interchangeable gowns, for her own chance to be seen. As the literal process of seeing collapses into the imaginative act of speculation, then, the gaze that might otherwise maintain the illusion of absolute distance between the subject and object of the look reveals itself as originating in a body. In the space of the waiting room, the distance that lends the gaze its power dissolves among a proliferation of identical hospital johnnies that mark each subject as object of the diagnostic gaze and render every look an act of self-surveillance.

If my analysis has begun to unveil the complexity of the medical waiting room as a cultural and representational space, it points also to the impossibility of unraveling the various threads of our experience there. Insofar as our experience of symbolic disempowerment in the waiting room frustrates the desire to split bodies into two "immutable" categories, it suggests the possibility of integrating diverse experiences of embodiment into cultural definitions of the subject that currently exclude the aging, the sick, and the disabled. Even as the waiting room breaks down the barriers between individual bodies and threatens to unveil our "wholeness" as an illusion, however, it does not necessarily begin to question the many and complex ways in which cultural definitions of "wholeness" have been constructed. Our "experience" of disability in the waiting room depends upon our symbolic vulnerability to cultural constructions of illness that themselves depend upon problematic equations between subjectivity and physical mobility, productivity, or narrative progression. Moreover, although time in the waiting room may render the healthy subject temporally suspended and temporarily unproductive, such symbolic vulnerability to cultural constructions of disability fails even to gesture toward knowledge of the physical incapacitation and overwhelming pain that many whose "living-moving" bodies are sick or disabled experience on a daily basis.

"Normality," Lennard Davis argues, "has to protect itself by looking into the maw of disability and then recovering from that glance" (1995, 48). Insofar as it delays—if not denies—such a recovery, the medical waiting room functions as a space where the impossibility of resisting symbolic immobilization contains at least the theoretical potential to mobilize us toward rewriting cultural assumptions about normality. In those endless moments of waiting—however many or few they might be—the supposedly "immutable" categories that divide bodies as whole and incomplete, normal and abnormal, healthy and sick, collapse into an experience of immobilization—literal and symbolic—that returns us to the shared vulnerability of our embodiment. For those of us lucky enough to escape (temporarily) the threat of illness or disability, our experience in the waiting room may be something, like Humpty Dumpty's fall, that rips us apart—something that disrupts not just our binary understanding of "normalcy" but our assumptions about what constitutes our own wholeness. For others of us, our escape from the waiting room may serve only to encourage us to put ourselves back together again as healthy, productive subjects, bound ever more tightly by cultural forms that obscure any glimpse of the body that lurks beneath. Perhaps it is our desire to leave the medical waiting room behind, to recover from the experience of looking into the "maw of disability" and seeing ourselves, that prompts many of us—patients and critics alike—to push past a space we prefer to think of as empty into a culture that defines us as healthy, productive, and whole.

{II}   THE BODY OF GRIEF

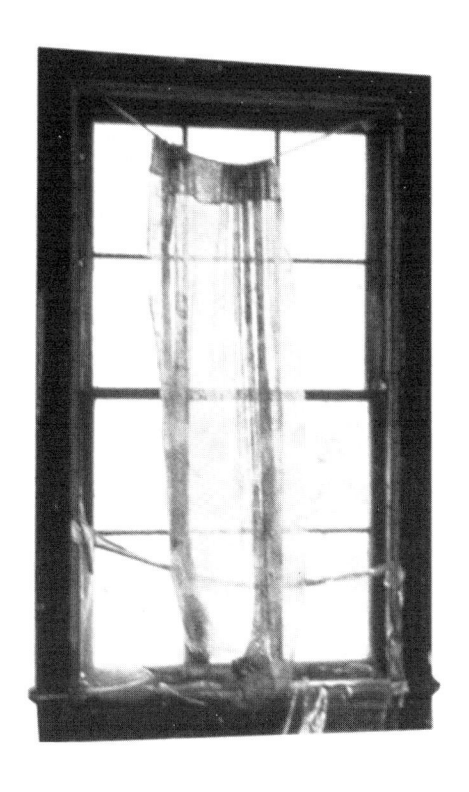

CHAPTER FOUR

∽

The Contours of Grief and the Limits of the Image

Hands

My father's hands were strong. Only a week before he died from a cancer that had spread throughout his body, he heard me in the bathroom next to the family room where he spent his final days lying on an improvised bed, heard me mumbling in frustration at a sink that kept dripping water. Before I even knew he was there, I felt his right hand—familiar, soft yet calloused, tanned from years of outside work— brush past my cheek as he effortlessly turned off the faucet that wouldn't budge. He was a quiet man, graceful in his moving, and often in my childhood the first announcement of his presence as I sat engrossed in a book or caught up in my thoughts was the feel of those strong hands on my shoulders, a touch so familiar it never startled me. Ten years after his death, my love for my father is intact, my memories of him still present. The pressure of his touch, however, is irretrievably gone. In trying to recollect the feel of his hands on my shoulders, I conjure images of touching so far from the sensation of touch that they only exaggerate its absence. Nothing that I read or knew before my father's death prepared me for this, most obvious of losses: the irretrievable sensation, the missing touch, the absent body that I sense but cannot locate, feel but cannot feel.

Given literature's reliance on words and images, literary representations of grief render the corporeal experience of loss with surprising frequency. Theoretical constructions of the mourning process, however, focus almost exclusively on psychological definitions of recovery that assume a disembodied subject. Turning to those theories of mourning after my father's death, I came away unsatisfied. In their discussions of the role that memory plays in recreating and then acknowledging the absence of the lost object, psychoanalytic and cultural theories charting loss often marginalize or ignore the way in which *feeling* is both an emotional and a physical phenomenon. In my experience, the loss of the body remains the thing left unspoken in prevailing theories of mourning. Perhaps the self-evident fact of bodily loss renders it resistant to theorization. In the months and years after my father's death, I asked myself repeatedly what *could* be said or known about the sensory absence with which I was repeatedly confronted. In the same way that the feel of my father's hands on my shoulders seemed lost to me—even memory incapable of rescuing that sensation from the realm of the intangible—the fact of bodily loss emerges as at once the most obvious fact of grief and at the same time the most unspeakable. What need is there to speak something that the grieving body experiences with such immediacy? What power is there in speaking something that exists in a corporeal realm where words have no power?

In leaving the embodied dimension of grief unspoken, however, theories of mourning not only reflect but enforce cultural assumptions that constitute the experience of loss as a strictly psychological phenomenon.[1] Calling for metaphors and models of subjectivity that acknowledge the implication of the subject in the object, theorists of the body and feminist philosophers have increasingly questioned psychoanalytic discourses that divide the subject into discrete categories of body and mind. Articulating such a position, Elizabeth Grosz emphasizes the need to create an intellectual language that avoids a discourse of polarization to develop instead an understanding of what she terms "embodied subjectivity" or "psychical corporeality." Such a formulation of identity would necessarily include a "psychical representation of the subject's lived body as well as of the relations between body gestures, posture, and movement in the constitution of the processes of psychical representations" (Grosz 1994, 23). Taking Grosz's argument to heart would entail acknowledging not only the way in which loss is experienced through the body—in the disruption of habit, the adaptation of posture, the absence of touch[2]—but revising prevalent theories of mourning to account for the complex ways in which embodied subjectivity complicates the psychological process of coming to terms with loss. A corporeal theory of grief, in other words, would not reduce my father's absence to the missed pressure of his hands on my shoulders, but would acknowledge and respond to the way the loss of that feeling shapes the feeling of loss.

At the center of James Agee's novel of one family's experience of grief,

A Death in the Family, a young boy confronts the dead body of his father, laid out for viewing in the family's living room. As he stares at that body, Rufus focuses on his father's hand: "The arm was bent. Out of the dark suit, the starched cuff, sprang the hairy wrist. The wrist was angled; the hand was arched; none of the fingers touched each other. The hand was so composed that it seemed at once casual and majestic. It stood exactly above the center of his body" (1998, 281). The reiteration of Rufus's desire to surge forward and touch his father's hand punctuates the narrative's careful and controlled visual inventory of the dead body. As the narrative reveals the limitations of Rufus's gaze—"He could just see over the edge of the coffin. He gazed at the perfect hand."—it tracks not only the child's literal distance from his father's body but Rufus's assimilation into cultural norms that legislate symbolic barriers between his living body and the motionless "hand he longed, in shyness, to touch" (282). Rufus's struggle to absorb the fact of his father's death and to respond to it appropriately is staged through the tension between vision and touch; as his gaze travels over the length of his father's familiar yet strangely inanimate form, Rufus polices his own desire to touch the hand that both is and is not his father's, to caress the familiar "hairy wrist" that looked, suddenly, as if it were "perfectly made of wax" (282).

The narrative's earlier portrait of the intimate, embodied interaction of father and son heightens the tension of this painful scene, in which the child struggles with the fact of his father's death and the impossible longing to return to the embodied interaction he associates with touch. As Rufus listens to the prayers of adults, he

> turned his eyes from the hand and looked towards his father's face and, seeing the blue-dented chin thrust upward, and the way the flesh was sunken behind the bones of the jaw, first recognized in its specific weight the word, *dead*. He . . . gazed once again at the hand, whose casual majesty was unaltered. He wished more sharply even than before that he might touch it, but whereas before he had wondered whether he might, if he could find a way to be alone, with no one to see or ever know, now he was sure that he must not. He therefore watched it all the more studiously, trying to bring all of his touch into all that he could see; but he could not bring much. (285)

Although the body of Rufus's father remains literally accessible in death, this scene traces its perceptual collapse into a mere object of the gaze. Rufus's tangible experience of his father's body—the strength of his arms, the warm scratchiness of his cheek, the smell of his armpits—contracts into a visual tunnel that locks Rufus into his gaze and renders the distance between father and son unnegotiable. Although Rufus is invited—even commanded—to look at his father's body, his internalization of a cultural prohibition against touching that familiar form pushes him into a desperate attempt to reestablish intercorporeality through the gaze. Despite the intensity of his look, however, Rufus's attempt to "bring all of his touch into all that he could see" fails, leaving the little boy alone in his own body. Rufus experiences the physical presence of his father's body as a taunting illusion; grief collapses multisensory intercorporeality into the strained dynamics of an intense looking destined never to break through into touch.

Given the fact that even the most forceful touch could never startle his father's body into response, what is perhaps most interesting about this scene is Rufus's need to police not merely his actions but his desire. When Rufus and his sister return for a final glimpse of their father's body, the narrative attributes Rufus's renunciation of the desire to touch his father to the crowd of people that surround the body. Under the "force of all the eyes" observing him and his sister, Rufus gazes upon a body so flattened and diminished by his look that it no longer seems to call out to be touched: "[His father] did not look as big as he really was, and the fragrance of the flowers was so strong and the vitality of the mourners was so many-souled and so pervasive, and so permeated and compounded by propriety and restraint, and they felt so urgently the force of all the eyes upon them, that they saw their father almost as idly as if he had been a picture, or a substituted image, and felt little realization of his presence" (292). Beneath the forces of "propriety and restraint" that Agee externalizes in this scene, Rufus's intercorporeal relationship with his father hardens into the subject/object dynamics of vision that he fought so hard to resist. The child's denial of "presence" in the body displayed before him represents not merely an acknowledgment of the literal impossibility of intercorporeality but a renunciation of the very longing to touch. As the animated body of his father stiffens into its representation as image, Rufus's "idle" response to his father's form serves as a veneer of protection against what he has so quickly come to experience as an impossible desire. By severing the connection between the living body he knew and the dead body before him, Rufus enforces a boundary that he cannot hope to dissolve and denies a desire he cannot hope to realize.

In grief, I will argue, the literal impossibility of reconnecting with an absent body is often exacerbated by cultural forces that deny the "propriety" of such desire. Whereas available models of mourning chart the healthy reconstitution of the subject through a psychological model that involves testing memory against reality, the very process of transforming lost bodies into images creates tensions that often define the experience of grief; in Agee's text, for example, traces of intercorporeality continue to surface even in the "picture" of his father that Rufus carries with him in his mind. In this chapter, I would like to explore the way that embodiment shapes the experience of grief, both its affect and its effects. By failing to fully acknowledge the extent to which we experience loss as a bodily phenomenon, I will contend, we not only dismiss the significance of intercorporeality but often doom ourselves to a "failed" mourning that returns us again and again to the unspoken absence of the body. The "substitution" of image for body that Agee represents necessarily involves a letting go of the intercorporeal aspects of human relationship, a loosening of the desire to touch and be touched. Whereas the disruption of intercorporeal bonds renders such a loosening not only inevitable but desirable, our desire to remake ourselves as whole within a culture that privileges mind over body can push us to obscure the embodied dimensions of grief, to deny our own desire for intercorporeality by replacing the body with its "substituted image" too quickly and too easily. My goal in this chapter is to expose some of the many ways in which mourning always remains entangled with a missing body the inaccessibility of which shapes the contours of our grief. In capturing the torment of a young boy's response to the presence of a beloved body he is forced to see but forbidden to touch, Agee encapsulates cultural assumptions about grief that deny the role of the body in loss and push the mourner to overwhelm the desire to touch with the consolation of image and memory. In the pages that follow, I use Merleau-Ponty's theory of the chiasm to consider the ways lost bodies vie with their imagistic counterparts to shape the dynamics of grief in Marilynne Robinson's *Housekeeping,* Roland Barthes's *Camera Lucida,* and the photography of Shellburne Thurber.

Unraveling the Chiasm

Maurice Merleau-Ponty's exploration of the role of the body in perception and experience has initiated what some critics have described as a "'Copernican revolution' within phenomenology and philosophy" (Evans and Lawlor 2002, 5). In *The Visible and the Invisible,* Merleau-Ponty defines "the thickness of the body" as "the sole means I have to go unto the heart of . . . things" (1968, 135); he uses the figure of the chiasm, which he describes as an intertwining, to image a reciprocal model of embodied perception that he figures as an intertwining of the embodied subject and the world. Insofar as the human subject always approaches the world through the locatedness of the body, Merleau-Ponty argues, perception must be understood as a dynamic, interactive process in which the subject can see and touch only insofar as it is seen and touched by the surrounding world. This notion of reversibility, Gail Weiss observes, "describes an ongoing interaction between the flesh of the body, the flesh of others, and the flesh of the world, a process in which corporeal boundaries are simultaneously erected and dismantled" (Weiss 2000, 204). The concept of intercorporeality is thus crucial to Merleau-Ponty's theory of chiasm:

> What is open to us, therefore, with the reversibility of the visible and the tangible, is—if not yet the incorporeal—at least an intercorporeal being, a presumptive domain of the visible and the tangible, which extends further from the things I touch and see at present. There is a circle of the touched and the touching, the touched takes hold of the touching; there is a circle of the visible and the seeing, the seeing is not without visible existence; there is even an inscription of the touching in the visible, of the seeing in the tangible—and the converse; there is finally a propagation of these exchanges to all the bodies . . . which I see and touch—and this by virtue of the fundamental fission or segregation of the sentient and the sensible which, laterally, makes the organs of my body communicate and founds transivity from one body to another. (Merleau-Ponty 1968, 142–143)

Merleau-Ponty's model locates the gaze in a body that can be seen and touched by the bodies that it sees and touches. He describes our relationship with the visible world in terms of a fleshly "intimacy"; we approach the world not by seeing it from a distance but "by palpating it with our look" (131).

By locating the basis of perception in intercorporeality, Merleau-Ponty not only stresses the implication of human experience in the body but exposes the impossibility of disentangling bodies from one another. As James Hatley argues in "Recursive Incantation and Chiasmic Flesh," one's flesh cannot be understood apart from its "intractable involvement" with the bodies of others.[3] The "transivity" of bodies that Merleau-Ponty describes frustrates any critical attempt to draw firm boundaries between the self and the other.[4] Hatley observes, "Given the chiasmic structure of one's identity, one cannot be oneself without already being the site of the interfolding of other bodies, of other beings into one's own embodied existence" (2000, 239). In this chapter, I explore what it means to understand grief as a response to the unraveling of the chiasm. Given that we know ourselves and others not only through but as our bodies, how is grief structured around the unfolding of two bodies once intertwined? In claiming that "every thought known to us occurs to a flesh," Merleau-Ponty stresses the impossibility of separating the sentient and the sensory worlds. Although the loss of a loved one's body disrupts the chiasmic relationship that defines Merleau-Ponty's model of perception, the gaps that grief exposes in the circle of intercorporeality necessarily return us to the lived body's status as a site of bodily interfolding. Grief unravels Merleau-Ponty's model of perception only to suggest the impossibility of understanding loss without it.

Although the loss of loved ones may not erase our memories of their embodied presence, it necessarily undoes a chiasmic structure that depends upon the balancing force of a body that pushes back against our own. Rufus's viewing of his father's body in *A Death in the Family* renders concrete a dynamic of chiasmic unraveling that prefigures the survivor's experience of the absent body in grief. Visualizable but untouchable and untouching, the lost body of a loved one taunts the survivor with its absent presence. In Agee's novel, the literal accessibility of the corpse only heightens Rufus's awareness of the broken circle of intercorporeality; as the little boy tries desperately to "bring all of his touch into all that he could see," the chiasmic relationship that Merleau-Ponty describes as "an inscription of the touching in the visible, of the seeing in the tangible" breaks down, returning Rufus to a one-directional visual apprehension in which his father's body exists only as "a substituted image." Grief solidifies the transformation of body into image that Rufus enacts through his response to the corpse; as his father's dead body is carried away, memory substitutes its own images of his father's form.

If American culture touts the consolation of memory and image as an answer to loss, understanding grief as an embodied experience demands acknowledgment not just of the failure of such images to render the body present but of their sustaining contribution to the taunting rhythms of grief. The verisimilitude of an image to a body taunts the viewer by asserting presence only to disrupt the exchange of intercorporeality that defines perception; a memory can be recalled but never held, the image of a body "seen" but never touched. Sartre defines the imagined object by virtue of that untouchability: "For the rest, the object as an image is an unreality. It is no doubt present, but, at the same time, it is out of reach. I cannot touch it, change its place" (Sartre 1948, 177–178). In Sartre's figuration, the act of touching and being touched differentiates our interactions with real bodies from the process of imagining. Grief tangles the mourner in a world of images that taunt and tantalize as they mimic embodied presence. In defining the image as that "which is absent from perception," Sartre observes: "It is but a mirage.... More exactly, the object as image is a *definite want*; it takes shape as a cavity" (179). The image of the absent body in memory expresses the mourner's desire without fulfilling it; the shape of memory constructs an outline that gestures toward the animating and embodied presence the image lacks.

The tension between the type of embodied perception that Merleau-Ponty defines as an intertwining and the mourner's construction of a missing body through the images of memory alone underlies the embodied experience of grief. Indeed, grief may be located in the space between the body and the image; as the "circle of the touched and the touching" that Merleau-Ponty describes is broken, the survivor's struggle to respond to loss may be mapped not only as a motion to reclaim healthy subjectivity but as a struggle to relocate the missing body through which the mourner's identity is constituted.

The difficulty of sustaining a model of grief that acknowledges the centrality of the body without resorting to a focus on the consolation of metaphor or image becomes evident in the argument of the one critic who has applied Merleau-Ponty's theory of chiasm to the experience of grief. Suzanne Cataldi's "Embodying Perceptions of Death: Emotional Apprehension and Reversibilities of Flesh" begins with the premise that grief "reveals how intimately woven, incorporated others are, into the fabric of our own lives. We cannot even begin to make sense of the pain of grief, which is . . . a pain of separation, unless we do suppose . . . some intercorporeal bonds" (2000, 197). Citing the importance of Merleau-Ponty's theory of flesh, Cataldi persuasively describes how the loss of a loved one's body disrupts our ability to complete habitual actions consciously or unconsciously directed toward the body of the other.

Cataldi's argument thus appears to offer a necessary supplement to psychoanalytic analyses that marginalize the role of embodiment in the experience of grief. Having acknowledged the painful disruption of embodied interaction as a significant aspect of grief, however, Cataldi backs away from her own observations to refocus attention on the consolation of emotion. Even as she suggests the crucial ways in which the loss of the body matters, Cataldi's argument begins to recuperate that loss through metaphorical language that would cover over the very gap she has exposed. By expanding "the circle of tactility" to encompass emotional as well as physical "touch," Cataldi attempts to define the withdrawal of intercorporeality as a form of touching. Our body, she argues, can be "emotionally touched or 'moved'" even by a dead body: "The 'objective' or perceptible sight of a dead body, for example, can be said to be horrify*ing* or heartbreak*ing*. And if a perception—a sight, a sound, a smell—is emotionally 'touching' us . . . then I believe that it is *ac*tivated enough to occasion . . .

transivities of meaning from one body to another—*even* if one of these bodies happen to be dead" (191). Instead of exploring how the inability to touch or be touched by the body of a loved one shapes the survivor's experience of grief, Cataldi shifts the definition of tactility in order to deny the enormity of its loss. In the attempt to show "how even live and dead bodies can be brought together, thought together, in the folds of *Flesh*" (189), she pushes the tangible reality of the body to the margins of her argument, replicating the perceptual models Merleau-Ponty worked to overthrow even in attempting to extend his claims. Within the metaphorical leveling of Cataldi's formulation, Rufus's desperate longing to touch and be touched by his father might be realized rather than aggravated by the "heartbreaking" sight of his father's dead body. In rerouting Merleau-Ponty's terms through a metaphorical system that pulls us away from the body, Cataldi extends his claims but undermines the most radical premise of his argument.

As he describes the embodied subject's relationship with the world in *The Visible and the Invisible,* Merleau-Ponty assumes a relationship between multidimensional beings that press against one another through their shared flesh: "It is the body and it alone . . . that can bring us to the things themselves, which are themselves not flat beings but beings in depth, inaccessible to a subject that would survey them from above, open to him alone that, if it be possible, would coexist with them in the same world" (1968, 136). Even if the corpse's physical presence lends it some claim to coexisting in the survivor's world, Cataldi's attempt to extend that claim to buried or cremated bodies reveals the tenuous scaffolding of her metaphorical bridge. In order to sustain such a model of worldly coexistence, Cataldi is pushed to argue that the very "stoppage of sense" a grieving individual experiences in relation to the absent body of a loved one is a form of touch. Through the notable absence of sensory interaction with the dead body, she claims, "we do, in a sense, remain 'in touch' with the dead" (198). Cataldi's use of the clause "in a sense" registers her argument's motion from materiality to metaphor. Having begun with a focus on intercorporeality based upon sensory exchange, Cataldi moves through the slipperiness of language to a model of intersubjectivity in which the subject, "in a sense," remains "in touch" with the dead; Cataldi's phrases invoke the material definitions of "sense" and "touch" even as their metaphorical deployment pulls us away from the terms of fleshly exchange.

In the conclusion of her argument, Cataldi returns to the grieving body to appropriate its material signs as testimony to the theory she constructs: "When memories blur and blot our vision, when we swallow that 'lump' in our throat, or hear that 'crack' in our voices, we can emotionally perceive that loved ones are behind it, that they are still there, still intermingled, intermingling with us, as they must have been—all along" (200). What most interests me about Cataldi's argument—which draws close to an acknowledgment of the absent body's significance in grief only to retreat from that knowledge—is its testimony to the strength of the cultural force that pulls us out of our bodies and pushes us to reconstitute ourselves through language, metaphor, and image as continuously whole. Cataldi's argument, which begins with Merleau-Ponty's focus on the necessity of embodiment, comes not only to collapse the distinction between materiality and metaphor but to equate imagery and embodiment. "Grief," she observes late in the essay, "can be imaged, embodied in various ways" (199). The comma in Cataldi's sentence signals grammatically an equivalence between the image and the body that her argument must assume if it is to fill the "gap" of grief that she opens up for view in the two paragraphs immediately preceding this sentence (198). In the pages that follow, I will attempt to trace the way grief shapes itself around the absent body, around a gap that I will locate in the space filled by Cataldi's comma, the space between the body and the image.

Images of Grief in Marilynne Robinson's *Housekeeping*

Recent work on grief continues to shape itself in response to Freud's theories of mourning, theories first articulated in his seminal essay "Mourning and Melancholia."[5] In that essay, Freud constructs a now famous narrative that describes the healthy subject's reaction to the loss of a loved one as a process of "reality-testing" that pits memories of the lost object against the reality of its inescapable absence. "Normally," Freud concludes, "respect for reality gains the day. Nevertheless its orders cannot be obeyed at once. They are carried out bit by bit, at great expense of time and cathetic energy, and in the meantime the existence of the lost object is psychically prolonged. Each single one of the memories and expectations in which the libido is bound to the object is brought up and hypercathected, and detachment of the libido is accomplished in respect of it" (1957, 244–245).

Kathleen Woodward's critique of Freud's narrative of mourning establishes a line of argument increasingly central to contemporary grief theory. Echoing the claim of Kathleen Kirby that "even in psychoanalysis, grief is that which is not or cannot be expressed," Woodward pushes to articulate "a discourse about mourning more expressive than that provided by psychoanalysis, a discourse that would combine the affective dimension of the experience of mourning with theoretical descriptions of mourning as a process" (Woodward 1990–1991, 94). Reacting against Freud's definition of "normal" mourning, Woodward describes his theory as follows:

> It is psychic work which has a precise purpose and goal: to "free" ourselves from the emotional bonds which have tied us to the person we loved so that we may "invest" that energy elsewhere, to "detach" ourselves so that we may be "uninhibited." Mourning . . . is slow, infinitesimally so, as we simultaneously cling to what has been lost and "test" reality only to discover that the person we love is no longer there. By "reality" Freud means primarily that we compare our memories with what exists in actuality now. (94–95)

Locating the most fascinating dimension of Freud's argument in his representation of the process of mourning "as a passionate or hyper-remembering of all the memories bound up with the person we have lost," Woodward describes Freud's focus on memory-work as compelling but "vague" (95).[6] Woodward's desire to reverse what she describes as Freud's marginalization of the affective dimensions of grief leads to her establishment of a kind of scholarship she describes as "Grief-Work," a scholarship that interrogates Freud's assumption that mourning must always come to an end, that affect should always be discharged (Woodward 1992–1993, 99).

In recent years other grief theorists have applied similar critiques to a range of texts and cultural contexts. In work that approaches mourning through a theological and moral perspective, Darlene Fozard Weaver examines how religious doctrine may "obscure the present and persistent inconsolability of . . . loss" (Weaver 2004, 34). Expanding Michael Moon's claim that Freud's model of mourning "may seem to diminish the process and to foreclose its possible meanings instead of enriching it or making it more accessible to understanding" (Moon 1995, 234), Sarah Brophy explores the idea of a resistant grief which does not conform to existing cultural models of loss. "While the psychic and cultural expectations of mourning work are such that one either has wisdom or does not, one mourns or is melancholic," Brophy observes, "for certain resistant grievers, such as the writers I investigate in this study, and such as myself, the narrative of mastery over grief does not match the experience of loss as it is written out" (Brophy 2004, 19).

Woodward's "affective grief," Brophy's "unresolved grief," and Weaver's "inconsolable loss" are all constructed so as to acknowledge the "present and persistent" experience of grief, removing it from Freud's tireless advance toward mental health. Implicit in their shared responses is a recognition of the body's role in grief that I would like to articulate and explore.

Although Weaver's attention to carnality broaches the centrality of embodied physicality to grief (she refers, for example, to the "special and embodied character of creaturely bonds"[41]), her discussion remains largely focused on emotional excess; Moon and Brophy address embodiment in terms of the erotic power of the lost body, but their arguments shift quickly to the political implications of homosexual erotics in relation to AIDS.

In accepting the challenge to supplement Freud's understanding of mourning with a more experiential account of grief, I would like to complicate the definition of subjectivity implicit in Freud's argument to locate the lost body of grief as the source of many of the tensions that Woodward and others identify. Whereas Freud's model of mourning focuses on the "psychic work" that allows us to "'free' ourselves from the *emotional* bonds which have tied us to the person we loved" (Woodward 1990–1991, 94, emphasis mine), at no point does Freud address the way in which the subject's relationship to the lost object is constituted *through the body* as well as through the psyche. Insofar as the death of a loved one severs not just emotional but physical bonds, grief is necessarily experienced by an embodied subject. Indeed, I will argue, factoring embodiment into Freud's psychological model further disrupts what Woodward has already critiqued as Freud's "mysteriously" smooth narrative of mourning.

Revisiting Freud's theory of mourning within a framework of embodied subjectivity exposes one fundamental source of the tension that Woodward locates in Freud's argument as she attempts to account for a sustained experience of grief that falls outside Freud's model of mourning and melancholia. Woodward's critique of Freud's model of loss claims:

> Inarguably for Freud, the most important aspect of this work of mourning is that it must come to an end. . . . Thus Freud defined mourning as a way of divesting ourselves of pain, of getting it over and done with.
>
> For Freud, melancholia by contrast is pathological. . . . It is denial of the reality of loss. . . . In this unequivocal distribution [between mourning and melancholia] I find a peculiar kind of piety, an almost ethical injunction to kill the dead and to adjust ourselves to "reality." In "Mourning and Melancholia" Freud leaves us no theoretical room for another place, one between a crippling melancholia and the end of mourning. (1990–1991, 95)

For Freud, the role of memory in mourning is to provide a form of recollected presence against which the absence of the lost object can be measured and eventually absorbed: "Each single one of the memories and situations of expectancy which demonstrate the libido's attachment to the lost object is met by the verdict of reality that the object no longer exists;

and the ego . . . is persuaded by the sum of the narcissistic satisfactions it derives from being alive to sever its attachment to the object that has been abolished" (1957, 255). As Woodward observes, in Freud's model "Mourning is represented as a dizzying phantasmagoria of memory. *Every* memory must be tested" (Woodward 1990–1991, 95). What Freud describes as the "intense" opposition between the presence of the lost object in memory and the absence of that object in reality not only fuels but constitutes the "work of mourning." If we understand presence as *embodied* presence, however, Freud's model is complicated by memory's limited ability to capture the multisensory experience of a lost body. In answering Grosz's call to extend theories of subjectivity to encompass psychical corporeality, a theory of loss that accounts for the body must begin by questioning Freud's declaration that, in memory, "the existence of the lost object is psychically prolonged" (1957, 245). Memory's images have no bodies—or rather, they have bodies that are disembodied: smooth rather than textured, untouchable and untouching. Given the image's primarily visual quality, its failure to hold onto the textured experience of the lived body exaggerates its already mediated representational status. Memory cannot speak the body's past presence without highlighting its present sensory inaccessibility; in doing so, memory participates in blurring the very dynamics of absent presence it should, in Freud's model, help to clarify.

Marilynne Robinson's novel *Housekeeping* (1982) provides a forum for redefining the relationship between memory and mourning as it traces a young girl's struggle to grow up in the shadow of repeated familial losses, including the death of her mother by suicide.[7] Having lived through the sudden deaths of their mother, grandfather, and grandmother, Ruth and her sister Lucille find themselves under the care of their maiden aunt, Sylvie, whose transient lifestyle renders her a questionable maternal substitute. The novel traces Ruth's growing bond with her aunt and her subsequent decision to escape with Sylvie when the town threatens to separate them. My interest lies not in that narrative of escape, however, but in the unrecuperated dynamic of loss which lurks beneath that narrative. Critics of *Housekeeping* tend to address the protagonist's response to her mother's death in terms that deemphasize the embodied dynamics of Ruth's grief by highlighting, instead, the psychic and symbolic implications of loss. Recognizing that "Ruth is repeatedly disappointed in the hope of maternal restoration" (King 1996, 571), Kristin King interprets Ruth's struggle to access her mother's absent form not within the context of an orphaned child's grief but as a "search for the undifferentiated wholeness of the pre-Oedipal Mother" (567); she reads the novel as a staging of tensions between the semiotic and the symbolic which always exist in the formation of (female) identity. If King's provocative argument casts Helen as the pre-Oedipal Mother and appropriates Ruth's grief for her mother as a means of articulating the complexity of the female subject's negotiation with the symbolic order, Marcia Aldrich's search for the "broader implications of Robinson's woman-centered novel" (Aldrich 1989, 132) leads her not merely to bracket the specifics of Ruth's loss but to subsume individual characters in the novel within one composite category: "The heroine of *Housekeeping*, by which I mean not any one character but a composite, is the mother. Some of the individual characters are biological mothers and some are surrogate mothers, but this heroine is the other in (m)other. . . . The novel is more interested in th[e] maternal bond and the process of mothering than in specific mothers" (132). In arguing that *Housekeeping* authorizes a typological rendering that collapses the distinction not merely between biological and surrogate mothers but between one character and the next, Aldrich reduces the characters in the novel to a narrowly defined signifying function and projects the disembodying tendencies of such an argument back onto the landscape of the novel itself. Aldrich denies not only the embodied aspects of Ruth's loss but the very fact of her grief: "Ruth, because she has refound her mother in Sylvie and experiences no real differences with Sylvie, neither searches for various substitutes for the mother's body, nor feels the absence of her original mother" (134). Aldrich's denial of the significance of Helen's death renders explicit the consequences of a disembodied criticism that would rewrite absence as presence. In highlighting the symbolic interchangeability of various maternal figures, Aldrich dismisses as irrelevant the specific, embodied terms of Ruth's loss.

Whereas Aldrich implies that the compensation of substitution—whether linguistic or symbolic—renders material presence irrelevant, Sian Mile positions the novel in active opposition to a materialist argument that would highlight the significance of the body. Claiming that "*Housekeeping* is a book which rejects not just the materiality of the body and the house but the materiality of all things," Mile argues that Robinson actively "refuse[s] the notion of a material definition of subjectivity" and "reject[s] . . . the necessity to . . . valorize the female body and use it as a defining feature of female subjectivity" (Mile 1990, 130–131). The arguments of King, Aldrich, and Mile represent the spectrum within which most critics have understood Ruth's loss of her mother in *Housekeeping*. In illuminating the symbolic implications of Ruth's experience, critics who trace the impact of her mother's death in psychoanalytic terms frequently bracket out the significance of embodied absence. Their analyses not only confirm Woodward's claim that "even in psychoanalysis, grief is that which is not or cannot be expressed," but point to the further critical marginalization of corporeal loss, a loss the significance of which some of Robinson's critics not only deprioritize but actively disavow. Whereas Mile cites the frailty and the perishability of the body as cause for "refus[ing] the notion of a material definition of subjectivity" in the novel, I will explore how *Housekeeping* critiques rather than conspires with Ruth's tendency to disentangle the material dimension of grief from her own subjectivity. As it calls attention both to the enormity of Ruth's embodied grief and to the impossibility of its symbolic recuperation, *Housekeeping* uncovers the implications of an ethos of disembodied subjectivity that many of the novel's critics uphold in their analyses. In arguing that Ruth's mourning represents not only "a search for the undifferentiated wholeness of the pre-Oedipal Mother" but an attempt to come to terms with the loss of Helen's specific, embodied presence, I will relocate Ruth's grief in the body to consider the ways the tensions of embodied subjectivity permeate and define her experience of loss. Ruth's grief, it seems to me, revolves around her frustrated attempt to evade the absent body that culture would have her disavow.

Housekeeping traces Ruth's "sustained" grief to its origin in an embodied dynamic of loss that Ruth is unable to overturn or even acknowledge. The novel documents the way grief pulls the subject out of an embodied relationship with the missing other to lock the mourner in a taunting world of images. Rather than invoking the spiritual and symbolic consolations proffered by Western cultural and religious traditions, Ruth's memories of her mother are painful exactly to the degree that they are numinous. Her apprehension of her mother through disembodied images offers neither the religious comfort of promised salvation nor the secular comfort of enduring memory. Instead, Ruth's memories mock the mourner by continually substituting the image for the thing. Ruth's meditations on her mother are obsessed with the fact of her missing body, a body that haunts every image Ruth's mind can construct but consistently eludes her grasp. Under the pressure of her own grief, Ruth continually refigures the consolation of memory not as a form of material transcendence but as a kind of haunting entrapment within the image. In a hallucinatory vision, she translates her mother's liberation from the material world into the nightmarish invulnerability of a body present but immaterial and inaccessible:

> What is thought, after all, what is dreaming, but swim and flow, and the images they seem to animate? The images are the worst of it. It would be terrible to stand outside in the dark and watch a woman in a lighted room studying her face in a window, and to throw a stone at her, shattering the glass, and then to watch the window knit itself up again and the bright bits

of lip and throat and hair piece themselves seamlessly again into that unknown, indifferent woman. (Robinson 1982, 162)

Ruth's horror in this passage results from the awareness that memory only *seems* to "animate" the images it constructs. Despite her reference to the bodily specifics—lip, throat, hair—of the woman she images here, neither physical violence nor emotional force can touch that "indifferent" mother figure. As the passage continues, the impossibility of sustaining an embodied image of her mother emerges in Ruth's tribute to the power of thoughts that, unlike bodies, cannot sink or be carried away: "Like reflections on water our thoughts will suffer no changing shock, no permanent displacement. If they were more substantial—if they had weight and took up space—they would sink or be carried away in the general flux. But they persist, outside the brisk and ruinous energies of the world" (162). The power of the image rests upon an immateriality that simultaneously defines its failure to do more than gesture emptily toward the embodied subject it would represent. In her grief, Ruth experiences memory as a violation that taunts her by parading images of her mother's body before her eyes but rendering that body invulnerable and untouchable.

Ruth's relentless quest to break through the veneer of image and memory to touch her mother's absent body highlights the way in which the fact of embodiment often shapes the experience of grief. As the process of mourning thrusts a subject further and further into the isolated arena of consciousness, disengagement from the tactile world exaggerates the mourner's experience of bodily loss. Although Ruth claims at points in the novel that she would be happy just to *see* her mother, here she explores the limitations of a visual epistemology that she associates with falsehood:

> Everything that falls upon the eye is apparition, a sheet dropped over the world's true workings. The nerves and the brain are tricked, and one is left with dreams that these specters loose their hands from ours and walk away, the curve of a back and the swing of a coat so familiar as to imply that they should be permanent fixtures of the world, when in fact nothing is more perishable. Say that my mother was as tall as a man, and that she sometimes set me on her shoulders, so that I could splash my hands in the cold leaves above our heads. Say that my grandmother sang in her throat while she sat on her bed and we laced up her big black shoes. Such details are merely accidental. Who could know but us? (116)

The body with the familiar curved back or the swinging coat that Ruth sees walking away in her dreams proclaims its presence, its necessity, in visual terms that constantly misrepresent by virtue of their seeming solidity. In fact, the "specter" figures that Ruth envisions represent only feeble shadows of the mother and grandmother whose bodies she once experienced in a multisensory, tactile way; unlike the visual images that taunt her through memory and dream, the song emanating from her grandmother's throat, the feel of her mother's tall shoulders beneath her, the cold leaves in which she splashed her hands, exist only conditionally—"Say that my mother. . . . Say that my grandmother . . . "—and in a past that cannot be retrieved. Whereas visual images of lost bodies mock her in their seeming presence, the tactile interaction of her own body with those bodies is so irrevocably absent as to call into question even the fact of its past existence. Grief undoes the chiasmic quality of perception that Merleau-Ponty describes as a circle in which there is "an inscription of the touching in the visible, of the seeing in the tangible" (1968, 143); images lock the mourner in a continual replaying of memory that renders the other's body present only as absence. Both untouchable and untouching, the dream bodies that Ruth constructs in her mind are, like the images Sartre describes, "phantom-objects [that] are fleeting and ambiguous; at once themselves and something other than themselves" (Sartre 1948, 188–189).

When Ruth, desperate for consolation, reports her willingness to emerge from the darkness and settle for the mere sight of her mother later in the novel, that assertion rings hollow: "If I could see my mother, it would not have to be her eyes, her hair. I would not need to touch her sleeve. There was no more the stoop of her high shoulders. The lake had taken that, I knew. It was so very long since the dark had swum her hair, and there was nothing more to dream of, but often she almost slipped through any door I saw from the side of my eye, and it was she, and not changed, and not perished" (160). Although Ruth tries to console herself with the possibility of her mother's return as a disembodied presence, the passage lingers over the intimate, sensory experience of the mother's body—the stoop of her shoulders, the feel of her sleeve—even as Ruth proclaims her willingness to sacrifice that tactile form of knowledge.[8] Ruth's negotiation with the fates unravels as the disembodied presence that she proclaims herself willing to accept collapses into a visual image that offers little more than the consolation of memory that she has already rejected. Only from an angle, for a moment, at a distance, can the image of her mother suffice before it reveals itself as a mocking reminder of absence. In the next sentence, Ruth acknowledges, "She was a music I no longer heard, that rang in my mind, itself and nothing else, lost to all sense, but not perished, not perished" (160). Present as the mother is in Ruth's mind, but "lost to all sense," it is exactly the angle of her shoulders and the feel of her sleeve that elude Ruth. Ruth's grief shapes itself around the embodied form that she can imagine but never experience. Trapped in a desire she continues to disavow, Ruth seems destined to circle around and around the corporeal loss that she refuses to acknowledge.

When Ruth enters the woods with Sylvie early one morning, the unspoken bodily dynamics of grief take shape through Ruth's imaginings of the statue of a woman she might have constructed had there been snow. Although Lot's wife "was salt and barren, because she was full of loss and mourning," Ruth declares the desire to remake her as a maternal figure adorned with flowers and surrounded by children who would "love and marvel at her for her beauty, and . . . laugh at her extravagant adornments, as if they had set the flowers in her hair and thrown down all the flowers at her feet, and they would forgive her, eagerly and lavishly, for turning away, though she never asked to be forgiven" (153). Imaginatively restoring the body of the mother, Ruth asserts the child's willingness to forgive her desertion and remakes the mother as a beautiful figure with rare flowers gleaming "in her hair, and on her breast, and in her hands" (153). The image Ruth constructs, however, emphasizes the limitations of the only maternal body she can now imagine, a body that sacrifices the warmth and sensory accessibility associated with a mother's breasts and hands for the "rare" beauty of a purely aesthetic form that invites the children to "come close" only "to look at her" and not to touch her: "Though her hands were ice and did not touch them, she would be more than mother to them, she so calm, so still, and they such wild and orphan things" (153). Once again, the form that Ruth erects as compensation for the loss of her mother's body returns the reader to its essential lack. Although we can direct emotion toward an image, Sartre observes,

> this tenderness does not rebound on the unreal object; it has not fed on the inexhaustible depths of the real: it remains cut off from the object, suspended; it occurs to reflection as an effort to rejoin that unreal gesture which remains beyond its reach and which it does not attain. What we seek in vain here is the receptivity, the *passion* in the sense given that term in the seventeenth century. One could speak of a dance before the unreal, in a manner that a corps de ballet dances around a statue. The dancers open their arms, offer their hands, smile, offer themselves completely, approach and take flight; but the statue is not affected by it; there is no real relationship between it and the corps de ballet. Likewise, our conduct before the object cannot really touch it, qualify it any more than it can touch us in return; because it is in the heaven of the unreal, beyond all reach. (Sartre 1948, 204–205)

The "receptivity" that Sartre describes invokes Merleau-Ponty's image of chiasmic reversibility as "a circle of the touched and the touching"; in contrast to such embodied transivity, the dance that Sartre describes here is poignantly disconnected. Ruth's appeal to the statue form may represent an attempt to lend dimension and texture to memory, to create a body that she can feel pressing back against her own. No matter how carefully Ruth's mind constructs the image of her mother's body, however, it remains untouchable and untouching, an image "beyond all reach." The body with hands of ice that Ruth imagines shaping represents less a restoration of her mother's absent form than a statue rendering of the all-too-present images of grief—images that recall, invoke, remember a body but cannot animate it.

Despite the initial cathartic outbursts of weeping that many mourners experience, grief remains primarily a disembodied process that exaggerates—not mitigates—the sudden isolation of one body from another. If, as embodied subjects, we experience ourselves always through and as our bodies, the kind of loss that tears a loved one away from a parent, child, or lover propels the survivor into a state of heightened psychic isolation that cannot be expressed physically. In "Experience," Ralph Waldo Emerson rails against the fact that, despite the overwhelming loss he feels after his son's death, he bears no bodily relationship to his own grief:

> The only thing grief has taught me, is to know how shallow it is. That, like all the rest, plays about the surface, and never introduces me into the reality, for contact which, we would even pay the costly price of sons and lovers.... In the death of my son, now more than two years ago, I seem to have lost a beautiful estate—no more. I cannot get it nearer to me.... This calamity... does not touch me: some thing which I fancied was part of me, which could not be torn away without tearing me... falls off from, and leaves no scar. (Emerson 1983, 472)

Emerson seeks a depth, dimension, texture in grief that would match the intensity of his embodied interaction with his child, but finds the disembodied experience of his loss doubly wounding. As Sharon Cameron points out in her analysis of the essay, Emerson's claim that loss does not touch him signifies not the absence of feeling on his part but the fact that "the feeling has no palpable consequences. Here 'consequences' seem imagined... as that particular bodily manifestation that affects the body of the mourner" (Cameron 1991, 212). Emerson's quest for a "penetrative" experience of grief reflects the degree to which he experiences both his love for and his loss of his son as an embodied subject. The link between subjectivity and embodiment that defines human relationship, however, seems somehow severed in the fact of grief, through a process which not only removes the body of a loved one but seems not to register that bodily absence in any material form. Like Robinson's protagonist, Emerson cries out to be physically touched, if not by the missing body of his dead son then at least by the grief that would mark his son's absence.

For Ruth, perhaps because of her youthful status, the physical and psychic isolation of grief propels her into a state of contingency in which she experiences her own body as an absence: "It was a source of both terror and comfort to me then that I often seemed invisible—incompletely and minimally existent, in fact. It seemed to me that I made no impact on the world, and that in exchange I was privileged to watch it unawares" (105). Despite the fact of a changing adolescent body that periodically breaks into sweat, convicting Ruth of "gross corporeality" (106), the experience of grief locks her away from the tactile world and questions the presence not only of her mother's body and her own but of those around her: "When we did not move or speak, there was no proof that we were there at all. The wind and the water brought sounds intact from any imaginable distance. Deprived of all perspective and horizon, I found myself reduced to an intuition, and my sister and aunt to something less than that. I was afraid to put out my hand, for fear it would touch nothing, or to speak, for fear no one would answer" (70). Having been propelled at an early age into the disembodied experience of grief, Ruth struggles to affirm both the presence of her own physical form and her ability to reach out and touch the bodies of others. Her feeling that she "made no impact on the world" and, in turn, could not be impacted by its touch, represents her internalization of an epistemology of grief that refuses expression through embodiment. Stressing the absolute separation of the individual and the "unreal object" of his or her imagination, Sartre observes, "the world of imagery is completely isolated, I can enter it only by unrealizing myself in it" (1948, 188). Ruth's failed struggle to intertwine her body with her mother's, to attain the "intercorporeality" that Merleau-Ponty describes, results only in further isolation; because she is unable to access the maternal body that lurks behind the "unreal object," Ruth's entrance into the "world of images" leads to a process of "unrealizing" that distances her from her own corporeality without lending her access to the maternal body that she imagines.

In her attempt to regain some form of sensory engagement with the bodies lost to her and the world around her, Ruth tries to negotiate the gap between body and mind, gesture and thought, the material and the immaterial, by casting them as part of a necessary continuum:

> To crave and to have are as like as a thing and its shadow. For when does a berry break upon the tongue as sweetly as when one longs to taste it, and when is the taste refracted into so many hues and savors of ripeness and earth, and when do our senses know any thing so utterly as when we lack it? And here again is a foreshadowing—the world will be made whole. For to wish for a hand on one's hair is all but to feel it. So whatever we lose, very craving gives it back to us again. Though we dream and hardly know it, longing, like an angel, fosters us, smooths our hair, and brings us wild strawberries. (152–153)

The forced logic of Ruth's reasoning here parallels the failed attempt at consolation represented by the maternal body whose "hands were ice." In attempting to claim grief as a sensory phenomenon—"when do our senses know any thing so utterly as when we lack it?"—Ruth only exaggerates the gap between desire and experience, absence and presence, image and body. The abstract possibility of desire as consolation crumbles under the force of manipulation required to lend longing a body and render it capable of smoothing her hair.[9] With the very immediacy and particularity of Ruth's final image, the kind of metaphorical compensation for grief that she would construct through language falls apart. Once again, Ruth experiences grief as an expulsion from the tactile world she associates with her mother's body and fails to reconstruct in other forms. Although she claims here that "we dream and hardly know it," the particular torture of grief for Ruth is her mind's continual substitution of the shadow for the thing and, despite her protests here, her own relentless awareness of the space between the two.

Insofar as it lends presence to an absent loved one, memory, we are often told, keeps that loved one "alive" in the mind's eye. Memory, however, taunts the grieving subject with images that figure presence only as they bespeak bodily absence. For Freud, the role of memory in mourning is to provide a form of recollected presence against which the absence of the lost object can be measured and eventually absorbed. As Ruth's struggles with memories of her mother reveal, however, the dynamics of embodied grief are aggravated rather than resolved by the presence of disembodied images which, in their lack of texture and tactility, figure the irretrievable loss of intercorporeality. Rather than invoking presence by echoing what was, images gesture toward a lost body that the image cannot hold and the mourner cannot touch. The testing of past presence against present absence that Freud describes in "Mourning and Melancholia" depends upon memory's ability to restore the missing object in imaginative terms. The failure of the imagination to capture the textured experience of embodied subjectivity, however, renders memory's untouchable image of the lost object not merely partial or limited but illusory.

Introducing the body into Freud's theory disrupts his narrative model of mourning, a model which casts the subject's motion toward recovery as a gradual process of measuring reality against memory in order to let go. Ruth's consistently frustrated attempt to locate her mother's body in images points to the revised role of memory in a corporeal theory of grief. In Ruth's struggle to come to terms with her mother's death, images body forth present absence rather than past presence. In speaking the presence of the lived body only in the context of its sensory inaccessibility, the disembodied image replaces the process of measuring what *was* against what *is*—so essential to Freud's narrative of successful mourning—with a collision of absences. In measuring memory against reality, the embodied subject is caught between lack and lack and finds itself spiraling into an experience of grief nameable under Freud's model only as melancholia.

Underlying Ruth's "melancholic" inability to move through the mourning process with the assistance of memory lies her fundamental need to return over and over again to memory in the effort to heal its lack. Throughout the novel, Ruth's repeated denial of her desire for her mother's body marks not just the impossibility of realizing that desire but the cultural unspeakability of such a desire itself. Like Rufus, whose response to the force and propriety of adult surveillance is to renounce the longing to touch the familiar body he must come to view only as "a picture, or a substituted image" (Agee 1998, 292), Ruth remains caught in an impossible desire that she continues to disavow. Given that Freud's theory of mourning focuses on the restoration of healthy subjectivity in the face of loss, what Woodward describes as its curious inability to acknowledge the "affect" of grief may be linked to its implicit assumption of a disembodied subject. What lurks at the margins of Freud's essay—what the essay itself disavows—is the urgency of the one loss that cannot be recuperated: the loss of embodied presence. If the healthy subject "is persuaded by the sum of the narcissistic satisfactions it derives from being alive to sever its attachment to the object that has been abolished" (1957, 255), the gradual willingness to release such a psychic bond follows in the wake of a severed attachment to a living, breathing child, husband, mother, or friend.[10] Focusing on the embodied experience of intercorporeal loss implies neither the primacy of the body over the psyche nor the marginalization of psychological models of experience. It does demand, however, a shift toward acknowledging that the sudden and unconsenting loss of intercorporeality necessarily shapes the psychic processes Freud describes. Kathleen Woodward's call for the interdisciplinary study of Grief-Work (Woodward 1992–1993) stands in opposition not only to psychoanalytic theories that mark sustained grief as illness but to cultural attempts to "comfort mourning" through attention to the consolations of memory or the reconstitution of bodily loss in spiritual terms. In such a context, the challenge of Grief-Work begins with the acknowledgment that the loss of the body as body cannot be recuperated and extends to an exploration of the way in which cultural tendencies to recuperate loss translate not only to the marginalization of embodied experience but to the unspeakability of embodied grief.

By the end of *Housekeeping,* Ruth's inability to sustain her mother's embodied presence through memory or to recuperate the loss of that presence within a spiritual framework leads her to construct a theory of mourning that upends traditional hierarchies of body and spirit to expose the corporeal loss around which the novel revolves. In Ruth's representation of Christ's death and resurrection, she embodies the act of remembering as a means of counteracting the incorporeality of images. Whereas Ruth associates memory with the mediated forms of words and images, she imagines acts of grieving so embodied, so multisensory, that the force of grief would propel the mourner's body into the realm of the image and lend a body to loss. "Memory," she states, "is the sense of loss, and loss pulls us after it" (194). In contrast to a narrative of psychologically successful mourning that propels the subject through memory toward healing, Ruth's representation focuses on a "mourning [that] would not be comforted" and a lack that cannot be filled:

> And when He did die it was sad—such a young man, so full of promise, and His mother wept and His friends could not believe the loss, and the story spread everywhere and the mourning would not be comforted, until He was so sharply lacked and so powerfully remembered that his friends felt Him beside them as they walked along the road, and saw someone cooking fish on the shore and knew it to be Him, and sat down to supper with Him, all wounded as He was. There is so little to remember of anyone—an anecdote, a conversation at table. But every memory is turned over and over again, every word, however chance, written in the heart in the hope that memory will fulfill itself, and become flesh, and that the wanderers will find a way home, and the perished, whose lack we always feel, will step through the door finally and stroke our hair with dreaming, habitual fondness, not having meant to keep us waiting long. (194–195)

Ruth draws upon the figure of Christ and the story of his resurrection to construct a narrative of grief that culminates not in the healthy reconstitution of the grieving subject but in the reembodiment of the lost loved one. In rejecting Christian ideology that privileges spirit over flesh, resurrection over incarnation, Ruth imagines failed mourning—"and the mourning would not be comforted"—not as melancholia but as a grief so penetrative that it not only exposes but fills the fundamental lack of memory's disembodiment. In Ruth's version of Christ's resurrection, Christ's friends experience the "lack" of his presence so "sharply" that memory materializes into flesh: "He was so sharply lacked and so powerfully remembered that his friends felt Him beside them as they walked along the road." If, as Emerson's essay reflects, part of the horror of grief lies in the absence of a bodily correlative for the emotional devastation the mourner feels, here Ruth imagines the "power" and the "sharpness" of grief assuming an almost physical force that lends tactility to emotion, binding feeling with feeling to restore chiasmic intercorporeality.

Ruth's hope that "memory will fulfill itself, and become flesh" emerges not out of a desire to know her mother as body only but out of the recognition that memory's images invoke presence only by sacrificing embodiment. A true resurrection, Ruth's parable suggests, would not echo and extend the work of memory to imply a transcendence of flesh into spirit. Rather, it would fill the lack that memory cannot address and culture cannot name, would address the loss that cannot be recuperated. Ruth figures embodied grief as a process that would penetrate images of loss with a sensory intensity capable of animating them. When Christ returns from the dead, the gift his friends receive is not his divine appearance but his return to mortal embodiment; the God who returns to them after his supposed death doesn't preach from on high but sits down to supper with them "all wounded as He was" (195). Unlike the dream woman that haunted Ruth with images of her miraculous invulnerability to physical force, the Christ Ruth represents consoles his friends with a wounded body that reassures them he is not merely a divine spirit or a creation of their imaginations. As Ruth describes the return of the perished in the flesh, she lingers on the hand of the body returned to her which, in the act of stroking her hair, would pull her out of the solipsistic fantasy world of loss and desire to ground her in the tactile experience of chiasmic embodiment. Ruth's revisionary invocation of Christ's reincarnation reverses the figurative leap made by Suzanne Cataldi as she argues that we continue to be "touched" by the dead. To feel, in the sense of experiencing an emotion, the *Housekeeping* passage implies, can bridge into feeling in a sensory arena, so that when Christ's friends "felt Him beside them as they walked along the road" their feeling could be confirmed by the physical act of touching. Such a vision lends purpose to the torturous and repetitive process of mourning by casting the work of mourning not within the trajectory of psychological recovery that Freud sketches but as a (necessarily failed) narrative of reembodiment that gestures toward an irrecuperable loss.

Camera Lucida and the Body of the Photograph

Committed as she is to a narrative of grief that fulfills itself only in reembodiment, Ruth seems destined to remain stuck in what Freud might designate the pathological rhythms of a failed mourning. Kathleen Woodward's critique of Freud's model of loss claims that "the most important aspect of this work of mourning is that it must come to an end. . . . Freud leaves us no theoretical room for another place, one between a crippling melancholia and the end of mourning" (Woodward 1990–1991, 95). Woodward introduces Roland Barthes's *Camera Lucida* as a text that represents a sustained mourning that falls short of crippling melancholia.[11] Her discussion of Barthes's text raises questions about how the "work" of mourning that Freud describes is accomplished, and suggests that the "completion" of that work is not always possible or even desirable. In this section, I would like to consider an element of Barthes's text that Woodward's analysis does not address. How, I will ask, is Barthes's grief shaped by tensions of embodiment that surface continually in his consideration of his mother's absence? If the images of memory taunt Ruth by invoking an embodied presence she can neither embrace nor escape, how do photographic images body forth the absent presence that Barthes struggles to hold in *Camera Lucida*?

Barthes's struggle to locate his grief assumes the form of a negotiation with images ranging from memory to dream to photograph. In figuring the attempt to find a successful representation of his mother as a form of muscular labor, Barthes emphasizes the contrast between his embodied presence and her immaterial inaccessibility:

> It was not she, and yet it was no one else. . . . straining toward the essence of her identity, I was struggling among images partially true, and therefore totally false. . . . For I often dream about her (I dream only about her), but it is never quite my mother. . . . I dream about her, I do not dream *her*. And confronted with the photograph, as in the dream, it is the same effort, the same Sisyphean labor: to reascend, straining toward the essence, to climb back down without having seen it, and to begin all over again. (Barthes 1981, 66)

Despite the figure of exertion he employs, Barthes's repeated engagement with images evokes the circularity of grief rather than the narrative process of mourning. Barthes represents the work of mourning as a process of physical "labor"—"climbing" and "straining"—that fails to register consequence in the immaterial arena of grief. The "intense immobility" of the photograph, its status as static image rather than animated body, not only renders it incapable of returning his mother to him but taunts him with a partiality that gestures toward an irretrievable presence the photograph can neither capture nor restore; "partially true," the images he contemplates are "therefore totally false." Erin C. Mitchell links the partiality of these images to Barthes's experience of mourning: "Barthes feels the pain of almost recognizing his mother in the images before his eyes; the photographs express the simultaneous absence and presence of his mother; photographs both compel and express his mourning" (Mitchell 2000, 330). Although Mitchell usefully highlights the significance of the mother's "simultaneous absence and presence" in the photographs Barthes considers, her conclusion that such images "both compel and express his mourning" leaves unexplored the complicated tensions that result from the image's role in Barthes's grief. Freud's narrative of mourning depends upon the process of measuring past presence against present absence; the images Barthes contemplates, however, disrupt that process by rendering his mother's past presence inaccessible. The consolation of representation dissolves into its opposite as imagistic presence only highlights embodied absence: "I dream about her, I do not dream *her.*" Barthes's inability to locate his mother's memory in the partiality of the image undercuts the productivity of his grief-work. The narrator of *Camera Lucida,* I would argue, finds himself stalled in a universe of images that speaks neither to his mother's presence nor to his apprehension of her loss. Reacting against Freud's formulation of the work of mourning as a motion toward reclaiming healthy subjectivity, Barthes describes his inability to move through the mourning process as a form of enforced immobility: "It is said that mourning, by its gradual labor, slowly erases pain; I could not, I cannot believe this; because for me, Time eliminates the emotion of loss (I do not weep), that is all. For the rest, everything has remained motionless" (75). His search in *Camera Lucida* is a search for an image of his mother that defies the immobility of the photograph and disrupts the immobility of grief to bring the body back to him.

In Part Two of the text, Barthes reports that he has found a photograph of his mother that captures her essence. Looking at that particular image of his mother as a child, he tells us, "I studied the little girl and at last rediscovered my mother" (69). Unlike all the other photographs he has viewed and discarded, this image, it would seem, appears somehow to convey his mother's being. The process by which it captures her essence, however, remains as mysterious as the photograph itself, which Barthes refuses to show the reader.[12] When he describes the effect of the image, his language is deliberately broad. Claiming that the picture "accords with both my mother's being and my grief at her death," Barthes goes on to say, "I could not express this accord except by an infinite series of adjectives, which I omit, convinced however that this photograph collected all the possible predicates from which my mother's being was constituted. . . . the Winter Garden Photograph was indeed essential, it achieved for me, utopically, *the impossible science of the unique being*" (70–71). Barthes's vague linguistic constructions emphasize the difficulty of conceptualizing a picture that "accords with" both his own grief—an almost inaccessible emotion—and his mother's being. Of what would such an accord consist? If the photograph he refers to "collected all the possible predicates from which my mother's being was constituted," how are we as readers to understand Barthes's conceptualization of the "predicates" of being? Does he refer here to elements of personality, emanations of spirit, or physical postures? Barthes's vague and uncharacteristically untheorized positing of the photograph's "essential" success raises questions about the power of the image to body forth the absent figure of the mother. Significantly, the image Barthes settles on embodies his mother's presence only in/as a body that Barthes himself never knew in intercorporeal terms; only the photograph of his mother as a child succeeds in figuring presence without embodying absence.[13] If the images that Ruth struggled to contend with were primarily memories floating through her mind, Barthes attempts to work through the immobility of grief by positing a material image—a photograph—that, in returning his mother to him, accomplishes what his own grief cannot.

The necessarily ambiguous language that Barthes employs to describe the Winter Garden Photograph's success, however, cannot wholly contain the tension between image and embodiment that he, like Robinson's protagonist, struggles to negotiate. Immediately after asserting in abstract terms the photograph's success at capturing his mother's broadly defined "being," Barthes falls into a meditation on the last days of his mother's life that locates her abstract identity in the experiential specifics of embodiment: "At the end of her life . . . my mother was weak, very weak. I lived in her weakness (it was impossible for me to participate in a world of strength, to go out in the evenings; all social life appalled me). During her illness, I nursed her, held the bowl of tea she liked because it was easier to drink from than a cup" (72). If the Winter Garden Photograph would locate his mother's presence in a single image defined by health and youth, Barthes's painful memories of his intimate, embodied relationship with his dying mother almost immediately overwhelm the "impossible" coherence of the image he withholds from representation. Barthes, then, quickly breaks out of this meditation on his physical/spatial connection to his mother's incapacitated body to assert a metaphorical tie between that experience and the photograph: "she had become my little girl, uniting for me with that essential child she was in her first photograph" (72). Barthes's two modes of reading the Winter Garden Photograph reflect the double-edged status of a text that operates, in Michael Moriarty's terms, as both a work of semiology and a work of antisemiology. Moriarty defines *Camera Lucida* as "a work of semiology in that it explores the photographic sign: of antisemiology in that instead of studying the interrelationships of signs within a system it looks through the individual sign to the referent (the real object)" (Moriarty 1991, 198). Barthes's endorsement of the Winter Garden Photograph as "accord[ing] with both my mother's being and my grief at her death" relies upon his semiotic reading of the image; the physically unfamiliar form of his mother as a child symbolically invokes the dependency she manifests in her final days even as it renders her aging, weakened body youthful and whole. My interest lies in the way the text's antisemiotic impulse disrupts the consolation of the image to gesture toward the familiar, fragmented body that Barthes reveals only to recover. Even as Barthes posits the wholeness of the representation he withholds, *Camera Lucida* testifies to the embodied dynamics of a loss that the Winter Garden Photograph can neither express nor recuperate.

In excluding his mother's lived body from the photograph that would contain all the "possible predicates" of her being, Barthes constructs and controls an idealized image haunted by the loss of an intercorporeality it fails to acknowledge. The tension between image and embodiment emerges early on in *Camera Lucida,* when Barthes defines the project of his text by asking, "What does *my body* know of photography?" (9, emphasis mine).[14] By locating the gaze in a body, Barthes dismisses the illusion of abstraction and objectivity that would render him a mere critic of photography.[15] He emerges, instead, as an embodied viewer interested in representation not for its own sake but for its capacity to body forth a referent. In looking at a photograph, Barthes admits, "Myself, I saw only the referent, the desired object, the beloved body" (7). Despite his semiotic exchange of bodies for symbols—the unfamiliar little girl of the photograph standing in for his weakened, aging mother—Barthes's quest to render present his absent mother demands that he supplement the "utopic" image he claims "accords" with his mother's being and his own grief; the image that would figure the essence of her being emerges as incapable of holding onto his mother's familiar form. His attempts to animate and embody the image result in *Camera Lucida*'s most poignant and irresolvable tensions.

Barthes initiates his antisemiotic project by establishing the photograph's function as evidence of the referent's embodiment, going so far as to claim that "photography's inimitable feature (its noeme) is that someone has seen the referent . . . in *flesh and blood*, or again *in person*" (79). Unlike other images (of memory, dreams, and so on), the photograph necessarily originates in the lived body. Although the image of Barthes's mother is neither animated nor three-dimensional, it testifies to her past presence in those terms: "In Photography," Barthes claims, "the presence of the thing (at a certain past moment) is never metaphoric; and in the case of animated beings, their life as well" (78). Barthes's need to turn to photography to assert what seems the most basic and obvious fact about his mother—that she was once present as a living, breathing being—reflects the power of grief to overwhelm the mourner's sensory experience of the world so thoroughly with images that it becomes a struggle to assert even the most obvious facts of past and present corporeality: that Barthes's mother once lived, that Emerson's body carries on without his son, that when Ruth reaches out with her hand there will be something to touch. Its assertion of past presence brings the photograph closer to the mourner's lost world of sensory experience but falls short of transporting him or her there; for this reason, Barthes describes the photograph as "neither image nor reality, a new being, really: a reality one can no longer touch" (87).

As Ruth's meditations made clear, however, the frustration of the mourner's ability to touch in many ways defines the experience of grief. Having "rediscovered" his mother in a photograph that establishes the fact of her past presence, Barthes struggles still to find a way to access in sensory terms the "reality" the photograph represents and evidences. Ultimately, what he demands of the Winter Garden image is no less than what Ruth demands of the images of memory: that they fulfill themselves in the flesh. Having begun by focusing on the "intense immobility" of the photograph and its parallel with the motionlessness of his grief, Barthes pushes his argument toward the assertion that "photography has something to do with resurrection" (82). Extending Sontag's idea that a photograph is "a material vestige of its subject in a way no painting can be" (Sontag 1977,

154), Barthes locates the possibility of resurrection in the photograph's ability to function as a medium through which he can once again touch the lost body of his mother:

> The photograph is literally an emanation of the referent. From a real body, which was there, proceed emanations which ultimately touch me, who am here; the duration of the transmission is insignificant; the photograph of the missing being, as Sontag says, will touch me like the delayed rays of a star. A sort of umbilical cord links the body of the photographed thing to my gaze: light, though impalpable, is here *a carnal medium,* a skin I share with anyone who has been photographed. (81)

Barthes breaks down the science of photography in order to turn the look into a touch, restoring the chiasmic quality of vision; as his gaze rests on his mother's photograph he images that contact as an opportunity to rub against her or "share" her skin. His emphasis on the way the "real" body imprints itself on the photograph and the photograph imprints itself on his own eye allows him to establish a connection with the image that is material, if "impalpable" and chronologically removed. The metaphorical "umbilical cord" that he describes is tenuous and thin, but constructed out of knowledge of chemical processes that render it, at least at some level, grounded in materiality. Ultimately, that cord connects Barthes's gaze with the body of his mother: "(Hence the Winter Garden Photograph, however pale, is for me the treasury of rays which emanated from my mother as a child, from her hair, her skin, her dress, her gaze, *on that day.*)" (82). Here, Barthes locates the value of the chosen image not in its ability to collect "all the possible predicates from which my mother's being was constituted," but in its material status as a "treasury of rays" that allows him to touch her hair and her skin. Whereas the Winter Garden Photograph "was indeed essential" for Barthes because it achieved the "impossible science of the unique being," these passages demonstrate the way in which that unique being connects not to an abstract conception of his mother's identity but to a material realization of her embodied presence on a specific day.

If the Winter Garden Photograph bears the trace of his mother's body, however, Barthes's attempt to reach through the image to retrieve her necessarily fails. Responding at first to the fact that his mother's face in the photograph is "vague, faded" (99) Barthes tries enlarging the photo to reveal smaller and smaller details: "I believe that by enlarging the detail 'in series' (each shot engendering smaller details than at the preceding stage), I will finally reach my mother's very being" (99). Ultimately, he acknowledges,

> I live in the illusion that it suffices to clean the surface of the image in order to accede to *what is behind*: to scrutinize means to turn the photograph over, to reach its other side. . . . Alas, however hard I look, I discover nothing: if I enlarge, I see nothing but the grain of the paper: I undo the image for the sake of its substance; and if I do not enlarge, if I content myself with scrutinizing, I obtain this sole knowledge, long since possessed at first glance: that this indeed has been: the turn of the screw has produced nothing. (100)

Locating the "substance" of the image in the form of his mother's corporeality, Barthes attempts to push past the surface of the photograph to retrieve the absent body that it marks. Neither tactile nor theoretical manipulation of the photograph, however, yields access to that missing form; notwithstanding the intensity of Barthes's struggle, the surface of the image is not the surface of his mother's body, nor the grain of the paper her skin. Although he "live[s] in the illusion" that photography "has something to do with resurrection," that connection, too, emerges as primarily metaphorical. If the missing body of his absent mother touches him through the photograph, as he claims earlier in the text, he cannot touch it in return: "I cannot penetrate, cannot reach into the Photograph. I can only sweep it with my glance, like a smooth surface. The Photograph is *flat*" (106). If, as Merleau-Ponty argues, "the thickness of the body" is "the sole means I have to go unto the heart of . . . things" (Merleau-Ponty 1968, 135), the flatness of the photograph marks its contents' exclusion from a world inhabited by bodies and "beings in depth" (136). Ultimately, then, the photograph's status as image renders it hauntingly equivalent to the mind's own images of grief, images that are "partially true, and therefore totally false" (Barthes 1981, 66).

Regardless of the degree of physical verisimilitude it offers, the photograph of a deceased loved one remains what Barthes describes as "a temporal hallucination" (115). As it renders his mother's presence verifiable but inaccessible, the Winter Garden Photograph taunts Barthes with a body that can be seen but not touched, identified but never experienced. For this reason, the photograph's status as "neither image nor reality, a new being, really: a reality one can no longer touch" emerges less as a slightly diminished form of the real than as a tortured form of the image, or what Barthes later describes as "a mad image, chafed by reality" (115). Like the constant, recurring images of grief that replace Ruth's embodied interactions with her mother, Barthes's photographs bring him painfully close only to deny him access. In her study of the workings of the mind in the process of imagining, Elaine Scarry defines imagining as "*not*-perception: it is instead the quasi-percipient, slightly percipient, almost percipient, not yet percipient, after-percipient of perceptual mimesis" (Scarry 1999, 66). The photograph, like imagining, takes us to the brink of perception and then pulls back; its freely offered visual access and historical verifiability screen the harsh way in which it denies tactile access or lived interaction.

Although Barthes describes the labor of grief as a failed attempt to see his mother again—"And confronted with the photograph, as in the dream, it is the same effort, the same Sisyphean labor: to reascend, straining toward the essence, to climb back down without having *seen* it [emphasis mine], and to begin all over again" (66)—his visual metaphor misrepresents a goal that cannot be achieved through vision alone. He wants not merely to see his mother but to touch her, smell her, reclaim her body. It is that sensory fullness that the photograph simultaneously recalls but excludes in its essential flatness, as Barthes acknowledges: "Surrounded by these photographs, I could no longer console myself with Rilke's line: 'Sweet as memory, the mimosas steep the bedroom': the Photograph does not 'steep' the bedroom: no odor, no music, nothing but the *exorbitant thing*" (91). This dynamic, characteristic of all photography, emerges as particularly troubling in the image of mourning when a body no longer accessible in experiential terms is rendered visually present. Presence, as Miles Richardson observes in "The Gift of Presence," "requires the presence of the body, but the body not as an object but as the self made flesh, equipped with the seeing hand, the listening eye, the comprehending ear, the beseeching mouth, and the empathetic skin" (2001, 264). As Barthes's text reveals, the static quality of the photographic image emerges as particularly poignant in the context of grief: "When we define the Photograph as a motionless image, this does not mean only that the figures it represents do not move; it means that they do not *emerge*, do not *leave*: they are anesthetized and fastened down, like butterflies" (Barthes 1981, 57). If photography exposes the ever present gap between the living-moving body and the body as image, grief lives in the space of that gap as a permanent condition. Although Barthes claims initially that the Winter Garden Photograph allows him to "rediscover" his mother, he cannot rescue her from the "flat" surface that transforms her living-moving body into an "exorbitant thing."[16] As Ruth discovers in *Housekeeping*, the image crumbles under the force of the mourner's attempt to hold on to the experience of embodied interaction with a loved one, leaving the grieving subject alone in a room with a head full of images or a handful of glossy paper. The conclusion of *Camera Lucida* unveils its own image of Barthes, "in the love stirred by Photography," turning not to embrace another body but to dance with the beloved image: "I passed beyond the unreality of the thing represented, I entered crazily into the spectacle, into the image, taking into my arms what is dead" (117).

Disembodied Spaces in the Images of Shellburne Thurber

If Barthes searches desperately through piles of old photographs to find one that might allow him to "tak[e] into [his] arms what is dead," the contemporary American photographer Shellburne Thurber uses her photography to document the impossibility of retrieving lost bodies in and through the image. Joann Blais describes *Camera Lucida* as "a text with an absent centre, an elegiac and empty room" (Blais 1994, 236). In photographing empty rooms, Thurber explores the possibility of representing grief by constructing images that gesture toward an "absent centre" which they, like *Camera Lucida*, refuse to represent. Thurber's photographs of empty and abandoned domestic spaces span decades and geographical distance but share a focus on the absence of the bodies that once animated the rooms her pictures represent. Thurber began taking photographs shortly after her mother's death. In an attempt to understand the mother that she never really knew, she used her camera to image the empty spaces that her mother had once inhabited (Donnelly 1999, 14). Another series of photographs emerged in response to the death of her favorite "aunt" (actually a close family friend); Thurber's grief led her to her aunt's home, where she captured a series of images that picture the once familiar rooms now empty but still haunted by her aunt's presence. Such images, in Timothy McElreavy's words, "work through mourning as a process of finding the deceased by no longer finding her. The empty bedroom with its elaborate wallpaper, veiled window, and mirror evokes Aunt Anna, figuring her ghost among the floral designs and reflective surfaces of her room. The photographs, however, show none of this; the projections that one might perceive in the image cannot literally be pictured there" (McElreavy 1999, 10). McElreavy's analysis points to the "absent centre" in the empty rooms Thurber photographs; the image "evokes" a missing loved one whose presence is reflected in the room's surfaces but whose body can never be found. The absence of the loved one's embodied form thus becomes, in many ways, the subject of the photograph. If Barthes's *Camera Lucida* traces his poignant but unsuccessful attempts to offset the failures of the visual image, Thurber's images dwell in the space of that failure as they constantly draw the viewer's attention to the tension between absence and presence, image and body, surface and depth.

In a recent series of photographs, Thurber expands her focus out from the empty spaces created by the death of her mother and aunt to abandoned interiors of the homes of strangers. In 1998, she traveled throughout the south to capture images of decaying houses and empty interiors. Despite the absence of a personal connection between the photographer and the past occupants of these spaces, these photographs function as images of grief that evoke families, lives, and bodies no longer present. Having sought out abandoned interiors and decaying houses, Thurber makes no attempt to recreate the living-moving bodies of those who once inhabited those spaces. Her photographs represent grief not by claiming to capture its lost object but by picturing the emptiness of spaces that once formed themselves around bodies no longer present. Thurber responds to what Sartre describes as "the essential poverty of images" (Sartre 1948, 209) not by attempting to embody the photograph but by highlighting the absence of bodies that the image cannot locate, animate, or hold onto. If Barthes's photographs claim to represent his mother's embodied form but strip the body of its animating qualities, Thurber's images reanimate the empty space the body leaves behind to unveil the limitations of the image.

Both *Housekeeping* and *Camera Lucida* document the failure of the image to hold onto the specificity of a missing body; Ruth's multisensory, textured experience of her mother's body collapses into the "anonymous" image of an untouchable woman, while Barthes confronts dream images and photographs that continually frustrate him in his desire to relocate his mother's specific, embodied presence. In both these texts, grief finds no solace in images that fail, of necessity, to hold onto the lost body in all its texture and specificity. In contrast, Thurber constructs a series of photographs that highlight irretrievable absence. Her images invoke absent bodies that never existed as presences for the viewer. In an exaggeration of the dynamics of grief, these images shape themselves around an aching absence disturbing not only in its inaccessibility but in its anonymity. If grief forms around the absent and irretrievable body, Thurber's images enact the form of grief without its content.

Whereas Barthes struggles to deny the limitations of the image and Ruth attempts to break through the image to access the absent body that it represents, Thurber refuses to compensate for the image's lack. Her images exist in the tension between what Barthes describes as the "flatness" of the photograph and what Merleau-Ponty designates the "thickness of the body." A long tradition of thought understands the photographic image as static, framed, motionless, "killed into art"; although the photograph captures life, such a tradition would argue, it does so at the expense of motion, tactility, texture. Photographs, in the words of Erin C. Mitchell, "transform human referents into mortified objects; both actual and virtual photography 'freeze' human beings as static images. Photographs reify the human being as object of the gaze" (Mitchell 2000, 325). As a result, the viewer is able to approach the image from a distance, to attain visual mastery, to capture the scene and render it comprehensible. The "real" world of the photograph can be seen but never accessed, witnessed but never touched; as Sartre observes, "the object as an image is an unreality" (Sartre 1948, 177). Thurber calls attention to the fact that her photographs are images by exposing their untouchability even as she heightens their tactile invitation. She creates a desire in the viewer to engage tactilely with them and even simulates bodily engagement but ultimately forces us to confront the failure of the image to achieve texture or human presence.

Despite the absence of bodies in Thurber's photographs, her images consistently foreground tensions of human embodiment. In an interview about this series, Thurber describes homes as surrogates for human presence and domestic interiors as stand-ins for the body (Donnelly 1999, 15–16). In the collapsing architectural spaces that she captures with her camera, isolated signs of past human presence emerge: a potholder left hanging on a crumbling wall, remnants of a lacy curtain on a broken window, a bar of soap covered with cobwebs next to an old metal sink. The conspicuous placement of these isolated artifacts in photographs of otherwise empty spaces exaggerates what Susan Sontag describes as the speculative viewing dynamic of photography in general: "The ultimate wisdom of the photographic image is to say: 'There is the surface. Now think—or rather feel, intuit—what is beyond it, what the reality must be like if it looks this way.' Photographs, which cannot themselves explain anything, are inexhaustible invitations to deduction, speculation, and fantasy" (Sontag 1977, 23). Arguing that the image extends such an invitation without supporting the viewer's quest for meaning, Sontag traces understanding to an apprehension of functioning that must be explained in time. If, as Sontag claims, "only that which narrates can make us understand" (23), the photograph invokes narrative speculation the image refuses to substantiate. The story or domestic history the viewer would construct from Thurber's images remains a fantasy which would function, like the work of the imagination Elisabeth Bronfen describes in *Over Her Dead Body*, to repair or mitigate a reality that otherwise threatens to destroy us. "In that it presupposes loss," Bronfen observes, "storytelling involves the work of mourning, with the . . . text transforming a narcissistic wound into a fictitious positivity" (1992, 350).

Although Thurber's images invite the viewer to construct a story of past presence, such presence is always shadowed by a loss foretold in the image's empty, abandoned spaces. Thurber's images thus reverse the work of mourning by generating fictions of past presence which only exaggerate the space of present absence. In "Stories," John Berger observes, "Before a photograph you search for *what was there*. . . . If there is a narrative form intrinsic to still photography, it will search for what happened, as memories or reflections do" (1982, 279). In Thurber's photographs, the "search for what was there" pushes the viewer to construct a story that continuously dissolves into a narrative of loss. My interest in Thurber's images lies not primarily in the narratives her photographs inspire the viewer to create but in the visual processes they push the viewer to enact. If storytelling, in Bronfen's terms, "involves the work of mourning," the gaze that Thurber's photographs construct undoes that work to return the viewer again and again to the lost body of grief. Even as they render bodies absent and inaccessible, Thurber's photographs mark the parameters of corporeal loss through a series of visual illusions that construct and then dissolve bodily presence.

Material signs of past presence in Thurber's photographs encourage the viewer to search for human forms amidst the clutter of these abandoned rooms, exaggerating what James Elkins describes as the human tendency to search out and identify bodily forms in any visual field. Prior even to conscious intuition, he claims, "we scan the visual field to see if it might harbor a body" (Elkins 1996, 130). What we want, he observes, is not just complete figures or smoothed outlines "but complete *bodies*. We need to see figures that are like bodies, and ultimately, we need the bodies themselves. When I see a form—any form, any shape at all—I am also seeing a body. I may be looking at only a smudge on a piece of paper, but I see it as a single form, a unit unto itself, a thing, a body. A lover is very different from a smudge, but ultimately I take an interest in every isolated smooth continuous object because I am interested in bodies" (129).

This tendency to "understand strange forms by thinking back to bodies" (129) is exaggerated in Thurber's photographs by the tensions they foreground between human presence and absence. Many of Thurber's images direct the viewer's attention to the paradox of absent presence that also defines the embodied experience of grief. In "Kill the Day," the opening poem of his recent collection, *The Painted Bed*, Donald Hall represents his grief over his wife's death through images of her body as it is lost to him, first as presence and then as absence:

When she died, at first the outline of absence defined
a presence that disappeared. He wept for the body
he could no longer reach to touch in bed on waking.
He wept for her silver thimble. He wept when the dog
brought him a slipper that smelled of her still.
In another summer, her pheromones diminished.
The negative space of her body dwindled as she receded
deeper into the ground, smaller and fainter each day,
dried out, shrunken, separated from the news of the day. (ll. 54–62)

Thurber's images evoke the sense of absent presence in part through a process of perceptual illusion that they initiate in the viewer. As Hall describes the almost unconscious gesture of waking to touch his wife's body, Thurber's images pull the viewer into empty space that is shadowed by human presence, not only in the artifacts and structures of abandoned rooms, but in what Hall describes as the "negative space of [the] body." Thurber creates that negative space by offering imagistic glimpses of a body that we, as viewers, wish to locate in the empty space of the abandoned rooms she represents. These rooms shape themselves around the body's absence, both in their visual rendering of a material unraveling that speaks to the body's breakdown and in their ghostly habitation by forms that echo the contours of the body.

Although the act of looking into someone's bedroom suggests the possibility of seeing their most intimate personal space, Thurber's "Chesson House: Bedroom corner with broken windows, view #1" (Figure 10) frustrates the possibility of such an intimate encounter through its rendering of an abandoned room stripped not only of human presence but of furnishings, identifiable artifacts, wallpaper and paint. This image is shot into the corner of the room, creating in the foreground of the photograph a triangle of "stuff" that frustrates the attempt of the gaze to focus, organize, and order the visually chaotic materials that include old cardboard boxes, broken window frames, and various types of building rubble. Unlike the single potholder or the lace curtain that signify human presence in the midst of absence, this debris-covered floor fails to signify itself as anything but materiality. As such, it also denies the gaze a literal place to settle or a metaphorical means to narrativize the image.

Caught up in the overwhelming irregularity of this preponderance of matter, the viewer searches for a focus and a familiar form. Here, the eye is pulled up from this pile of indistinguishable materials not only by the light that shines through the windows on either side of the corner but by the fact that "the eye prefers smoothly bounded objects that are more like

FIGURE 10

bodies to shattered collections of things that cannot be thought of as bodies" (Elkins 1996, 159); in this image, the gaze is drawn toward a piece of black material caught up in or suspended from the left window, its visual presence emphasized not only by the starkness of its color against the light but by its disruption of the image's one claim to order, the almost symmetrical placement of the two windows on either wall. The visual motion of the eye as it is pulled up and to the side of the photograph is exaggerated by the real or perceived motion of the cloth, the edges of which blur in shadow or movement. This lack of clarity and illusion of motion, along with the absence of any clear explanation about how the cloth might be suspended from the window, construct an initial impression—however fleeting—of a hunched body moving through the window and out of the room.

In animating this material, Thurber turns it into a piece of clothing that provides what Hall describes as an "outline" that gestures toward an absent human body whose presence the viewer witnesses as already gone. Defining the body as "a thing that is in perpetual motion until the moment of its death," Elkins extends the visual search for bodies to the desire for bodies in motion: "Once we have seen a body, or imagined one, or found a body metaphor to rest content with, then another desire becomes visible: we also want bodies to move, to be alive" (132). In the midst of crumbled plaster, collapsing cardboard boxes, and broken window panes, this cloaklike fabric bespeaks the presence of a human form that disappears before it emerges. Its apparent motion both supports its animation and contributes to its ghostliness; as the viewer's gaze steadies, the body we glimpse resolves itself into an intelligible, inanimate form.

Even as Hall reaches out for a body that fails to materialize, then, the viewer of Thurber's photographs glimpses a bodily image that recollects an animated form. Although that form quickly resolves itself into object materiality, the image remains haunted by the viewer's glimpse of the human body, a body now present only as absence. Thurber's image thus recreates the rhythms of desire that Hall describes as he reaches out to the empty space that should be filled by his wife's body, or that C. S. Lewis invokes when he describes grief as the constant frustration of habitual impulses directed toward the missing loved one (Lewis 1961, 39). If the psychoneurological phenomenon of subjective contour completion explains the "urge to make a continuous shape out of the pieces of our visual world" (Elkins 1996, 128), the success of Thurber's photographs may be due in part to their ability to exploit the parallel between that common perceptual phenomenon and the misperception of grief. Describing the desire to see the world "in analogy with the body" as "perhaps the most primal desire of all," Elkins concludes his description of visual process with language that seems applicable to the experience of grief: "We prefer to have bodies in front of us or in our hands, and if we cannot have them, we continue to see them, as afterimages or ghosts. It is an exquisite and complicated subject, the way our eyes continue to look out at the most diverse kinds of things and bring back echoes of bodies" (132). Thurber's photographs make no attempt to render the former inhabitants of the abandoned rooms visually accessible or fully present; instead, her images are filled with "echoes of bodies" that recreate the frustrated desire of grief without providing access to its missing object. Images of the body in these photographs are constructed as "afterimages" that represent the inaccessibility of bodies that we can never have "in our hands." As the gaze becomes narrativized, the breakdown of the image into time renders the viewer doubly susceptible to the loss that narrative would repair. The process of temporarily perceiving human presence only to correct that illusion with an acknowledgment of absence locates the viewer in a narrative of disposses-

FIGURE 11

sion that she experiences as well as observes. The freedom to generate and project stories is undercut by a series of perceptual illusions that fragment and disempower the gaze, returning it to its origin in a seeing, touching body incapable of penetrating the photograph's slick surface.

The contrast of building material and fabric also works to create echoes of the human body in Thurber's "Gholson Homeplace: Upstairs hallway with window and torn curtain" (Figure 11). In this image, the viewer's focus—constructed both through camera angle, texture, and light—is the single window in the hallway. The ceiling's peeling paint and the cracked sheetrock on the walls render the single lace curtain suspended in a drooping fashion on the window a poignant reminder of past human presence. In their discussion of memory and the body, Bloomer and Moore describe the way in which embodied experiences "leave their impression on the walls and forms of the interior and endow the rooms with artifacts which give us access to previous experiences" (50). That "access," of course, is limited and perhaps illusory, in the same way that the curtain's echo of the body is illusory in this image. The angle of the shot, the presence of light it catches streaming in from outside, and the particular way the folds of the curtain gather combine to construct this piece of fabric as clothing rather than curtain. Variations in the fabric's color and density create the visual illusion of a solid bodily form beneath the curtain: in the light and from that angle, a waist and two long legs seem only barely disguised by the play of lace fabric around them. The fleeting glimpse of a body suspended in front of the window where no body could be is less a failed illusion, perhaps, than a successful rendering of the way that perception filters through grief as the mourner searches for a body now present only as "the outline of absence." The body in Thurber's photographs, like the lost body of grief, is present only *as image,* as what Sartre describes as the "imagined object": "This passive object, kept alive artificially, but which is about to vanish at any moment, cannot satisfy desires. But it is not entirely useless: to construct an unreal object is a way of deceiving the desires momentarily in order to aggravate them, somewhat like the effect of sea water on thirst" (Sartre 1948, 178). The brilliance of Thurber's photographs of loss relates to the way the viewer's desire is constructed through deception and "aggravated" through perception, so that he or she imaginatively creates and then loses a presence never really known. Corey Creekmur defines "the desire to reanimate what has been stilled" (Creekmur 1996, 77) as the central impulse behind both photographic interpretation and the experience of mourning. Thurber's art explores that parallel as it both constructs and frustrates the viewer's desire to animate the empty spaces it represents. As the imagined body we glimpse reveals itself as image, the viewing process enacts the taunting rhythms of grief that Hall associates with his wife's death: "When she died, at first the outline of absence defined / A presence that disappeared."

In grief, the transivity of bodies that Merleau-Ponty describes along with the intertwining of vision and touch collapses into the taunting placement of the survivor's isolated body in a world of images that can neither touch nor be touched. Although Hall remembers sex with his wife as a chiasmic intertwining located in "the crossing place of bodies," his dreams are haunted by visions of her embodied form—"Now he dreamed again of her thick and lavish hair, / of her lush body wetting and loosening beside him" (ll. 137–138)—that resist materialization. Even as he tries to hold onto his wife's embodied presence through memory, Hall only loses her again and again. In grief, the "reversibility" that Merleau-Ponty defines as the mark of intercorporeality collapses into the subject/object dynamics of the unreciprocated gaze:

> He remembered ordinary fucking that shone like the sun
> in their household solar system, brighter than Jesus,
> than poetry, than their orchard under the mountain—
> the crossing place of bodies that regarded each other
> with more devotion the more they approached her death
> until they were singular, gazing speechless together
> while she vanished into open eyes staring all night.
> In the day's crush and tangle of melted nails,
> collapsed foundation stones, and adze-trimmed beams,
> the widower alone glimpsed the beekeeper's mask
> in high summer as it approached the day they built,
> now fallen apart with bark still on its beams,
> nine layers of wallpaper over the dry laths—
> always ending, no other ending, in dead eyes open. (ll. 139–152)

The poem's insistent return to the image of Jane lying with "dead eyes open" marks the way in which her inanimate body taunts Hall with a form of absent presence that mocks his experience of her as an embodied subject. Death unravels chiasmic intercorporeality to taunt the survivor with a subject present only as disembodied image and a body present only in its object form. With Jane's death, the lovers—who "were singular, gazing speechless together"—are locked away from one another, forced to split into subject and object of the gaze. If Hall's memories of intercorporeality resist materialization, Jane's open-eyed corpse lacks what Grosz describes as "psychical embodiment" (1994, 23); as Elkins observes, "If I look into someone's eyes and think of the fact that the eye is nothing but a rotating sack of fluid, then an eye becomes an unsettling thing: I see the eye but it does not see me. What *sees* is . . . the person connected to the eye, but the eye itself is just tissue" (1996, 48). Trapped in the tensions of embodied subjectivity, Hall "awakened daily to the prospect of nothingness / in the day's house that like all houses was mortuary" (ll. 18–19). Hall describes himself not only as a body crushed by and tangled up with the materials of a house that will not hold, but as a solitary seer whose vision portends only loss.

Hall's final images of unraveling rooms and collapsed structures recall the poignancy of Thurber's photographs, which also implicate the viewer in a material world animated by the perception of loss. As Hall's reader imaginatively peels back "nine layers of wallpaper over the dry laths," the painful dynamics of stripping away the marks of human presence are complicated by the way the poem dissolves the opposition between matter and that which animates it. Both Hall's poem and Thurber's photographs render material decay painful by introducing echoes of human embodiment into the midst of images of collapsing structures. As the room falls apart around the grieving widower in "Kill the Day," images of the industrial and the nonhuman ("melted nails" and "collapsed foundation stones") are not only "tangled" up with object signs of human presence—"nine layers of wallpaper over the dry laths"—but haunted by the connection between objects and organisms, growth and violability: "the day they built, / now fallen apart with bark still on its beams."

Thurber exploits that connection in her images not only by documenting the slow unraveling of material decay in the rooms she photographs but by exaggerating the viewer's desire to engage with the image in sensory terms. The "thickness" of Thurber's photographs is especially surprising given the content of her images. The abandoned spaces that she captures are not only uninhabited but largely devoid of furnishings and artifacts. These "empty" spaces, however, keep failing to be nothing. In part, Thurber's images achieve perceptual depth by capturing the textured status of the abandoned rooms she photographs; her images visually differentiate multiple layers of exposed material in places where we have come to expect uniformity and flatness. As she unveils the complex and varied material composition of the structural conventions of the room—its floor, its ceiling, its walls—Thurber pushes us to look for texture in places where we would least expect it. In "Chesson House: Bedroom corner with broken windows, view #1" (see Figure 10), the very walls of the room invite touch; peeling paint reveals cracked plaster which uncovers torn sheetrock which exposes wooden beams with dark spaces between them. As the viewer's eye pushes past the surface layer of the wall to penetrate its depths, awareness of its literal "thickness" and differentiated textures exaggerates the tactility of what was once a smooth surface. As the abandoned room decays, it reveals the complexity and variety of its material components. The motion of decay is captured in simultaneous form as the unraveling of the room is figured in the different colors, textures, and layers exposed here.

The photograph's revision of the wall's flatness as a kind of thickness or depth is thus echoed in the transformation of the static physical environment into an empty room surprisingly in motion; the room peels, crumbles, shifts before our eyes. The same is true of Thurber's "Gholson Homeplace: Upstairs hallway with window and torn curtain" (see Figure 11). The photograph is shot at a slight angle to include not only the window in the wall but the peeling paint above. The pieces of paint or plaster that hang suspended from the ceiling seem barely attached; they threaten to unleash themselves at any moment. The rough texture of that disengaging surface throws into counterpoint the fragility of the lace fabric suspended just below. As things fall apart, peel, and crack, as light moves through the window and catches in the curtain, the material of the room seems surprisingly animated.

The engaging, tangible composition of Thurber's photographs also moves the viewer around as he or she is pulled into texture and dimension, the gaze distracted by clutter and mess. Although we tend to experience the gaze as disembodied, Thurber's photographs denaturalize the processes of focus and visual organization to return us to a physiological definition of vision that emphasizes the motion of the eye rather than the power of the gaze. In "Chesson House: Bedroom corner with broken windows, view #1" (see Figure 10), the viewer's gaze is set in motion by piles of garbage that refuse visual differentiation or symbolic organization. The eye's focus is scattered by the triangular foregrounding of debris as the viewer's gaze collapses onto a floor covered with rubble, cardboard boxes, broken window frames, and building materials. Unlike the single potholder or the lace curtain that signifies human presence in the midst of absence, this debris-covered floor fails to signify itself as anything but materiality. As such, it also denies the gaze a literal place to settle or a metaphorical means of rendering the image stable or coherent. As paint peels and sheetrock crumbles, visual boundaries between objects waver and fail until it becomes virtually impossible to organize or even identify the material objects in the corner. These representations have a physicalizing impact on the viewer that results in part from the gaze's inability to define a focus that anchors and centers. Thurber denaturalizes the physiological processes of seeing to restore the viewer's awareness of looking as a sensory process. In *The Body Postured,* Alphonso Lingis argues that the gaze is always embodied: "Sensing is not a passive reception of impressions on our sensitive surfaces. Sensing is a behavior, a movement, a prehension, a handling. To feel the tangible, the smooth, the sticky, or the bristly, the touching hand has to move across it with a certain pressure, a certain pacing and periodicity, a certain scope of movement. But the look, too, in order to see the red of the dress has to focus, to move across its expanse with a certain pressure and scope and periodicity" (Lingis 1996, 61). Looking at Thurber's images denaturalizes the notion of the all-powerful, disembodied gaze. As the things in Thurber's photographs are animated—existing in potential motion as they fall apart, peel, or crack—the clutter and mess of the photos unsettles the gaze, setting it into motion and locating it in the viewer's body.

If the tensions of grief emerge out of an embodied subject's inability to reach through the image to touch a lost body, Thurber's photographs invoke the viewer's desire to touch but consistently return him or her to the limitations of the image. In perceptually constructing images of the body that immediately reveal themselves as mere images, her photographs unveil the illusion of accessibility with which Barthes struggles throughout *Camera Lucida.* Thurber not only shows the viewer the absent body that can't be shown but continually forces the viewer into a multisensory body through which access to the visual image must be partial and frustrated. In so doing, she recreates the dynamics of grief even as she exposes the impossibility of "comforting" a mourning that is embodied.

In "Chesson House: Abandoned bed with dark window" (Figure 12), Thurber invokes the very tangibility and depth that the photograph, as image, can never realize. Although the viewer accesses this image through the gaze, the composition of the photograph consistently alludes to an experience of texture and dimension that belies the flatness and the smoothness of the image. In addition to unveiling the literal "thickness" of the walls—crumbling wallpaper, cracked sheetrock, wooden frame—this photograph further disrupts the viewer's perception of the wall's flat plane. The strong vertical and horizontal lines of the image constructed by the wall, the bed frame, and the window create a kind of referential grid against which the materials in the photograph constantly strain. In the lower left corner of the image, a cracked section of wall erupts into the space of the bedroom and toward the viewer; in the right center of the frame, a large piece of ripped wallpaper violates the vertical plane established by the wall and the bed frame to push forward and catch the viewer's gaze. As the wall collapses inward, then, the window pulls the viewer back into a dark cavernous hole where we glimpse the frame of the house's roof

FIGURE 12

against a backdrop of total blackness that frustrates the desire to bind the image by locating its boundary in a final vertical plane. The photograph both presses upon the gaze and refuses to contain it by violating the boundaries of the visual planes it seems to establish and lending the illusion of perceptual depth to an image that is necessarily flat. The remains of the ripped blind in the corner of the window exaggerate its failure to maintain the boundaries of privacy by reminding us that what is revealed should be covered; the image disturbs not only by opening the private space of the bedroom to public view but by "seeing" through a window that swallows the gaze instead of redirecting it toward an outside world. In a similar way, the apparent dimensionality of Thurber's image flouts the viewer's seeming immersion in a three-dimensional world by inviting us to move into a representational space that can be accessed only through vision.

If, as Sartre argues, the image is defined by the fact that it is "present, but, at the same time, out of reach" (Sartre 1948, 177–178), Thurber also flouts the untouchability of the image by rendering its visual contents surprisingly tactile. In contrast to the smooth, impenetrable surface of the photograph itself, the contents of Thurber's "Chesson House: Abandoned bed with dark window" are not dirty (a quality that can be represented easily in visual terms) but gritty, rough, and textured. The juxtaposition of materials in this image invites not only visual but tactile apprehension. In the lower left corner, the protruding section of cracked wallboard pushes against a pile of sheets with a satiny sheen, while the sagging mattress, stained pillow, and lumpy comforter in the foreground scrape against the rough textures of the crumbling plaster found not only on the wall and ceiling but in the pieces of gritty rubble collected on the bare mattress.

The tension between the embodied viewer and the disembodied image is exaggerated by the photograph's ghostly evocation of bodily presence. A twisted wire hanger in the upper right corner of the frame and a pile of sheets discarded on the floor beside the bed recall the room's past status as a place where someone dressed, slept, lived. Insofar as the viewer imaginatively reanimates the bedroom's space, he or she is pushed to acknowledge the fundamental bodily absence around which the room revolves; not surprisingly, then, the shot is centered not on the bed itself but on the humped form of the dirty comforter draped across the bed where a body might otherwise be found. In its visual recollection of the absent body, the comforter not only plays a trick on the viewer, but introduces the imagined/absent body into the literal decay of the crumbling room. The impact of the room's physical collapse—its peeling plaster, fallen sheetrock, cracked and exposed walls—is heightened by the viewer's imaginative introduction of a body into the scene; as the gaze surveys the already intimate space of the bedroom, the imaginative press of human skin against the dirty, debris-covered mattress emphasizes the violation of personal space. Having momentarily reintroduced a missing body into the bedroom, the viewer experiences that visual illusion not as a form of imaginative rescue but as an almost physical immersion in the dirt and detritus of the abandoned room's decay. The photograph is haunted by a body present in its absence, a missing body that cannot be retrieved but through which the viewer experiences the textures and sharp edges of the room's material decay.

The viewer who responds to this image, then, enters its space not only through the gaze but through the imagined experience of the body's touch. As Merleau-Ponty observes, we see only as flesh, necessarily immersing ourselves in the things we see and touch as a body: "*as* tangible [the body] descends among [things], *as* touching it dominates them all and draws this relationship and even this double relationship from itself. . . . This bursting forth of the mass of the body toward the things . . . this pact between them and me according to which I lend them my body in order that they inscribe upon it and give me their resemblance, this fold, this central cavity of the visible which is my vision, these two mirror arrangements of the seeing and the visible, the touching and the touched, form a close-bound system that I count on" (1968, 146). Thurber's photographs invoke the "close-bound system" of bodily perception and intercorporeality that Merleau-Ponty describes only to close down mutual exchange. The layers of texture in the abandoned rooms she images call out to be touched as well as seen, but remain, in Sartre's terms, mere "mirage." If, as Merleau-Ponty argues, the "thickness of the body" defines the experience of perception, Thurber's images invoke the viewer's embodied response only to unravel the intertwining of the visible and the tangible, leaving us, like Barthes, cradling only images in our hands.

Thurber exploits the parallel between photographic image and memory, between the texture of a room and the materiality of a body, to pull her viewer into an experience of grief in which the awful tensions of embodiment rip apart the "fold" that Merleau-Ponty describes as an intertwining of subject and object. Her photographs recreate the dynamics of grief by returning the viewer to the material location of the object body and simultaneously locking the viewing subject out of tactile engagement with either the image or the body that image invokes as absence. If Merleau-Ponty celebrates the body's status as "a being of two leaves, a thing among things and otherwise what sees and touches them" (1968, 137), Thurber's images dwell in the friction generated by our "double-belongingness to the order of the 'object' and to the order of the 'subject'" (137).

Embodied subjectivity not only renders us, like the materials of the abandoned rooms Thurber photographs, susceptible to crumbling and decay, but forces us to witness that loss again and again as our minds construct the absent presence of bodies we can no longer hold through images we are unable to touch.

Remembering the Body

In "The Body Remembers: Grieving and a Circle of Time," Patricia Hentz, a specialist in psychiatric nursing and ethics, documents the results of her qualitative study of women in mourning. In the context of current research on the cognitive and affective aspects of grief and mourning, Hentz's work demonstrates the need for "attention to how one's body experiences the loss and the memories it has encoded" (Hentz 2002, 161). Her research testifies not only to the importance of the body in the experience of loss, the way in which "the experience of the lived other" contributes to the dynamics of grief, but to the isolating consequences of a culture that obscures the embodied dynamics of loss (168). Again and again, Hentz documents the feeling—shared by almost all of her subjects—that their grief refuses containment within the "normal" parameters of loss because their experience of absence forms itself around a missing body and manifests itself not just in consciousness but in motion, habit, and posture. Pressured to ignore the embodied dimensions of a loss too unwieldy to force into a cultural narrative of psychological recovery, the participants in Hentz's study experienced a grief exaggerated by social norms that silenced and isolated them: "This study has challenged our knowing of grief and mourning and has uncovered an aspect ignored and often denied: the body's memory and its role in grief and mourning. Traditional models of grief counseling with emphasis on cognitive, emotional, and behavioral outcomes need to be revisited. Participants in this study spoke of feeling that they were not heard. Their experiences did not fit into existing paradigms" (171).

Hentz's research points to the practical as well as the theoretical implications of scientific and cultural paradigms that exclude or marginalize the role of the body in grief. Although the incontrovertibility of bodily loss renders its acknowledgment painful and difficult, the failure to incorporate the corporeal dynamics of loss in theories of grief implicitly reinforces the embodied subject's experience of isolation and fragmentation in the face of embodied loss. Insofar as the indisputability of the body's loss in death obscures the complexity of relinquishing a presence that not only shapes but constitutes our own embodied subjectivity, our culture's failure to "hear" the body's experience of grief pressures us, like Robinson's protagonist or Barthes's narrator, to disavow the corporeal dimensions of loss. Cultural and critical failures to mark the significance of the lost body's absence may push us toward recovery built on a discursive ground which continually threatens to give way beneath the force of embodied absence. In his poem "As from a Quiver of Arrows" (1998), Carl Phillips explores the question of the body's role in grief. Beginning with the question of how to sustain or remember the body in the face of its irrecuperable absence, the poem interrogates the narrative motion of mourning through metaphors that spatialize and embody the experience of loss. For the poem's speaker, the attempt to detach the dynamics of grief from the realm of intercorporeality fails, returning the mourner to the site of an absent body inextricable from his own. As the object referent of the poem's opening question—"What do we do with the body" (l. 1)—shifts from the absent presence of the lost body to the speaker's own animate form, the poem gestures toward all that is unclaimed or unspoken in familiar cultural constructions of grief. Confronted with the impossibility of restoring or even "remembering" the missing touch of the lost body, Phillips's speaker locates that absent presence in his own interrupted gesture. Reaching out toward an emptied space that returns him to his isolate corporeality, he turns to his own body as a register of loss to ask, in the haunting simplicity of the poem's final line (l. 40), "What will I do now, with my hands?"

CHAPTER FIVE

∞

Teaching the Body to Talk

The Language of Grief

This chapter explores two contemporary novels—Carolyn Parkhurst's *The Dogs of Babel* (2003) and Don DeLillo's *The Body Artist* (2001)—that address the way the bereaved subject enters a world of signs in a failed attempt to recuperate the embodied dimensions of loss. If the construction of mourning as a psychical and linguistic process often marginalizes the lost body of grief, that body returns in these novels to assert the embodied dimension of a loss that refuses to be contained in the realm of the psyche or in the space of signification. The body of grief emerges in these texts in strange forms and in strange places, in a dog that refuses to speak the details of its owner's death and a ghostly little man clad only in underwear who appears out of nowhere to mouth the words and repeat the gestures of the dead. The narrative isolation and projection of corporeality onto animal or supernatural form reflects a rupture that emerges under the pressure of loss. That rupture, I will argue, speaks to the irresolvable tensions that result from the culture's construction of artificial boundaries that divide the body from the embodied subject and displace the experience of grief from the culturally sanctioned language of loss.

In her reading of *Camera Lucida,* Joann Blais images the writing subject of Barthes's text as suspended between two divergent relationships to representation, which she describes in terms of the intellectual and the primitive: "In *Camera Lucida* the writing subject moves rapidly from the posture of an inquiring intellectual to that of an ambivalent amateur of photographs and (disappeared) bodies, nostalgically wanting to become a primitive individual, 'without culture'" (Blais 1994, 232). The refusal of language that she attributes to the narrator of *Camera Lucida* parallels the grieving subject's refusal to move past the fact of the absent body into the compensation of representation. Insofar as the bereaved subject enters the cultural discourse of mourning, he or she must bracket out the body, stepping into the "disincarnate" position of the "'good' cultural subject [who] 'speaks' and allows himself to be identified by that speech" (232). As I discussed in the last chapter, psychoanalytic theories of mourning often reinforce the importance of leaving the body behind to assume the position of the speaking subject. Not surprisingly, then, depictions of grief often become entangled with explorations of the act of representation, the process through which a subject would articulate, resist, or recuperate loss through the mediation of the sign.

In "The Precession of Simulacra," Baudrillard documents a twentieth-century cultural shift from a utopian faith in the power of representation to an era of simulation which renders the real indistinguishable from its representation in a system of signs. Representation, in Baudrillard's argument, depends upon the fundamental axiom of "the principle of equivalence of the sign and of the real" (1994, 6). All Western culture, he contends, once depended upon the "utopian" belief "that a sign could refer to the depth of meaning, that a sign could be exchanged for meaning and that something could guarantee this exchange" (6). Simulation, by contrast, stems from "the radical negation of the sign as value," the collapse of distinction between the "true" and the "false," the "real" and the "imaginary" (6). "By crossing into a space whose curvature is no longer that of the real, nor that of truth," Baudrillard observes, "the era of simulation is inaugurated by a liquidation of all referentials. . . . It is a question of substituting the signs of the real for the real" (2).

This chapter explores two contemporary novels that address the failure of both the promise of representation and the culture of simulation to speak to the embodied dynamics of loss. In tracing a linguistics professor's failed attempt to compensate for his wife's death by teaching his dog to talk, *The Dogs of Babel* exposes language's inability to embody past presence. The protagonist's failed experiments with canine language acquisition reflect his desperate efforts to render his wife's death intelligible through language. In trying to teach his dog to talk, Parkhurst's protagonist would displace rather than represent his embodied grief; by ushering loss into the realm of signification, he attempts to heal the gap of representation and rescue the lost body through language. *The Body Artist* situates the embodied dynamics of its protagonist's grief within a postmodern culture that threatens to dissolve the distinction between absence and presence, the sign and the thing itself. Caught off guard by the sensory immediacy of her husband's absence, DeLillo's bereaved protagonist moves into the space of her own psyche to interact there with a simulacrum of her husband's presence, an odd, ghostly figure that ultimately exposes rather than fills the gap between representation and embodied presence. Turning to language and performance as a means of speaking to a lack they would not only access but recast through representation, the protagonists of these novels attempt to negotiate the embodied dynamics of loss through opposite but equally ineffectual attempts to enter a world of signs, leaving their bodies behind.

Words and Flesh in Carolyn Parkhurst's *The Dogs of Babel*

In their theorization of incorporation, Nicholas Abraham and Maria Torok provide a spatialized model of mourning that appropriates the body as a means of imaging a dynamics of loss which they conceptualize in purely psychic terms. My interest in their argument lies in its simultaneous marginalization and appropriation of embodiment. Although their theories of loss focus exclusively on psychic operations, their metaphorical use of the body to explain the dynamics of mourning allows issues of corporeal loss marginalized in their psychoanalytic models to find their way back into the terms of their argument. Introduced by Abraham and Torok as a tool for explicating psychic processes, the body invoked as a vehicle of metaphor enters their argument from the margins to exert the pressure of materiality on their theorization of loss. Abraham and Torok define incorporation as "the refusal to reclaim as our own the part of ourselves that we placed in what we lost" (Abraham and Torok 1994, 127). Because it assumes a disembodied subjectivity, their argument never explicitly acknowledges the body as a part of the self, or the unraveling of the chiasm as a dimension of loss. Instead, their argument explores the way in which "incorporation reveals a gap within the psyche; it points to something that is missing" (127). In attending to the something that is missing, however, Abraham and Torok's argument also gestures toward other gaps, including the missing body that is invoked through metaphor in their theory.

In "Mourning or Melancholia: Introjection versus Incorporation," Abraham and Torok not only revise Freud's understanding of incorporation but render their theory of unsuccessful mourning in surprisingly spatial and embodied terms. Although they focus exclusively on "loss sustained by the psyche," they define incorporation, one response to such loss, as the fantasy of introducing the lost loved one "into one's own body" (126). Loss that cannot be acknowledged as such, they argue, leads to a process whereby the words that cannot be uttered are "swallowed along with the trauma that led to the loss. Swallowed and preserved. Inexpressible mourning erects a secret tomb inside the subject. Reconstituted from the memories of words, scenes, and affects, the objectal correlative of the loss is buried alive in the crypt as a full-fledged person, complete with its own topography" (130). If, as I argue in chapter 4, memory's incapacity to represent the past embodied presence of the lost loved one necessarily disrupts the model of successful mourning that Freud sketches, Abraham and Torok's theory of incorporation revolves around the survivor's fantasy of realizing the presence of the lost loved one in markedly literal and embodied terms; in this fantasy, the act of swallowing initiates a process of "reconstituting" from memory a "full-fledged person, complete with its own topography," a person now "buried alive in the crypt." Buried but alive in the mourner's body, that person haunts the grieving subject not just psychically but physically, "making him perform bizarre acts, or subjecting him to unexpected sensations" (130).

If we choose to think of this oddly physicalized "ghost of the crypt" as a marker of the embodied dimensions of loss (what Abraham and Torok call its "objectal correlative"), it is not surprising that its incorporation is also linked to antimetaphor in their theory. Stripped of metaphor, grief leads us back to embodied loss and a loved one whose "reconstitution" through memory's words, scenes, and affects is as much a fantasy as reincarnation. That a literalizing fantasy of incorporation should return us to the body is not surprising; what is surprising, however, is the absence in Abraham and Torok's theory of any acknowledgment of tensions between literal (that is, embodied) loss and their metaphorical deployment of embodied images to describe a "fantasy" that "implement[s] literally" an act of swallowing they mean for us to read figuratively. If "the magic of incorporation" depends upon "demetaphorization (taking literally what is meant figuratively)," the process of metaphorization (making figurative what is also literal) governs Abraham and Torok's argument. Despite their exclusive focus on what they describe as "intrapsychic situations," Abraham and Torok not only deploy material and spatial metaphors with frequency but introduce numerous examples of bodily acts in the course of their argument. Those acts are of interest to them primarily in metaphorical terms; for example, "the literal ingestion of foods becomes introjection when viewed figuratively" (128). As their spatialized and embodied figures of psychic processes continually rub up against their depictions of corporeal acts, however, the physical body shadows the figures that they construct. Despite the theoretical persuasiveness of their argument that necrophagia represents "a form of language" that functions as a preventive measure of anti-incorporation, for example, I would argue that Abraham and Torok's repeated references to "the actual eating of the corpse" subvert the figurative coherence of their material image of incorporation by offering a glimpse of the dead body's immediacy that disturbs and disrupts their psychic model.

One might then conceive of the spatialized and corporeal images of incorporation for which Abraham and Torok are famous as figures that are themselves haunted by the ghost of an embodied understanding of grief they cannot escape through metaphorization. If representation emerges as a substitute for the presence of the mother's body, reading Abraham and Torok in this way might also suggest a correlation between the antimetaphorical nature of incorporation and Abraham and Torok's expression of that response to grief through spatialized figures that locate the dead in the mourner's *body*. Within such a reading, the embodied loss that cannot be recuperated through image or metaphor might be said to assert itself in the very image of incorporation that figures the grieving subject's resistance to metaphor. Rather than push such a connection to an extreme, I would like to use it as a springboard to think about possibilities for envisioning a theory of grief that acknowledges the body's loss without subsuming it within metaphor. Shifting focus toward what is excluded from theories of psychic loss, how might we reintroduce the body into theories of grief in a manner that would allow us to conceive of an antimetaphorical impulse which emerges not as a refusal to acknowledge loss but as a refusal to speak loss in a certain way? If it is possible to understand the experience of grief within an epistemology of the body, in other words, how might such an epistemology shape the language within which the embodied subject articulates loss?

Carolyn Parkhurst's *The Dogs of Babel* offers an extended meditation on language, grief, and embodiment that raises questions about Abraham and Torok's language-based theory of mourning. The narrator of *The Dogs of Babel*, a linguistics professor whose wife inexplicably falls to her death from a tree in their own backyard, responds to his grief by devoting himself to uncovering the story of her final hours. As he collects and interprets a series of clues, he undertakes a linguistics project that his friends and colleagues greet with skepticism; in the attempt to garner testimony from the one witness to his wife's fall, Paul Iverson devotes himself to teaching their dog, Lorelei, to talk. Paul attempts to frame his project in scholarly terms, invoking scientific studies and citing experiments that range from simple linguistic analyses of canine vocalization to the mutilating surgeries of a pseudoscientific group invested in physiologically altering the voice boxes of dogs. Using the unlikely scenario of teaching a dog to talk as a device for exploring the relationship between language, grief, and embodiment, Parkhurst's novel identifies and unsettles prevailing cultural assumptions about corporeal and linguistic forms of mourning. The widower's desperate struggle to intellectualize and control his overwhelming grief by teaching his dog to talk reflects a cultural injunction to rename and recast embodied loss within forms of language that render it symbolic. Paul's need to project the experience of embodiment onto his dog even as he attempts to usher that dog into language reflects the tensions associated with culture's disavowal of embodied grief; the linguist's attempt to teach his dog to talk marks not only his desire to recreate her as a linguistic subject but his desire to render his own grief subject to the compensation of representation. Whereas Abraham and Torok focus on patients who construct psychic crypts out of the words of loss they refuse to utter, *The Dogs of Babel* questions the assumptions of psychological and cultural models that locate health and coherence in the translation of loss into language.

In Paul, Parkhurst develops a character who begins with language and works backward through words before he can experience loss. Paul embraces representation without marking its secondary status; he demands that language not only speak the secrets of the dead but, in doing so, offer a remedy for grief. Underlying Paul's effort to unearth the details of his wife's death is a thinly veiled hope that the story he receives will somehow both represent and repair loss. Paul's literalized (mis)understanding of the compensation of representation pushes arguments about the necessary articulation of loss to a parodic extreme. In following Paul's language-based quest to its inevitably failed conclusion, the novel uses Paul's experiment to trace the limits of language's ability to recuperate or even express the embodied dimensions of loss. The linguist throws his considerable energy into piecing together the story of how his wife, Lexy, died; he reads the signs left behind in her absence intensely, metaphorically, attempting to construct through them a narrative with the power to render Lexy's death intelligible. Attempting to crack the code created by the rearranged order of books on their bookshelves, Paul accumulates clues based on the placement of letters and words in the books' titles. Even as he responds to loss as a puzzle that can be solved by language, however, Paul continually betrays the embodied nature of his grief and its resistance to the compensation of language.

Although Paul's attempt to teach his dog to speak emerges out of the understandable need to know why and how his wife died, his desperate project reflects a larger attempt to reconfigure the body so that it is subject to the powers of language. Abraham and Torok's focus on the recuperative power of language locates the sensory dimension of loss within a literalizing pathology where the body, swallowed whole by the mourner who refuses language, haunts the crypt. In *The Dogs of Babel*, the embodied absence of Paul's wife haunts his linguistic project. His only access to her occurs in a dream that seems to restore sensory presence—in the dream, Paul happens upon his wife in the kitchen cutting an onion so strong it makes his eyes sting—but collapses into a reiteration of corporeal absence: "The dream gets strange after that—there's something else, something about how Lexy needs her body back, the body I buried. I don't know how we're going to get it back for her" (208). In contrast to Lexy's missing corporeality, the presence of the couple's dog is imaged in terms that exaggerate her sensory immediacy and physical accessibility; Lorelie's panting, drooling presence not only interrupts Paul's story repeatedly but returns him to his own body as he buckles under her "dense, heavy weight" (113), leans against her "great, furry heft" (217), cringes at her "endless, keening howl" (4), is heated by "the rough warmth of her neck" (113). Paul's desire to lend his dog a voice emerges not only out of the hope of filling in the details of his wife's death, but out of the desire to fill the hole left by the absence of his wife's embodied form: "Dogs are witnesses. They are allowed access to our most private moments. They are there when we think we are alone. . . . If they could tell us everything they have seen, all of the gaps of our lives would stitch themselves together" (14). The dog's status as embodied, inarticulate witness, Paul implies, allows it not only to access inaccessible and intimate spaces but to own a form of knowledge Paul locates in the gaps of representation.

As he suggests that a dog's speech would fill not only the gaps of narrative but "all of the gaps of our lives," Paul reveals the impossible terms of his investment in animal "telling," an investment more fully disclosed in his dream that Lorelei speaks to him. In that dream, the dog agrees to "tell [Paul] everything [he] need[s] to know" in exchange for a piece of meat (87); rather than providing a narrative of his wife's death, however, Lorelei leads him directly to his wife's body. After accepting Paul's bribe, the dog

> grabs it with her teeth and charges out of the room. I jump up and run after her. When I catch up with her, she's in my office, lying in front of a door I've never seen before.
> "She's in there," says Lorelei, her mouth full of meat.
> I open the door. Inside is a small closet. Lexy sits huddled on the floor.

> She's dressed in a blue nightgown. She is very thin. "What took you so long?" she says. (87)

Although Lorelei speaks to her master, her mouth is filled with more than words and her words are more than supplements to absence; echoing her embodied gesture, Lorelei's language literally reveals Lexy's body, a thin, "huddled" body hidden in a closet in Paul's book-filled study. If grief is a puzzle that can be solved by language, the linguist's dream reveals that his quest to teach Lorelei to speak is anchored in the fantasy of an articulation so revelatory it not only stitches up the gaps of narrative but reconstructs the embodied presence of the dead. Paul's fantasy taps into what Baudrillard charts as a long-standing but displaced cultural belief in representation as "the visible and intelligible mediation of the Real. All Western faith and good faith became engaged in this wager on representation: that a sign could refer to the depth of meaning, that a sign could be exchanged for meaning and that something could guarantee this exchange" (Baudrillard 1994, 5). Paul's reaction to loss is to fantasize the creation of a sign he might exchange for the lost object; on the other side of language's door lies a body waiting to be rescued through representation.

In lending his dog the power of language, Paul would give voice to the embodied dimension of his own loss, finding a way to articulate—and, in his fantasy, to heal—a dimension of grief resistant to the compensation of representation. Lorelei's resistance to filling her mouth with words reflects her immersion in a tactile, sensory world where disembodied language has no hold. If Abraham and Torok image the cryptophore's rejection of language in terms of the empty mouth that "reverts to being the food-craving mouth it was prior to the acquisition of speech" (Abraham and Torok 1994, 128), Paul fantasizes in Lorelei a being who, in speaking with her mouth full, bypasses representation in favor of a material referentiality that renders presence palpable.

Whereas "language acts and makes up for absence by representing, by giving figurative shape to presence," Lorelei's function in the novel is to trample, knock down, or move through the constructions of language. Early in the novel, Lorelei interrupts a long conversation between Paul and Lexy in which the two of them analyze the language and imagery of a narrative with symbolic echoes of their own relationship: "There was a series of soft thuds from the staircase as Lorelei loped down to join us. She came over to the couch and jumped up, insinuating her large, dense body into the small space between us" (62). Here, Lorelei literally disrupts the couple's exchange of words about words by "insinuating" her large body between them. Later in the novel, Parkhurst uses Lorelei's presence to stage a kind of grief resistant to the compensation of language, a grief that returns us from the figurative shapes of representation to the forms, smells, and textures of the body. If the human body as construct exists only in opposition to the subject of language, culture, and consciousness, the novel's canine body naturalizes the isolation of corporeal experience from its psychical counterpart.

As Paul assembles his linguistic scholarship and struggles to justify in intellectual terms his project to teach Lorelei to talk, he also documents her embodied response to his wife's loss:

> This morning, I find [Lorelei] in the bedroom, sleeping stretched out on one of Lexy's sweaters. I must have left the closet door open, and I can only assume that Lorelei, drawn by the scent of Lexy's perfume, her hair, her skin, still lingering on her clothes, jumped up and tugged at the garment until she had freed it from its slippery, padded hanger. I don't take the sweater away from her. Instead, I walk quietly out of the room and leave her to breathe in her memories, whatever they might be. (63)

As Lorelei presses her nose against the lingering scents of her owner's body, she appears to experience Lexy's absence as a sensory presence. Paul's desire not to disrupt this scene emerges from his respectful acknowledgment of his exclusion from this nonlinguistic form of compensation for loss. If Lorelei, on the one hand, embodies a dimension of Paul's grief that cannot be expressed through words, her experience of animal embodiment also remains inaccessible to him. Whereas Lorelei's ability to "breathe in" memories of the lost body stems from her capacity to identify and absorb the scent of hair and skin still lingering on clothing, Paul's memories of Lexy can be imaged and articulated but not experienced in multisensory terms. For him, the "slippery, padded hanger" on which his wife's sweater once hung possesses a tactile immediacy that his most beloved memories of his wife fail to attain. In his own recollection of Lexy's embodied presence, Paul must struggle to physicalize his memory of intercorporeality:

> The day was warm, and we drove with the windows open. Breeze on my arms as I drove. Savor it now, the day, the breeze. Run the memory of it over your tongue. Speak it aloud; there's no one listening. Say "sun" and "hot" and "day." Close your eyes and remember the moment, the warm pink life of it. Lexy's body in the seat next to mine. Her voice filling the car. Let it wash over you. It ends soon enough. (48)

The memory work recounted in this passage revolves around the attempt not to articulate past experience but to reembody it, to supplement the mind's labor with the texture and force of physical sensation. Trapped in a consciousness that taunts him with a presence he can access only in imagistic and linguistic terms, Paul struggles to lend the "figurative shape" of representation an experiential body; his grief at the loss of "Lexy's body in the seat next to mine" forces him to remember intercorporeality only insofar as he closes his eyes and imagines it. For Paul, the body's sensory immediacy becomes, ironically, its most inaccessible aspect. Working backward from representation, he begins not with his experience but with the words that represent it; in voicing those words, running memory over his tongue, he attempts to supplement the images of memory with a tactility borrowed from speech. As he speaks aloud, saying the words "sun" and "hot" and "day," the linguist inhabits the border where language and body meet, a border he identifies earlier in the novel as he points out "the double meaning of both the English 'tongue' and the French *langue,* which refer both to the physical tongue and to language" (10–11). Moving from sense to sound, Paul strives to compensate for representation's failure to compensate for loss by materializing language, rerouting its signifying function through the body to supplement the immateriality of words. If introjection involves channeling grief through language to fill the emptiness of the mouth with words, Paul locates the value of such words not in the power of representation but in the way they can be traced back to affirm the embodied existence of the mouth that would utter them.

Paul's focus on the mouth's articulation of sounds takes words out of the realm of referentiality, pushing them back into the bodies that form them. Abraham and Torok structure their model of grief around "swallowing" words or literalizing their meaning; while they locate the primary image of loss in the physical mouth, the words that fill the mouth *stand in for* the mother's breast in representational terms. Paul's struggle to articulate a language of grief literalizes Abraham and Torok's metaphor of "swallowing" words in the attempt to acknowledge and speak to dynamics of bodily loss. The words Paul utters, were they to stand in for the missing breast, would invoke the child's experience of that breast in all its sensory immediacy, rather than figuring the lost breast as simulacrum of maternal love. In speaking words that restore memory to his tongue, Paul hopes not just to image or represent past experience but to touch and taste "the warm pink life of it." Passing through this fantasy of embodied speech, he struggles to reach into the space of language and come away holding the body otherwise lost to him.

In the guise of searching for a means of teaching his dog to speak, Paul gives voice to his simultaneous immersion in and consciousness of the bodily experience he would represent. Acknowledging that Lorelei's vocal cords are not well suited to making the sounds of human speech, Paul devises a typewriter system with visual symbols rather than letters on the keys. When that motion from linguistic signification to pictorial representation fails, Paul considers switching senses to develop a "scratch-and-sniff keyboard" with a different scent assigned to each key. Although the keyboard idea fails to allow Lorelei to communicate in human terms, the formulation of the idea lends Paul the imaginative license to articulate *his own* unspoken experience of loss:

> It occurs to me that maybe the visual cues are a problem. Sight is not her best sense. Maybe I need to assign a different scent to each key. A scratch-and-sniff keyboard. But how do I sum up how Lexy smelled to Lorelei? Rub her sweater on the keys? Spray her perfume, dab her hair gel, smear her lipstick on a palette, and mix them all together? What of Lexy's own unadorned scent, the scent beneath all those other scents she added to her body? I can't re-create that. (Oh, but if I could! If I could lift up an atomizer and spray that scent into the air!) (141)

Although the idea of adapting human systems of signification for canine use is farfetched, what is most striking in this description is the linguist's absolute failure to envision, much less implement, the transfer from human to canine-friendly language system that he claims to desire. The awkwardness of Paul's imaginative foray derives largely from his own resistance to the assumptions of the scientific experiment he imagines. He does not try to break down the world of scents into individual units, or define a semiotic structure of smell, or imagine a workable keyboard layout. Neither does he imaginatively confront the pragmatic difficulties that emerge from the comical image of a dog's heavy-nailed paws or broad, moist nose engaged in the fine motor work of typing on a keyboard, however large. Instead, Paul imagines his own hands spraying and mixing and smearing essences from his wife's body, then smelling them himself. The tactile blending of scents Paul imagines (mixing Lexy's scents on a "palette") resists the universalizing and signifying communicative function the typewriter is supposed to serve to call attention, instead, to his wife's distinctive, sensual, and unrepresentable smell.

The failed typewriter experiment offers Paul imaginative license to explore dimensions of his grief namable only in the context of a corporeal figuration of mourning relegated to his dog. The passage strays from its designated focus on the practical and theoretical elements of canine linguistics into a series of asides culminating in a parenthetical outburst that finally acknowledges the driving subtext of Paul's desperation: not the difficulty of teaching a dog to talk but the impossibility of signifying his own embodied loss. The imagined act that begins as a language experiment mediated by a writing instrument pushes into a lingering attention to his wife's lost body that manifests itself in narrative accumulation. Having imagined himself, like Lorelei, pressed against cloth that pressed against Lexy's body, Paul unleashes a string of images that move into closer and closer contact with the lost body he grieves. As the narrative accumulates increasingly intimate images of bodily contact—sprayed perfume, dabbed hair gel, smeared lipstick—the passage blows Paul's cover, stripping away not only the authority of academic distance but the representational functions of language. Caught gesturing, finally, toward what can't be represented or recuperated—"Lexy's own scent, the scent beneath all those other scents"—Paul retreats into the parenthetical, where he (momentarily) acknowledges the embodied loss that his elaborate academic project would obscure: "I can't re-create that. (Oh, but if I could! If I could lift up an atomizer and spray that scent into the air!)" (141).

Even as he turns to language to render coherent the experience of loss, Paul finds himself returned again and again to his desiring body and his dislocated grief. In trying to "liberate" language from the body, cultural discourses perpetuate acts of violence that parallel the mutilating canine surgeries of the novel, as Paul's history reveals: "I became a linguist in part because words have failed me all my life. I was born tongue-tied in the most literal sense: the tissue connecting my tongue to the floor of my mouth was short and thick, limiting lingual movement. . . . I was born with a tongue not meant for speaking, and despite all artificial attempts to loosen it, it has stayed stuck in place at every important moment of my life" (38). Paul's study of language emerges out of a desire to compensate intellectually for "lingual movement" limited physiologically by the shape and texture of his tongue tissue and expressively by the limits of representation. Despite "all artificial attempts" to sever the connection between words and the body that utters them, the anatomy of language, as Paul's tongue-tied status reveals, is invariably linked to the physiology of speech.[1]

Recognizing that words are caught up in the bodies that would articulate or apprehend them, Paul attempts to exploit that link through a hermeneutical system that renders language's referential quality subject to material metaphors of manipulation. The language game Paul plays as a child involves taking a word and rearranging its letters to see what other words it might contain: "The point wasn't so much to count the number of words that I found, but it was more to see what those words revealed about the word they came from. It was like magic to me, like a secret code to crack" (118). The "magic" of Paul's linguistic exercise depends upon the notion that language not only represents but embodies reality; Paul attempts to "crack" the "secret code" of words in order to access their vaulted meanings. In manipulating the letters of a word to create other words, Paul sees himself as revealing inherent meanings rather than constructing new meaning out of arbitrary signifiers: "I find myself playing the game now, writing down names and seeing what they can tell me. Look inside *Lorelei* and you find *roll* and *lie,* two very doggy verbs, two things she does very well. But look further and you'll see she carries within her a story to tell (see, there it is—*lore*) and a *role* she herself plays in that story" (118–119). Although he describes his activity as a "game," the satisfaction Paul derives from it depends upon the idea that language is not, as Wittgenstein's famous metaphor of the language game implies,[2] a series of arbitrary signifiers deployed within a structure shaped by merely conventional rules. Paul's material metaphors for linguistic manipulation—"Look inside Lorelei," "look further and you'll see"—lend depth and spatial presence to words, inferring that they can be peeled apart to reveal the essential truth within. Paul's grief manifests itself in his increasingly urgent desire to make words into things that can be manipulated to reconstitute the experience they represent; beginning with language, Paul reads backward into experience, affording words not only representational but epistemological power.

Lamenting the "disconcerting" fact that his name holds "a wealth of words" almost all of which "have to do with the life of the body" (119), Paul acknowledges the impossibility of using language to achieve immaterial subjectivity: "Try as I might, I cannot escape this body of mine that breathes and beats and lives" (119). His attempt to uncover language's hidden meanings by rearranging the individual letters that make up words not only returns him to the fact of his embodiment but depends upon a material model of constructedness that would transform arbitrary signifiers into objects that can be touched, stacked, broken open. Letters are not things that can be manipulated by the hand to make other things. If language, like subjectivity, is implicated in embodiment, representational constructs emerge out of an embodiment they are powerless to affect. While the abstractions of language are accessible only through the mediation of the senses, the immateriality of language renders the mere accumulation of words powerless to defend against loss.

The Dogs of Babel documents Paul's eventual success in cracking the code of Lexy's final linguistic messages to him: although he never teaches Lorelei to speak, he not only locates the words Lexy wrote on the inside of the dog's collar, but deciphers the message she spelled out through the words in the titles of the rearranged books on their shelves. As he pieces together her words, Paul, like the analyst Abraham and Torok describe, turns to those words to decipher the meanings hidden within them. "Psychoanalytic listening," Abraham and Torok write,

> consists of a special way of treating language. Whereas normally we are given meanings, the analyst is given symbols. Symbols are data that are missing an as yet undetermined part, but that can, in principle, be determined. The special aim of psychoanalytic listening is to find the symbol's complement, recovering it from indeterminacy. From the beginnings of psychoanalysis to the present, theoretical efforts have been aimed at finding rules that will permit us to find the unknown missing complement, in other words, the fragment that "symbolizes with"—or, we might say, that "cosymbolizes." (1986, 79)

Even after he solves the language puzzle that his wife leaves for him, Paul continues struggling to decode her words in order to locate their symbolic complement. If the analyst is charged with "not backing down from cosymbols no matter how concealed they may be" (Parkhurst 2003, 79), the novel reveals Lexy's message as part of a multilayered system of language which, no matter how many layers Paul peels off, has no solid foundation that might be "recover[ed] . . . from indeterminacy." Paul cracks the code of her text only to discover another text hidden beneath it; Lexy's story, when given voice, merely mouths phrases borrowed from another narrative to deflect further Paul's search for originary meaning.[3] The linguist constructs a coherent narrative around that cryptic code that enables him to imagine the reasons for a death that he comes to regard as suicide: "I find myself at a loss now. . . . There are no more puzzles to figure out, no more clues to follow. . . . And yet I can't seem to let it go. I sit here in my house, the house of Paul, with all my clues around me, and none of them seem to help. No matter how I lay them out, none of them seem to be able to tell me how to go on living" (256). In cracking the code of Lexy's linguistic messages to him, Paul pieces together her words without coming any closer to understanding, accepting, or undoing her loss. The narrative's focus on material and spatial terms emphasizes the limited scope of Paul's hermeneutic success. Paul manipulates the shapes of representation only to find that "no matter how [he] lay[s] them out," the figurative shape that emerges continues to evoke absence rather than presence. Squatting in the midst of an ever-widening circle of signs, the linguist remains untouched by their compensation for loss while the analyst "recovers" but cannot resuscitate the symbol's complement: the embodied presence that haunts the figurative shape of representation.

Rather than using language to represent that which he has lost, substituting words for material presence, Paul must relinquish his hold on words in order to experience his own grief. The linguist finds himself unable to acknowledge absence until he gives up the idea that he can locate and preserve presence through language, abandoning what Baudrillard describes as the "utopian" principle of "the equivalence of the sign and of the real" (1994, 6). As he attempts to piece together Lexy's story, Paul confronts the possibility that his desperate struggles to decipher the linguistic and interpretive puzzles of his wife's death implicate him in a mere diversionary tactic; his final rendering of Lexy's narrative figures language as a game capable not of clarifying or compensating for loss but merely of distracting from it. Addressing Lexy, Paul imagines her final contemplation of her death: "Your only worry is about Paul, about the pain you'll cause him. But you know he'll get through it. You leave him a note, written in book titles, a message in a collar, a puzzle for him to work out. Something to make him forget his grief" (255). In this rendering, the puzzle of language is imaged as a mere diversion for Paul. The activity of working out the puzzle emerges as an end rather than a means; the process of articulating and analyzing Lexy's words and acts distracts Paul from loss without stitching up the gaps of his life.

If Lexy anticipates the need to distract Paul from his grief through a series of words and stories that the linguist would decipher and decode, she also anticipates the way her loss will open up a gap that representation cannot fill. Although Lorelei consistently refuses to talk, her animal presence speaks to the sensory dynamics of embodiment that partially constitute Paul's experience of grief. As he focuses on adapting his dog's voice for human speech, Paul comes ultimately to recognize Lorelei not as the medium for Lexy's story, but as the complement to it: "You leave him a note, written in book titles, a message in a collar, a puzzle for him to work out. Something to make him forget his grief. And Lorelei—you leave him Lorelei. That's all that's left to do" (255). Insofar as Lorelei helps to fill in the gaps of grief's narrative, she does so not by articulating a coherent story of Lexy's suicidal motivations but by pressing her body against Paul's as he struggles to piece together the puzzle of his wife's words. Fearing that his dog, too, has been taken from him, Paul finally observes, "What I want most, more than all of life's secrets revealed, . . . is to crawl into bed and to feel the comfort of Lorelei's great, furry heft beside me" (217). The "comfort" that Paul's dog offers derives not from her ability to replace Lexy's embodied presence or compensate for it through the substitution of language but to recall Paul to a tactile, spatial, sensory dimension of his own embodiment that he loses not only in Lexy's absence but in the absence of a discourse capable of naming that dimension of his experience in any but animal terms.

In approaching absence solely through language, this linguist turns to words as a means of denying rather than expressing embodied loss. Before he can speak his grief, he must locate himself and his loss in a material realm which he acknowledges only through the mediation of Lorelei's sensory experience. Seeking clues from his dog to piece together as symbols, Paul must discard the conventions of psychoanalytic listening to hear the story she tells through the lens of a bodily experience of grief he locates only in her animal presence. Although Paul "cannot say" how the loss of Lexy's embodied presence disrupts his own experience of the world, he figures that disruption partially in the narrative he attributes to Lorelei, whose location in the cultural space of embodiment authorizes her sensory experience of loss. Acknowledging that "the story [Lorelei] chooses to tell . . . may not be the one I want to hear" (141), Paul observes:

> Maybe she wants to tell me about a single moment of summer grass, looking for something to chase, the feel of damp earth on bare paws. . . . The loneliness of the door closing, leaving her alone in the house. The patient waiting beneath the table, the smell of dinners not meant for her, the thrill of being in the right place at the right time when the human fingers slip and a piece of meat falls to the floor. The drool-induced terror of pulling up in front of the vet's office. The sweet sadness of Lexy gone, the constant vigil for her return. Seeing things happen and not knowing why. The smell of other dogs. The softness of couch cushions. The satisfying give as a pillow rips apart in her teeth. The hunt. The sun. Rolling in the dirt. (142)

The more Paul focuses on teaching Lorelei to verbalize her story in human terms, the more he directs us to the very sensory, bodily experience he would purport to have his dog transcend. Here, Paul's revised imagining of his dog's "story" finally allows the body to enter, and disrupt, the desired coherence of Lorelei's narrative. In this version of Lorelei's "story," the power of narrative collapses into "moment[s]" of embodied experience that escape placement within an organizing structure; the dog's inability to order events or assign a logic of cause and effect—"Seeing things happen and not knowing why"—results in her immersion in a world she cannot control. The projected story that would render Lexy's death intelligible—offering representational presence to stand in for embodied absence—fragments into units of sensation without apparent cause, effect, or connection, giving voice to an experience of dislocation and loss that Paul comes to name only through a story that he projects onto his dog's presence.

In imagining Lorelei as outside of language, Paul attempts to extricate himself from a disembodied grammar of loss. His imagining of Lorelei's experience stresses its resistance to placement within a symbolic structure, testifying to a dimension of embodied presence that is not recoverable through language. Abraham and Torok describe the literalizing pathology of incorporation as "the refusal to acknowledge the full import of the loss" (1994, 127); *The Dogs of Babel* ultimately insists that loss's full import cannot be measured outside the context of embodied grief. In attempting to speak his own embodied loss, Paul perpetuates the very opposition between mind and body, culture and nature, which his experience of grief problematizes. Observing that "Everything is both manufactured and natural in man," Merleau-Ponty concludes, "there is not a word, not a form of behaviour which does not owe something to purely biological being—and which at the same time does not elude the simplicity of animal life" (1962, 189). Paul's tendency to figure embodiment by reducing it to animal terms reflects not only a series of cultural assumptions that marginalize the human body but a desire to locate its elusive forms in terms that render it susceptible to manipulation. If his many attempts to voice the sensory dimensions of loss throughout the novel occur through the mediation of an animal presence associated with corporeality, his sole effort to acknowledge his chiasmic relationship with Lexy casts embodiment within a material language that is similarly reductive. Parkhurst's protagonist literalizes the notion of shared embodiment through a metaphor of organ transplant that renders intercorporeality in biological terms:

> I have heard that sometimes when a person has an operation to transplant someone else's heart or liver or kidney into his body, his tastes in foods change, or his favorite colors, as if the organ has brought with it some memory of its life before, as if it holds within it a whole past that must find a place within its new host. This is the way I carry Lexy inside me. Since the moment she took up residency within me, she has lent her own color to the way I see and hear and taste, so that by now I can barely distinguish between the world as it seemed before and the way it seems now. I cannot say what air tasted like before I knew her or how the city smelled as I walked its streets at night. (49)

Paul's transplant metaphor locates his wife's presence not within the walls of an artificially bounded space in his body, but as a life-sustaining organ that penetrates systemically to alter his sensory experience of the world. Whereas Abraham and Torok develop a spatialized model of incorporation that highlights the need to keep the lost loved one "outside [our] bodily limits" (1994, 129), this passage depathologizes the idea of "residency" by replacing the image of the encrypted other with the image of an implanted organ that sustains the body's functioning.

Paul's rare attempt to document the extent of his embodied loss exposes the inadequacy of his own linguistic fantasy of recuperation; his fantasy of bodily memory, however, renders intercorporeality in purely physiological terms. In describing the impossibility of reducing the lived body to its constitutive aspects or unraveling the body from space, Merleau-Ponty emphasizes the importance of conceptualizing embodiment in terms of "bodily synthesis" (1962, 149). Describing bodily spatiality as "the deployment of one's bodily being," Merleau-Ponty observes, "our body is not primarily in space: it is of it" (149, 148). Although the language of spatial location in this passage emphasizes the need to place Paul's relationship with Lexy in the body, his attempts to do so rely upon a materialistic and even mechanistic model of intercorporeality that imagines Lexy's "residency" in Paul as a series of boxes inside boxes: his body contains a transplanted organ which contains memory of its past life. Even as the passage highlights the difficulty of unraveling the lost other from the survivor's experience of the world, Paul's attempt to describe "the way I carry Lexy inside me" emerges as a materialist fantasy incapable of grounding or replacing the fantasy of language pressured by Paul's experience of embodied grief. The artificial tenor of Paul's transplant metaphor and the reduction of memory to an organic phenomenon—a thing within a thing that can be physically transplanted—call attention to his attempt to naturalize a notion of residency that locates the body in space rather than rendering bodily synthesis. Paul finds himself suspended not only between experiences of grief named as human and animal, but between discourses of words and things, subjects and objects, that fail in opposing ways to represent his experience of loss.

In the concluding paragraph of *The Dogs of Babel*, Paul reaches into the novel's circulating proliferation of words and body parts not to stitch together "all the gaps of our lives," but to acknowledge the impossibility of his own desire for coherence. Opposing the sensory and linguistic fragments accessible to him with the irrecuperable synthesis of his wife's embodied presence, Paul finally gestures toward the enormity of his loss:

I remember my wife in white. I remember her walking toward me on our wedding day, a bouquet of red flowers in her hand, and I remember her turning away from me in anger, her body stiff as a stone. I remember the sound of her breath as she slept. I remember the way her body felt in my arms. . . . I try to remember the woman she was and not the woman I have built out of spare parts to comfort me in my mourning. (260–261)

The five-time repetition of the phrase "I remember" in this passage interrupts the construction of a single, coherent representation of Lexy to offer, instead, a series of piecemeal, fragmented sensory recollections that complicate even as they echo Paul's imaginings of Lorelei's experience. Listing memories of the body that offer a visual ("I remember my wife in white"), auditory ("I remember the sound of her breath") and tactile ("I remember the way her body felt") sensation, Paul responds to his grief by accumulating memories that gesture toward a bodily synthesis they cannot capture. His reference to Frankenstein is double-edged. In exposing the constructedness of "the woman I have built out of spare parts to comfort me in my mourning," Paul undercuts the idea that memory's work can be understood in wholly organic *or* symbolic terms; he critiques both a vision of the body that would render corporeality as the sum of material parts and a vision of language that would assert linguistic coherence without acknowledging representation's lack. As Merleau-Ponty observes, "I do not bring together one by one the parts of my body; this translation and this unification are performed once and for all within me: they are my body itself" (1962, 150). Paul's fragmentary recollections of Lexy acknowledge the impossibility of restoring the unification enacted in and through her living-moving body. Attempting neither to turn corporeal absence into representational presence nor to reduce Lexy to the sum of her material parts, Paul offers a series of memories that intermingle emotion with the sound of breath and the stiffness of the body, invoking the psychical as well as the physiological experience of an intercorporeality memory can neither restore nor recreate.

The Dogs of Babel figures Paul's resistance to the incoherence of loss not only in the impossibility of an experiment that would lend language to a dog but in the need to image as animal the tactile, sensory dimensions of his own grief. The fractured polarization of sensory and linguistic experience played out through Lorelei's presence reflects the difficulty of negotiating an embodied experience of grief that resists both objectification and metaphorization. If Paul's trajectory in the novel begins with the compensation of representation and moves him through the sensory particularity of the material body, it ends not in his ability to teach the body to talk but in his willingness to speak an embodied grief that refuses the consolation of language. Abraham and Torok locate the sensory dimension of loss within a literalizing pathology where the body, swallowed whole by the mourner who refuses language, haunts the crypt. If such a focus locks the lost body within the linguist's closet, Paul's ability to "acknowledge the full import of [his] loss" (Abraham and Torok 1994, 127) demands that he disclose the material presence that is closeted by representation. In such a case, pulling the lost body from the closet functions not as an act of material resuscitation but as an opportunity for acknowledging the collapse of embodied presence into its material and symbolic forms. Working backwards from the synthesis of his own symbolic constructs to the fragments he has stitched together, Paul acknowledges that language's remedy for loss situates presence in the realm of the imaginary, a realm in which representation's figurative shapes may conspire with the disavowal as well as the disclosure of embodied loss.

The Ghost of the Body in Don DeLillo's *The Body Artist*

In *The Ends of Mourning*, Alessia Ricciardi traces a genealogy of mourning from Freud to Lacan in order to illuminate what she describes as the twentieth-century's failure to develop a hermeneutics of loss; this failure, Ricciardi observes, "results in a problematic philosophical and ethical condition that I define as being beyond mourning" (2003, 4). Arguing that the shift from Freud's contingent and historical view of loss to Lacan's vision of lack as a defining condition of psychic life underlies psychoanalysis's changing conceptualization of subject/object dynamics, Ricciardi situates the Lacanian view of lack in the context of the economy of a hegemonic postmodern culture that erases the specificity of the historical object to accept loss as an unresolvable trauma. Although I might question the ease with which Ricciardi adopts Lacanian theory as an index of the assumptions of hegemonic postmodern culture, her argument that the shift to a Lacanian understanding of lack "marks the cultural obsolescence of the ethical significance of mourning" (68) raises important questions about the cultural impact of denying the material dimensions of loss. In response to contemporary theories of loss that strip mourning of its historicity, Ricciardi cites the need to reconstruct "the specificity and ethical urgency of loss" (47). Restoring the specificity of loss, I will argue, entails not only acknowledging its historically specific object but positioning both subject and object in a dynamic of embodied intersubjectivity. Postmodern attitudes about the body contribute to and complicate not only the "postmodern politics of transience and detachment" that Ricciardi critiques but the postmodern subject's very experience of the immediacy of loss (46).

In opposing Freud's historically specific object of loss with Lacan's notion of lack as a structural component of the functioning psyche, Ricciardi positions what she describes as Freud's modernist methodology against a Lacanian construction of mourning as "a social formality, the impossible but obligatory work performed at the level of the symbolic order to fill the hole in the Real" (7).[4] Marking a significant shift in the way that psychoanalysis as a discipline conceptualizes mourning, Ricciardi posits that "the question of mourning, despite being officially answered and resolved, reemerges, at times, in the contemporary imagination with the disquieting force of a cultural enigma" (4). The question of mourning, I would argue, emerges over and over again in the contemporary imagination not *in spite of* its theoretical "resolution" but exactly because that resolution fails to speak to the embodied subject's lived experience of grief.

In the pages that follow, I will explore the way Don DeLillo's *The Body Artist* situates the embodied dynamics of its protagonist's grief within a postmodern culture that is "beyond mourning." DeLillo's focus on the issue of embodied loss, I will argue, not only reflects its recurring significance as a cultural concern but links "the disquieting force" with which it returns to the unresolved presence—and absence—of the body. Situated in a postmodern landscape defined by the collapsed realms of representation and reality, DeLillo's protagonist is forced to renegotiate her world by the pressure of a grief that continually asserts its specificity and urgency against the backdrop of a postmodern understanding of mourning. Lacan's model of desire, Ricciardi observes, originates

> in an enlightened acceptance of loss as the condition of psychic functioning. There is indeed no place for romantic nostalgia in this model, but rather only for a continuous "performance" of loss that is practiced at the synchronic level of the signifying chain, in the absence of any imaginary consolation, and that supplies the basis of a postmodern politics of transience and detachment. The Lacanian subject knows that the different, "historical" objects of desire are only simulacra. (46)

In adopting as its protagonist a performance artist, *The Body Artist* weighs the notion of mourning as "a continuous 'performance' of loss" against the urgency and specificity of embodied grief. Insofar as DeLillo's protagonist has absorbed a "postmodern politics of detachment," she responds to the death of her spouse in the space of signification; as she does so, she tests the limits of language and performance in a culture of representation. The continued "performance of loss," rather than shielding the postmodern subject from the impact of death, renders DeLillo's protagonist oddly vulnerable to a grief she is unable to acknowledge or affect.

By apprehending specific objects of desire as mere simulacra, the postmodern subject enters a universe of representation which, in asserting the unknowability of presence, implicitly posits the insignificance of absence. Turning to performativity as a means of understanding a lack she would recast through representation, the body artist attempts to detach herself from the embodied dynamics of a specific loss for which she has no language; in that process, however, she is forced to confront a material simulacrum of her husband's presence that exposes rather than fills the gap between representation and embodiment. In the postmodern landscape *The Body Artist* inhabits, the incontrovertibility of death emerges as the least accessible rather than the most immediate aspect of mourning. Under the pressure of a devastating and specific loss, theoretical self-consciousness about the constructedness of presence translates not into a sophisticated acceptance of lack but into a desperate demand that the compensation of representation extend into the material landscape of embodied absence. If "the different, historical objects of desire are only simulacra," the bereaved, desiring subject reaches into the realm of the linguistic and the performative not to represent but to reconstruct a presence always already inaccessible. *The Body Artist* traces the way in which that subject reemerges with empty hands.

∞

At the time of its publication, *The Body Artist* evoked reactions of confusion, frustration, and even indignation among reviewers attempting to understand and evaluate a short novel that in many ways seems to defy explication. Although the novel begins with a clear plotline and identifiable characters—the first chapter represents in minute detail the interactions of Rey Robles and his wife, Lauren Hartke, as they gather in the kitchen in their rented country home for breakfast—the suicide death of Rey after the first chapter leaves the novel to follow Lauren through a landscape of grief that critics describe as eerie, disturbing, even creepy (Caldwell 2001, Luce 2001). As Lauren returns to the house she shared with Rey, she discovers a strange little man in his underwear who seems to have been hiding in the house. That man, whom Lauren comes to name Mr. Tuttle, speaks only in disjointed sentences that contain oddly familiar echoes of past conversations. Drawn to this man who repeats not only the words but the inflections and the body language of her dead husband, Lauren struggles to make sense of a presence that critics describe variously as a ghost, an "externalized embodiment of her loss" (Adams 2001), and an incoherent figure who speaks only gibberish (Wittmershaus 2001).[5] If the critical attempt to name Mr. Tuttle occupies the most space in the novel's early reviews, critics' frustrations with their inability to do so successfully often emerge in extremes of praise or blame for a novel that many come to associate with the difficulties, the limitations, or the rewards of postmodernism. Maria Russo describes the novel as "that kind of expert mindfuck" (Russo 2001); Eric Wittmershaus observes, "There is something unmistakably Zen about this novel" (Wittmershaus 2001), while Maureen Corrigan sees *The Body Artist* as an example of "post-modernist self consciousness about self consciousness" (Corrigan 2001). As it situates Lauren's grief in an isolated summer home inhabited only by herself and a strange ghostly figure who may or may not be real, *The Body Artist* explores the way in which the experience of loss reinstitutes corporeal boundaries that the postmodern landscape would fade, blur, or even erase. Grief becomes the structure through which DeLillo maps the limits of a poststructuralist sensibility that would destabilize materialist assumptions and emphasize the constructedness of the body.

The Body Artist begins by depicting the way lived experience blurs the boundaries between Lauren's immaterial consciousness and her material surroundings but goes on to chart the way grief painfully reconstructs those boundaries. In the wake of her husband's death, memory taunts Lauren with the formless form of Rey's absent presence, a presence that overwhelms her consciousness even as it refuses to materialize. Grief emerges as the ultimate test of the postmodern landscape; it replicates postmodernism's collapse of material and immaterial worlds only to enforce with painful immediacy the boundaries that separate imagination from lived experience. As DeLillo introduces the fact of embodied loss into a postmodern landscape, he suggests that lived experience locates itself within the material spaces of body and world even as it constructs and transgresses the boundaries that define those spaces. The novel figures grief as an expulsion from embodiment into hyper-consciousness that tests the limits of the imagination and translates its freedom into a form of psychical constraint.

The novel's first chapter locates the reader for twenty-two pages in a narrow spatiotemporal landscape the parameters of which it painstakingly details and simultaneously disrupts. As it renders the domestic routines of a married couple over breakfast, the chapter hovers attentively over the simplest routine acts, breaking down the process of buttering toast or pouring orange juice into a series of steps that trace the body's motions and the mind's trajectories in minute detail. In interweaving physical acts with the play of the mind, the chapter highlights the constructedness of sensory perception and destabilizes the grounding of the body to depict the way lived experience blurs the boundaries between Lauren's immaterial consciousness and her material surroundings: "She looked past the bowl into a space inside her head that was also here in front of her" (25). Even in its simplest acts of representation, the narrative brackets physical acts with the words which construct them. As Lauren prepares breakfast, the toaster's lever "sprang or sprung" (12); the narrative interrupts its representation of Lauren's experience to highlight the mediating presence of language. Even as words interrupt acts, faulty perceptions undermine the sensory basis of bodily knowledge to destabilize assumptions of physiological grounding. At several points in the novel, constructs of the imagination collapse into moments of misperception which render the senses as unreliable as the imagination. In driving by a man sitting on his porch, we are told, Lauren "saw him complete" (72). Seconds later, the "man" whom Lauren "knew" with such certainty is revealed to be a paint can on a board balanced between two chairs (72). The novel questions the distinction between perception and representation; insofar as the eye "tells us a story we want to believe" (82), Lauren's literal vision of the man emerges as no less constructed than her narrative rendering of him.[6]

If *The Body Artist* deconstructs the illusions of knowledge in all forms, the novel's first chapter introduces a compensation for such loss of stability. Having blurred the lines between fact and fantasy, the novel traces Lauren's transgression of those conventional boundaries through imaginative acts that would liberate her from the constraints of time, space, and embodiment. As Lauren fixes breakfast and reads the morning newspaper, she drifts between worlds that occupy equal weight in the narrative rendering of her experience. She "was here and there," looking for the honey jar for her tea and having a conversation with a doctor in a news story: "She sipped her tea and read. She more or less saw herself talking to a doctor in the bush somewhere, with people hungry in the dust" (26). The phrase "more or less" glosses over the distinction between lived and imagined experience, suggesting a casual continuity between fictional and actual worlds that emerges repeatedly in the first chapter:

> You separate the Sunday sections and there are endless identical lines of print with people living somewhere in the words and the strange contained reality of paper and ink seeps through the house for a week and when you look at a page and distinguish one line from another it begins to gather you into it and there are people being tortured halfway around the world, who

speak another language, and you have conversations with them more or less uncontrollably until you become aware you are doing it and then you stop, seeing whatever it was in front of you at the time, like half a glass of juice in your husband's hand. (21)

As Lauren engages in conversation not only with her husband but "with people living somewhere in the words" of the newspaper she reads, *The Body Artist* disassembles the frames that contain and distinguish textual from extratextual worlds; in this world of "post-modernist self-consciousness about self-consciousness," Lauren must consciously struggle to wrest herself out of participation in "the strange contained reality of paper and ink" in order to perceive in literal terms: "then you stop, seeing whatever it was in front of you at the time, like half a glass of juice in your husband's hand."

If the first chapter moves into and out of Lauren's head, intermingling perception, reflection, imagination, and action, the rest of the novel pulls back, not to shore up the empirical foundation that it has deconstructed, but to acknowledge the complex dynamics of embodied intersubjectivity that shape the parameters of lived experience. In their lives together, Rey's embodied presence serves as a point of reference for Lauren's thoughts, words, and actions; answering his question in a distracted way, she "went to the stove, got the kettle and filled it from the tap. He changed stations on the radio and said something she missed" (14). Although Lauren's attention to her husband in this scene is only partial, focused as she is on the morning's mundane tasks and the flow of a consciousness not limited by her immediate surroundings, Rey's embodied presence serves as a point of reference around which she organizes time, space, and thought. Even as she misses his comment or chides him for not knowing that she dislikes orange juice, she moves through the day unconsciously accommodating his presence; the narrative's attention to the subtle dance of bodies in space as Lauren makes way for Rey's approach to the counter renders visible the give-and-take dynamic of a relationship in which the two characters literally and metaphorically pivot around one another: "She'd had to sort of jackknife away from the counter when he approached to get a butter knife" (14). The narrative's claim—"this is how you live a life even if you don't know it" (14)—hinges on the ambiguity of the referent for "this"; unspecified, *this* comes to encompass not just unexamined habits and thoughts, bodies and words, but the impossibility of separating one from another in the complex structures of lived experience through which embodied subjects construct themselves in relationship to one another. If consciousness, in Merleau-Ponty's terms, "is being-towards-the-thing through the intermediary of the body" (1962, 138–139), Lauren's memories of Rey recall a chiasmic exchange that emphasizes the impossibility of separating words, bodies, thoughts, and sensations in the blur of embodied intersubjectivity: "They'd gone upstairs and dropped into a night of tossing sensation, drifts of sex, confession and pale sleep, and it was confession as belief in each other, not unburdenings of guilt but avowals of belief, mostly his and stricken by need, and then drowsy sex again, two people passing through each other, easy and airy as sea spray, and how he'd told her that she was helping him recover his soul" (63). Although this passage invokes categories of "sensation" and "soul," its impact is to blur the boundaries between body and consciousness, self and other; the lovers' "drowsy," "drift[ing]" sex occurs in a state somewhere between sleep and wakefulness, where their multisensory, multidimensional knowledge of one another assumes the form of words and acts that transgress the boundaries between bodies and selves, rendering the lovers "two people passing through each other." "We are caught up in the world," Merleau-Ponty observes, "and we do not succeed in extricating ourselves from it in order to achieve consciousness of the world" (1962, 5).

With the sudden loss of her husband's embodied presence, however, Lauren's multifaceted interactions with him collapse from the world into the space of her consciousness; after his death, we are told, "the world was lost inside her" (39). If Lauren's ability to engage in conversation with characters in news stories in chapter 1 emerges as a form of imaginative freedom, a breakdown of space/time barriers that would allow her to transcend the limitations of the real world, grief locks her in the space inside her own head. What many critics describe as the "eerie" quality of *The Body Artist* emerges in part out of the novel's sudden inversion of the imaginative flexibility Lauren exercises early in the novel. Grief strains the limits of Lauren's consciousness, replacing imaginative mobility with the pressure of determining how much absent presence the imagination can hold. After Rey's death, Lauren continues to feel what she can no longer feel; the embodied presence through which she continues to negotiate her own body image emerges, like a phantom limb, as a presence registered only in misperception:[7] "She stepped slowly through the rooms. She felt him behind her when she was getting undressed standing barefoot on the cold floor, throwing off a grubby sweater and she half turned toward the bed" (35). Still pivoting around Rey's embodied presence, Lauren experiences his death as a perceptual distancing through which she "feels him" just outside the boundaries of her senses; unable to disengage herself from intercorporeality, she continually brushes up against her husband's absent form. Merleau-Ponty locates in the action of the hand reaching out to touch "a reference to the object, not as an object represented, but as that highly specific thing toward which we project ourselves, near which we are, in anticipation, and which we haunt. Consciousness is being-towards-the-thing through the intermediary of the body" (1962, 138–139). As the object of Lauren's reach dissolves into absence, she is forced back into a consciousness that holds her husband's presence only in representational terms. The imbalance created by Rey's sustained presence in her head and his sudden withdrawal from her body's reach causes Lauren to stumble. As she gets out of her car, her dislocation results in a near collapse imaged as "a small helpless sinking toward the ground, a kind of forgetting how to stand" (35).[8]

If Lauren's posture depends upon the reference of her husband's embodied presence, her experience of that presence before his death is merely habitual. When Rey is alive, Lauren experiences the smell of her husband's cigarette smoke as "part of her knowledge of his body. It was the aura of the man, a residue of smoke and unbroken habit, a dimension in the night, and she lapped it off the curled gray hairs on his chest and tasted it in his mouth" (21–22). In the wake of his absence, however, the "residue" of Rey's body drifts everywhere, lingering in a consciousness whose spaces it cannot fill. Trapped in the house she shared with him with only memory for company, Lauren struggles desperately to pull Rey out of her consciousness and locate him in familiar surroundings: "When she was downstairs she felt him in the rooms on the second floor. He used to prowl these rooms talking into a tiny tape recorder, smoke in his face, reciting ideas about some weary script to a writer somewhere whose name he could never recall. Now he was the smoke, Rey was, the thing in the air, vaporous, drifting into every space sooner or later, unshaped" (34–35). Lauren's feeling that Rey paces above her on the second floor registers the disconnect between their emotional proximity and his material inaccessibility; figuring him as just out of reach, she attempts to locate him in space and time so that she might render intelligible the collapse of presence into absence. If the novel's postmodern attention to the constructedness of knowledge and perception destabilizes the ground of materiality, Rey's death restores the significance of embodied presence by demonstrating the impact of his material absence. As the solipsistic experience of grief pressures Lauren's consciousness, the reader is trapped along with her in a mental/narrative space unable to contain the enormity of her loss; the first chapter's facile manipulation of inside and outside, consciousness and body, subject and world, fragments painfully as the novel focuses with grim determination on the expansion of a bereaved consciousness that pulls the outside world in, contracting and circumscribing the very surroundings that Lauren once transcended in her imaginative autonomy.

Experiencing her own body as "foreign and unfamiliar" after her husband's death (35), Lauren attempts to reenter the world by turning to the discipline of exercises that would ground her in her body:

> After the first days back she began to do her breathing exercises. There was bodywork to resume, her regimen of cat stretch and methodical contortion. She stuck out her tongue and panted in tightly timed sequence, internally timed, an exactitude she knew in the bones that were separated by the disks that went rat-a-tat down her back.
>
> But the world was lost inside her. (39)

Resuming a regimen that tones and shapes and orders, Lauren attempts to restore her placement within the conventions of time and space by returning to the reference point of her own body. Instead of reconnecting her to the external world, however, her bodywork reveals the impossibility of embracing "life lived irreducibly as sheer respiration" (59). Her attempt to get the world out of her and put it back into space assumes the form of self-immolation. Using emery boards, files, clippers, and creams, Lauren pares her body down as if to wear away the form that traps the world, history, consciousness, within her: "This was her work, to disappear from all her former venues of aspect and bearing and to become a blankness, a body slate erased of every past resemblance" (86). Described by one critic as "a body artist who tries to shake off the body—hers anyway" (106), Lauren uses her performance art to move from one body to another, aesthetically distancing herself from a corporeality that she would resignify through posture, gesture, costume, and affect. Speaking about the role of her body in her performance work, Lauren tells an interviewer, "'I taught it to do things other bodies could not. It absorbs me in a disinterested way. I try to analyze and redesign'" (107). If her lived relationship with Rey blurred the boundaries between self and other, body and consciousness, Lauren's response to his death involves "closing off" the points of interface that would render her vulnerable to loss: "It was necessary to alter the visible form, all the way down to the tongue. She was suppressing something, closing off outlets to the self, all the way down to the scourings at the deep end of the tongue, concealed from human view. The mind willed it on the body" (99–100). Lauren's attempt to blunt the loss of chiasmic intercorporeality assumes the form of theoretically distinguishing the mind from the body in order to render materiality a mere tool of subjectivity. The "something" that Lauren "suppress[es]" through her clippings and scourings and filings of her body, however, is her own knowledge of the impossibility of rendering consciousness manipulable through a material form capable of mechanistically "closing off outlets to the self." Moving back and forth from a world only body to a body only text, Lauren attempts to negotiate the impossible dilemma of embodied grief through exaggerated polarities that speak to the dislocation and fragmentation of embodied subjectivity in the shadow of loss.

If Lauren's vigorous exercise regime and rigorous body modifications offer little consolation for the loss of her husband's embodied presence, her grief leads her to the opposite extreme as she collapses into the passivity of staring at her computer screen for countless hours, mesmerized by images sent from a direct feed video cam positioned at the edge of a two-lane road in Finland. Watching images of Kotka engulfed in the blackness of the Scandinavian night for hours as the day goes on around her, Lauren is drawn not to the activity the screen reports—"the dead times were best"—but to its assertion of continuing presence despite the difference of time, the loss of light, the absence of motion:

> It was interesting to her because it was happening now, as she sat here, and because it happened twenty-four hours a day, facelessly, cars entering and leaving Kotka, or just the empty road in the dead times. The dead times were best.
>
> She sat and looked at the screen. It was compelling to her, real enough to withstand the circumstance of nothing going on. It thrived on the circumstance. It was three in the morning in Kotka and she waited for a car to come along—not that she wondered who was in it. It was simply the fact of Kotka. It was the sense of organization, a place contained in an unyielding frame, as it is and as you watch, with a reading of local time in the digital display in a corner of the screen. Kotka was another world but she could see it in its realness, in its hours, minutes and seconds. (40)

Lauren's focus on the "realness" of this virtual image suggests the compensation it provides for the dislocation of her grief, a grief defined by the tension between virtual presence and material absence. Trapped in the space of her own mind with a man whose overwhelming virtual proximity suggests a reality that is merely illusory, Lauren takes comfort in a virtual feed anchored in time and space despite its seemingly surreal quality.[9]

If Rey's embodied form continually eludes Lauren as she struggles to locate him just behind, above, around her, Kotka exists "facelessly," independent of any perception of it. Though in "another world," the "compelling" quality of Kotka derives from its existence beyond the realm of circumstance or thought, in a grounded material realm that calms Lauren's shaken sense of stability: "It was simply the fact of Kotka." If, as Merleau-Ponty observes, the "body is the pivot of the world" (1962, 82), Lauren's lived experience of Rey is formed around and through a knowledge of him that is sensory as well as symbolic, habitual as well as intellectual. With the sudden loss of that pivot, Lauren spirals around and around in a consciousness that struggles to locate grief in corporeal form, to "organize time until she could live again" (39). Kotka offers her a "sense of organization" that stems in part from a disembodied status that renders it unchangeable and invulnerable. Haunted by the sudden loss of her husband's embodied presence, Lauren takes comfort in the mesmerizing virtual presence of "a place contained in an unyielding frame."

When Lauren suddenly discovers a strange, small man sitting on the edge of a bed in her house wearing only his underwear, she lightheartedly contemplates the possibility that he is a virtual being that has stepped out of her computer screen into her home (47). Although critics have suggested that Mr. Tuttle, as Lauren comes to name the man, is Rey's ghost, or an "externalized embodiment of [Lauren's] loss," none of the novel's readers has focused on the way Mr. Tuttle's presence speaks to the embodied dynamics of grief that the novel charts. This odd little man, who looks nothing like Lauren's husband, speaks in unintelligible phrases that more than one critic has probed for critical significance. Lamenting the inconsistencies of a symbolic figure that seems to lack interpretive coherence, Eric Wittmershaus complains, "It's almost as if DeLillo has too-successfully conveyed the emotional vulnerability and scattered-to-the-four winds emotions that accompany grieving. . . . Simply put, [Mr. Tuttle's dialogue] is gibberish" (Wittmershaus 2001). If Wittmershaus's frustrated attentiveness to the sense of Mr. Tuttle's words yields only fragmentation, I would like to suggest that the "sense" of Mr. Tuttle's presence lies in the realm of the sensory.[10] Although Rey's presence after his death is only virtual—his existence confined to the images that swarm in Lauren's head—Mr. Tuttle supplements Rey's virtual presence by resituating Lauren's loss in the realm of the material. Grief limits Lauren's access to her husband to the realm of the representational; Mr. Tuttle, however, not only eats and sleeps in Lauren's home but renders Rey's gestures, inflections, and habits with sensory immediacy, offering the momentary illusion of access to a lost loved one whose embodied presence remains inaccessible.

Despite critics' tendency to describe Mr. Tuttle as a ghostlike figure, the novel repeatedly images Lauren's response to the small man whom she discovers sitting in his underwear on a bed in her house in bodily terms: "She stood looking at him, two *bodies* in a room (87, emphasis mine). Although Lauren demands that Mr. Tuttle articulate his history and explain his presence, his words function not as signs but as vocalizations that embody meaning. Unable to decipher their content, Lauren describes Mr. Tuttle's words as a "song" or "pure chant" (77) that pulls her out of her mind into his body. Leaning toward him, "She felt an easing in her body that drew her down out of laborious thought and into something nearly uncontrollable" (76). In contrast to the representational quality of memory, the sensory immediacy of the familiar voice that emerges out of the small man's body gradually asserts itself as *real*. Although Mr. Tuttle speaks to her,

> It was Rey's voice she was hearing. The representation was close, the accent and dragged vowels, the intimate differences, the articulations produced in one vocal apparatus and not another, things she'd known in Rey's voice, and only Rey's, and she kept her head in the book, unable to look at him. (62–63)

Hearing the sudden "bell-clap report of Rey's laughter," Lauren differentiates the "clear" sound of his voice from a recording or a "communication with the dead" to assert instead that "it was Rey alive in the course of a talk he'd had with her, in this room, not long after they'd come here" (63). As Lauren struggles to emerge from a realm of grief that renders her husband's presence merely representational, she focuses on the distinction between a vocal replication of Rey's voice—"the representation was close"—and the seemingly impossible resurrection of it: "It was Rey alive." If her experience of loss blocks Lauren's attempt to navigate the boundary between perception and representation, the significance of Mr. Tuttle's presence lies in his ability to restore the immediacy of Rey's presence: "It did not seem an act of memory. It was Rey's voice all right" (89). Functioning as a supplement to the disembodied images of grief, Mr. Tuttle's words give voice to Rey's presence in sensory terms: "She began to understand that she could not miss Rey, could not consider his absence, the loss of Rey, without thinking along the margins of Mr. Tuttle" (84). As the virtual body of grief rendered material, Mr. Tuttle functions not as Rey's ghost but as the opposite, as a materially present form that incarnates Rey's gestures and inflections in order to outline in sensory terms his bodily absence.

Even as he mimes Rey's voice and enacts Rey's gestures, Mr. Tuttle bodies forth a language that provides what one critic describes as "'the onomatopoetic rhythm of signification without the sign.'"[11] "Minus an identity and a language," Mr. Tuttle participates in a dialogue devoid of expressive or referential function. Generating a stream of empty phrases and incoherent sentences, he produces language as if it were a product of the body alone: "The words ran on, sensuous and empty" (77).[12] If Lauren's memories of Rey taunt her by rendering the presence of his words in the absence of the context provided by his worldly existence as a speaking subject with "a certain style of being," Mr. Tuttle's presence restores the rhythms, inflections, and gestures of Rey's speech without the presence of animating subjectivity. Rather than lending sensory form to memory's immaterial outlines, Mr. Tuttle's familiar inflections and gestures reveal what Merleau-Ponty describes as the inextricability of the psychical and the sensible in intercorporeal communication:

> The sense of the gestures is not given, but understood, that is, recaptured by an act on the spectator's part. The whole difficulty is to conceive this act clearly without confusing it with a cognitive operation. The communication or comprehension of gestures comes about through the reciprocity of my intentions and the gestures of others, of my gestures and intentions discernable in the conduct of other people. It is as if the other person's intention inhabited my body and mine his. . . . I become involved in things with my body, they co-exist with me as an incarnate subject, and this life among things has nothing in common with the elaboration of scientifically conceived objects. In the same way, I do not understand the gestures of others by some act of intellectual interpretation. (Merleau-Ponty 1962, 185)

Although Mr. Tuttle renders Rey's words and gestures materially, at no point does he "become involved in things with [his] body." Although materially present, he is "minus an identity, a language, a way to enjoy the savor of the honey-coated toast she watches him eat" (66–67). Lauren's attempt to penetrate the "pure chant" (77) Mr. Tuttle produces results only in frustration as she struggles to decode his "unadjusted" words: "There's a code in the simplest conversation that tells the speakers what's going on outside the barest acoustics. This was missing when they talked. There was a missing beat. It was hard for her to find the tempo. All they had were unadjusted words" (67). Rather than rendering Lauren's memories embodied, Mr. Tuttle's dislocated words further Lauren's sense of "losing touch"(67) with Rey "as an incarnate subject"; if Rey "inhabits [her] body" and she his, Mr. Tuttle's "unadjusted words" ultimately speak only to the absence of the intercorporeal dynamic that Merleau-Ponty describes as "reciprocity."

In returning her husband's voice to Lauren in sensory terms, Mr. Tuttle merely exposes the very paradox of embodied loss his presence might appear to resolve: "There was something raw in the moment, open-wounded. It bared her to things that were outside her experience but desperately central, somehow, at the same time" (64–65). If the wound that Mr. Tuttle's presence exposes is the irrecuperable experience of embodied loss, Mr. Tuttle's sensory proximity seems to promise a means of stitching up those very gaps. In the same way that Lauren turns to the mirror to access the man whose image she used to glimpse reflected there, she attempts to retrieve her husband's embodied presence by working backward from the sound of his voice now emerging from an unfamiliar body linked to a "virtual" presence: "She looked at [Mr. Tuttle], a cartoon head and body, chinless, stick-figured, but he knew how to make her husband live in the air that rushed from his lungs into his vocal folds—air to sounds, sounds to words, words the man, shaped faithfully on his lips and tongue" (64). Rey's existence in this unfamiliar body assumes a sensory immediacy that Lauren constructs as part of a physiological narrative she hopes to trace back to its origin in "the man" whose embodied subjectivity she once took for granted.

Like the man in her head, however, the man in Mr. Tuttle's body emerges as tauntingly partial. Although Lauren is enticed by the illusion of Rey's presence, her attempts to access her husband continue to fail. Having witnessed his familiar gestures, listened to his voice, heard his laughter, Lauren tries to bring Rey back by reducing herself to a sensory receptor and isolating the sensory experiences that would lend her access to him. In her desperate attempt to locate familiar sound and gesture in embodied presence, "[Lauren] looked. She was always looking. She could not get enough" (87). Hearing Rey's voice emerge from Mr. Tuttle, "She tried to concentrate on strict listening. She told herself to listen." (63) As the novel explores in the first chapter and elsewhere, the impossibility of isolating the physiology of sensory experience from its implication in a system of consciousness and knowledge renders the idea of mere looking or "strict listening" impossible. Defining flesh as neither biological nor "psychic" material, Merleau-Ponty stresses the inseparability of consciousness and the body, replacing "age-old assumptions that put the body in the world and the seer in the body" (1962, 138) with a model of mutually constituting fleshly exchange.[13] Just as Lauren's lived interactions with Rey "drift" from sensation to confession, her attempt to access her husband's presence by opening a series of Chinese boxes that would contain the body in the world and the man in the body—"air to sounds, sounds to words, words the man"—fails to restore her intercorporeal relationship with Rey. Although Lauren begs Mr. Tuttle to speak to her in a voice she recognizes as her husband's, the sensory accessibility of sound and gesture that would seem to render Lauren's images of her husband real only highlight his embodied absence:

> She wasn't watching [Mr. Tuttle] now. She was looking at the backs of her hands, fingers stretched, looking and thinking, recalling moments with Rey, not moments exactly but times, or moments flowing into composite time, an erotic of see and touch, and she curled one hand over and into the other, missing him in her body and feeling sexually and abysmally alone and staring at the points where her knuckles shone bloodless from the pressure of her grip. (51)

Rather than restoring Lauren's chiasmic exchange with Rey—an exchange DeLillo describes in Merleau-Pontyean terms as "an erotic of see and touch"—Mr. Tuttle's presence merely directs her back to the site of her loss, where she replays that erotic over and over. As Lauren "curl[s] one hand over and into the other," the overlay of her hands mimics the cradling action of a chiasmic exchange with Rey.[14] Caught up in the impossible goal of framing indistinguishable moments, disentangling interwoven bodies and separating out the dynamics of psychical corporeality, Lauren collapses into a form of self-embrace that exaggerates the rupture of sentient materiality to offer a painfully solipsistic mimicry of chiasmic intercorporeality.

Torn from the contextualization of embodied interaction, Rey's words and gestures assume in their redeployment a dislocated flatness that belies their sensory immediacy. Mr. Tuttle's "nearly intimate" presence bespeaks the possibility of a conjoining it cannot realize (42). Locked in a house with a man to whom she talks, with whom she walks, around whom she circles, Lauren remains locked out of the simplest form of access his proximity would imply. Her desire to reach out to him—"She wanted to touch him" (68)—implies a need to render accessible his dense material presence: "He seemed barely there, four feet away from her" (68). In one of the novel's most poignant lines, Lauren reveals the agony of living in painful proximity to a stranger who mouths Rey's words only to swallow them in an unfamiliar form. Having unsuccessfully searched Mr. Tuttle's eyes for signs of immaterial presence, Lauren turns to him. "She said, 'Why do I think I'm standing closer to you than you are to me?'" (87). The paradoxical dynamic Lauren describes marks the tension between material proximity and chiasmic intercorporeality; whereas Lauren hurls herself into relationship with the stranger who both is and is not Rey, Mr. Tuttle stands apart, his mechanistic unresponsiveness to Lauren marking a distance she cannot negotiate through perceptual means. Mr. Tuttle's physiological recreation of her husband's speech, inflection, and gesture pushes past representation into reality without rescuing Rey's presence from the realm of the virtual.

Ultimately, then, Mr. Tuttle embodies not Rey's presence but its taunting inaccessibility. In "The Ghost of Embodiment," Edward S. Casey uses the figure of the ghost to mark the way the lived body haunts models of embodiment that attempt to disentangle and dichotomize the figure of the body as a matrix of nature and culture: "Without embodiment, culture would be schematic in the pejorative sense of empty or sketchy. It would be a ghost of itself. By the same token, the body, were it not to bear and express culture, to implicate and explicate it, would be itself a ghost: an exsanguinated shadow of its fully encultured liveliness" (1998, 37). Haunted by the disembodied image of memory, Lauren struggles to locate her husband in Mr. Tuttle's form, "in the material place where Rey lives in him, alive again, word for word, touch for touch" (102). Suspended between the ghostly image and its simply material counterpart, however, Lauren collapses in the attempt to integrate and to embrace Rey's embodied presence:

> Rey is alive now in this man's mind, in his mouth and body and cock. Her skin was electric. She saw herself, sees herself crawling toward him. The image is there in front of her. She is crawling across the floor and it is nearly real to her. She feels something has separated, softly come unfixed, and she tries to pull him down to the floor with her, stop him, keep him here, or crawls up onto him or into him, dissolving, or only lies prone and sobs unstoppably, being watched by herself from above. (89–90)

Lauren's encounter with Mr. Tuttle uncovers rather than heals the fracture of embodied presence she experiences in her grief. The feeling that "something has separated, softly come unfixed," speaks both to the dissolution of intercorporeality in the face of loss and the sudden withdrawal of Rey's embodied presence despite his sustained existence in the landscape of her consciousness. Haunted by both presence and absence, unable to reach what she can literally touch, Lauren herself becomes suspended between matter and image, action and imagination. In struggling to reach "the material place where Rey lives in him," she effects the detachment of her body from her consciousness to "see herself" crawl toward the body which she simultaneously acknowledges as "the image." "Nearly real to her," Mr. Tuttle exists, along with her grief, in the space between representation and reality. Her attempt to access him, figured as a process of physical wresting described in conditional or hypothetical terms, emerges as a desperate effort to locate Rey's presence that belies the simple claim with which she begins. Rather than embodying the image of Rey in her memory, Mr. Tuttle renders it purely material; as Lauren "tries to pull him down to the floor with her, stop him, keep him here," she struggles to access in physical terms the embodied dimension of a loss that is neither material nor immaterial.

Describing the logic of coimplication that defines body and mind, body and society, nature and culture, Casey objects to models of stratification that locate the social over or upon the somatic. The alternative language he proposes echoes the language of this passage, in which Lauren "crawls up onto him or into him, dissolving." "The body," Casey observes, "remains in the center; it is the congenial or compliant other side of the social subject, its intimate in-side as it were. . . . It is a question not of this versus that but of this in that" (1998, 36). If poststructuralist models of grief locate meaning in language and culture, the restoration of the body to the "center" of such models implies not the reduction of subjectivity to materiality but the reintroduction of a concept of experiential embodiment that forsakes Cartesian polarities. Casey observes, "The body was bled out and abandoned by Descartes not just because he did not recognize its status as 'lived,' . . . but also . . . because he did not concern himself with its cultural and social dimensions. But it will not do, either, to reduce the lived body in turn to an object or product of discourse, as has happened in post-structuralist thought. This, too, renders the body a spector of itself, a paper-thin textual entity: it is to refuse to recognize the body as at once insinuating and insinuated, permeating and permeated" (37). Neither "permeating nor permeated" by the experiential world in which lived bodies exist, Mr. Tuttle's body mimics Rey's inflections and gestures without allowing Rey to live in them or Lauren to access them. If the meaning of a gesture, in Merleau-Ponty's words, "is not behind it, [but] is intermingled with the structure of the world outlined by the gesture" (1962, 186), Mr. Tuttle's gestures outline only the parameters of absence.

Lauren's inability to access Rey through Mr. Tuttle leads to an acknowledgment of the embodied depths of her own grief. Although Lauren's performance art textualizes the phenomenon of mourning, the apparent ease with which she moves into and out of others' bodies belies the tenacity of an experience of grief which her theatricality cannot ultimately wrest from its location in the "woven fabric" of her own embodied existence: "Why not sink into it? Let death bring you down. Give death its sway. Why shouldn't the death of a person you love bring you into lurid ruin?" (118). Grief assaults Lauren with a devastating force that overwhelms not only the theatricality of her body art but her psychic attempts to "accommodate" her husband's death. Momentarily, she embraces the fall into "lurid ruin" against which she has instinctively defended herself throughout the novel. She "sink[s] into" an acknowledgment of the immediacy of loss, locating the limits and effects of her grief in a series of ideas that she "held," as she once held Rey, "every way she was. Eyes, mind and body. She moved about the town's sloping streets unnoticed, holding these ideas, buying groceries and hardware and playing through these thoughts to a certain point, in the long hall, among the locks, tools and glassware" (118). The narrative attention to Lauren's movements locates the play of consciousness not merely in the landscape of "the town's sloping streets" but in the space of a body in a long hall, a body that holds and *is* matter—like the locks, tools, and glassware Lauren manipulates—even as it refuses to be reduced to the realm of the material.[15]

If the novel's opening chapter emphasizes the constructedness of meaning and the power of consciousness to transcend the limits of time and space, Lauren's experience of grief demands her recognition of what Merleau-Ponty describes as the "perpetual incarnation" of existence (1962, 166). As the material supplement to Lauren's immaterial images of Rey, Mr. Tuttle exposes not the insignificance of bodily presence but the impossibility of separating out the "woven fabric" of embodied subjectivity. Lauren's failure to hold onto Rey in either a sensory or a psychic realm forces her to push the limitlessness of imagination documented in chapter 1 to its logical conclusion: "Why should you accommodate his death? Or surrender to it in thin-lipped tasteful bereavement? Why give him up if you can walk along the hall and find a way to place him within reach? Sink lower, she thought. Let it bring you down. Go where it takes you" (118). Rejecting both the promise of sensory immediacy offered by Mr. Tuttle and the models of psychic accommodation proffered by a culture invested in containing the parameters of loss, a desperate, grief-stricken Lauren refuses the consolation of representation, demanding instead that consciousness "sink" into the world to shape the material realm in which it is located. The radical conclusion of *The Body Artist*, then, brings Lauren "down" to what is at once the most obvious and the least accessible fact of grief in a postmodern landscape: the unalterable loss of embodied presence.

As the novel's final chapter traces Lauren's attempt to locate her husband's body, then, it figures that body not simply as a sensory, material form that would project Rey's presence into space and time but as what Merleau-Ponty describes as the perpetual incarnation of existence: "In this way the body expresses total existence, not because it is an external accompaniment to that existence, but because existence realizes itself in the body. This incarnate significance is the central phenomenon of which body and mind, sign and significance are abstract moments" (1962, 166). Merleau-Ponty's inversion of classical hierarchies of mind and body turns models of identity inside out not by privileging the body over the mind but by recasting the very categories of mind and body as abstract manifestations of incarnate existence. The loss of intercorporeality after death emerges within such a frame not merely as the loss of a corporeal form on which the content of subjectivity could be written, but as the loss of a world in which the abstractions of body and mind could be incarnated. When, in the novel's conclusion, Lauren hears a noise upstairs in her house, she moves toward her room, "because that's where Rey was intact, in his real body, smoke in his hair and clothes" (123). Lauren's quest for Rey's "real" body here figures not only her fundamental desire to undo loss, but her longing to resituate his familiar presence in an incarnate form.

Refusing to "yield to the limits of belief" (124), Lauren makes one last effort to locate her husband's "intact" form as she rounds the corner to her bedroom. As her mind wills the incarnation of Rey's image, Lauren attempts to supplement the motions of consciousness through the imaginative performance of a series of bodily memories that relocate her in relation to Rey's "real body":

> She knew how it would happen, past the point of playing it through, because she refused to yield to the limits of belief.
>
> Once she steps into the room, she will already have been there, now, at night, getting undressed. It is a question of fitting herself to the moment, throwing off a grubby sweater, her back to the bed. She stands barefoot, raising her arm out of the sweater and striking a hand on something above. She remembers the hanging lamp, totally wrong for the room, metal shade wobbling, and then turns and looks, knowing what she will see.
>
> He sits on the edge of the bed in his underwear, lighting the last cigarette of the day.
>
> Are you unable to imagine such a thing even when you see it?
>
> Is the thing that's happening so far outside experience that you're forced to make excuses for it, or give it the petty credentials of some misperception? (124)

Lending her own body as the material form through which her fantasy might be incarnated, Lauren adopts a series of postures and positions that reflect her desire not merely to accommodate but to enact the familiar landscape of intercorporeality. If rescuing Rey's embodied presence from the realm of absence is simply "a question of fitting herself to the moment,"

Lauren figures that process of bending to her vision in habitual terms that involve measuring her body's reach against the familiar spatial configurations of a room that includes not only a bed, an outstretched arm, and a low-hanging lamp, but the missing body around which her own form pivots: "They are two real bodies in a room. This is how she feels them, in the slivered heart of the half second it takes to edge around the doorpost, with hands that touch and mouths that open slowly. His cock is rising in her slack pink fist. Their mouths are ajar for tongues, nipples, fingers, whatever projections of flesh, and for whispers of was and is, and their eyes come open into the soul of the other" (124–125). If, as Merleau-Ponty claims, perceptual habit is "the coming into possession of a world" (1962, 153), however, Lauren's imaginative performance of the habitual sequence of memory only perpetuates her world's unraveling. Regardless of the intensity of her imagining, reflected in the narrative's lingering over the enumeration of "tongues, nipples, fingers, whatever projections of flesh," these manifestations of Rey's body remain projections of Lauren's mind. If the grounding of the body is insufficient to stabilize perceptual objectivity, the projections of the mind dematerialize in the absence of corporeality.

Having acknowledged the necessary interweaving of body and mind, sense and imagination, in the experience of embodied subjectivity, Lauren must also acknowledge the way in which her fantasy of Rey's return lacks a form that no amount of imaginative force can supply: "She stopped at room's edge, facing back into the hall, and felt the emptiness around her. That's when she rocked down to the floor, backed against the doorpost. She went twisting down, slowly, almost thoughtfully, and opened her mouth, oh, in a moan that remained unsounded" (125). Ultimately, what Lauren confronts before she rounds the corner into her empty bedroom is not the fact of Rey's embodied absence but the existence of spatial, temporal, and corporeal boundaries that locate—simultaneously lending form to and restricting—the play of her own mind. Merleau-Ponty observes, "I am not in space and time, nor do I conceive space and time; I belong to them, my body combines with them and includes them" (1962, 140). As Lauren approaches the empty bedroom, the agonizingly slow way in which she "rocks down" to the floor documents the painful process of recombining with space and time. If the chiasm involves "the coiling over of the visible upon the seeing body, of the tangible upon the touching body," Lauren's reintroduction to space marks the unraveling of her chiasmic intercorporeality with Rey; as she backs against the doorpost, the narrative images her collapse to the floor as a slow "twisting down" that emphasizes her painful entwining with the emptiness of space.[16]

Earlier in the novel, the narrative considers, "If there is no sequential order except what we engender to make us safe in the world, then maybe it is possible, what, to cross from one nameless state to another, except that it clearly isn't" (85). In rendering the obvious—"except that it clearly isn't"—as a final qualifying clause, this sentence mimics the structure of Lauren's experience of grief. That structure is also replicated in the dramatic conclusion of *The Body Artist*, which builds toward the realization of a fantasy that collapses in the light of day. In the novel's postmodern landscape, the incontrovertibility of death emerges as the least accessible rather than the most obvious fact of loss. The dramatic climax of this novel of grief literally reveals nothing as Rey's widow enters their bedroom several months after his death to see that her husband still is not there:

> She thought she would not bother looking in there. It was pathetic to look. The room faced east and would be roiled in morning light, in webby sediment and streams of sunlit dust and in the word *motes*, which her mother liked to use.
> Maybe it was all an erotic reverie. The whole thing was a city built for a dirty thought. She was a sexual hysteric, ha. Not that she believed it. (125–126)

Even as she continues to place words on the same plane as things, to shift between and among various models for constructing meaning, Lauren must disavow a delusion of reincarnation no more or less fantastical than a rendering of grief as erotic reverie; if the Freudian diagnosis of sexual hysteria would figure the landscape of her loss symbolically as "a city built for a dirty thought," Lauren turns from that symbolic rendering to supplement the vision of what the mind creates with a focus on what the eye sees: "The room was empty when she looked. No one was there. The light was so vibrant she could see the true colors of the walls and floor. She'd never seen the walls before. The bed was empty. She'd known it was empty all along but was only catching up. She looked at the sheet and blanket swirled on her side of the bed, which was the only one in use" (126). As it charts the collapse of Lauren's fantasy of the body's return, the novel's conclusion introduces a language that implicitly recalls vision's physiological grounding; in the vibrancy of morning sunlight, Lauren sees "the true colors of the walls and floor." The invocation of this essentializing adjective functions, I would argue, not to undo the novel's constructivist assumptions but to establish a baseline frame of reference that delimits the spectrum of possibility within which meaning might unfold. Trapped not only by Rey's absence but by the theoretical promise of undoing that loss, Lauren ultimately acknowledges the limits of her imagination as she turns, instead, to a pragmatic model based in a shared experiential world. The theoretical inaccessibility of the body outside of linguistic and hermeneutic structures fails to guarantee its opposite; Lauren's efforts to reconstruct Rey's "real body" through language and imagination delay her confrontation with an embodied loss that emerges in this postmodern landscape as oddly inaccessible. Only in the novel's conclusion is Lauren able to perceive what she can no longer see or touch. In *The Body Artist,* then, the trajectory of mourning is imaged not as a psychological process that involves testing memory against absence but as a literal act of perception that involves stripping away the compensation of language and imagination to see what is not there. For Lauren, "catching up" to the fact of Rey's embodied loss entails not only recognizing his physical absence—"The bed was empty"—but acknowledging her inability to span the distance of that absence through the power of either consciousness or habit.

In probing the resistance of grief to the consolations of the imagination, *The Body Artist* ends where it begins, but with a difference. The novel stages the impossibility of recuperating embodied loss against the backdrop of a world which dissolves the boundary between absence and presence. If the logical extension of the constructivist universe in which we live is the textualization of the world, the shock of grief in a culture beyond mourning is not the fact of loss but its resistance to the recuperation of language, image, and imagination. Defining current theoretical interest in the body as a response to recent language-based understandings of experience, Daniel Punday observes, "After a decade of suspicion about language's ability to refer to anything beyond itself, the body has emerged as a site where the power and problems of reference play themselves out" (Punday 2003, 1). For Lauren, grief entails working through a focus on language and the constructedness of meaning to access the fact of embodied loss. The theoretical coimplication of imagination and perception fails to guarantee the image's transfer from the realm of the mind to the realm of the body, despite their chiasmic twining. *The Body Artist* charts the geography of Lauren's grief in the context of a critique of essentialism, interrogating the idea that the elimination of the body as the grounding for meaning might find its logical extension in the blurring of the corporeal parameters of loss. Whereas Merleau-Ponty in *The Phenomenology of Perception* argues for the need to acknowledge the body as "the unperceived term in the centre of the world" (1962, 82), *The Body Artist* looks back at Merleau-Ponty's theories from the vantage point of the twenty-first century to mark the difficulty of perceiving the absence as well as formulating the presence of the body in our midst.

"Our minds," Thomas De Zengotita observes in his characterization of life in the twenty-first century, "are the product of total immersion in a daily experience saturated with fabrications to a degree unprecedented in human history" (De Zengotita 2002, 35). Defining the time in which we live as an "era of simulation," Jean Baudrillard documents how the breakdown between the "true" and the "false," the "real" and the "imaginary," immerses us in a world defined by "the murderous power of images, murderers of the real" (Baudrillard 1994, 5). Asserting what has become a wearying commonplace of contemporary cultural theory, Baudrillard and De Zengotita position the contemporary subject as an adept consumer of images in a simulated world. If, as I argue in the previous chapter, culturally sanctioned models of mourning implicitly exclude the significance of the lost body, the mourner's immersion in a contemporary image culture necessarily heightens and complicates tendencies to disavow the embodied dynamics of grief. Nudged by such cultural dynamics, culturally sanctioned theories of mourning which have a profound investment in the power of language to represent loss may move further and further away from the acknowledgment of its reality. The compensation of representation comes to lie not in the *expression* of absence but in the irrelevance of presence in a world defined only by the inescapable presence of simulation. As representations dissolve into simulacra, the talking cure may emerge as a series of self-supporting fabrications.

The language Baudrillard uses to describe our "era of simulation" suggests how the disembodied dynamics of existing models of loss extend the cultural logic of a world in which images have no reference: "It is no longer a question of imitation, nor duplication, nor even parody. It is a question of substituting the signs of the real for the real, that is to say of an operation of deterring every real process via its operational double, a programmatic, metastable, perfectly descriptive machine that offers all the signs of the real and short-circuits all its vicissitudes. Never again will the real have the chance to produce itself—such is the vital function of the model in a system of death, or rather of anticipated resurrection, that no longer even gives the event of death a chance" (2). This passage uses death as a figure of the real only to document its erasure. The ease with which Baudrillard makes the breathtaking claim that death no longer has "a chance," since "anticipated resurrection" entirely trumps the real, demonstrates how easily the fact of embodied loss may be subsumed within the realm of imaginary fabrications. Only in such a culture of simulation would the obvious assertion that the dead cannot be reembodied become controversial, counterintuitive, or naïve. The entrance into a culture of simulation demands leaving one's body behind or, in the case of grief, denying the immediacy of embodied absence. In an image culture in which "everything is already dead and resurrected in advance" (Baudrillard 1994, 6), the immediacy of embodied loss becomes subsumed within the realm of representation, relegating bodily presence to the domain of the primitive or the nostalgic and rendering the fact of absence—"The bed was empty"—strangely inaccessible even in the light of day.

CHAPTER SIX

Objects of Grief

The Object Embrace

A year ago, shortly after her hundredth birthday, my grandmother died in the same home she had lived in for over sixty years. Well into her mid nineties, widowed for decades, she planted her own vegetable garden, made Sunday breakfast for her great-grandchildren, and mowed her large lawn on a riding tractor. Often, when I came to visit her I would find her on the ladder cleaning gutters, on her knees in the dirt of her flower beds, or on that tractor, a tiny wrinkled woman wearing an old straw hat and dirty Keds sneakers with Peds.

After she died, my sister and I each chose a piece of jewelry from her jewelry box, an antique satin-lined case filled with brooches and pearls and sapphire earrings that she almost never wore. I didn't know what I was looking for until I found it: a slender gold watch with a small round face and an expandable accordion band. Unlike some of the other pieces of jewelry in the box, the watch I chose was neither beautiful nor handcrafted, but inexpensive, mass-produced and battered with use. My grandmother wore one like it her whole life long; when, after years of constant wear, one watch ceased to work, she would buy another, often the same make, always the same simple style. The watch I have—the one she wore for most of the last decade of her life—still runs, though it's marked with the wear of my grandmother's body and the labor of my grandmother's life. The glass face is rough with scratches, its once smooth surface so scarred by use that some of the numbers beneath are hard to decipher. As my grandmother aged, she grew thinner and thinner; even from my earliest memory, the watch that encircled her wrist slipped along her forearm with her every motion. When she reached for my hand, it slid toward me as well. When she brushed my long hair for minutes at a time, hairbrush and watch would often collide with a gentle click that was part of the rhythm that nearly always made me close my eyes. Even in rare moments when she sat still, my grandmother's watch dangled at her wrist, so that when I saw her without it—washing dishes in the sink, stepping into the bath, the late days of her life when she could no longer see or know the time—her body seemed unfamiliar, her right arm pale and unadorned. All metal and glass, the watch wears the past in the worn finish of its pressure points, the darkened flecks of gold, its scratched surfaces and unevenly burnished back. Tracing the cool slide of its familiar surface with my hand, I can almost feel my fingers slipping onto the papery thin texture of my grandmother's soft, translucent skin.

It is this imaginative yearning for the watch to remain contiguous with her skin, for the object to serve as a material bridge to a lost body, that made me choose it initially and that makes it still something I find myself touching and turning over in my hands. Here is incontrovertible proof of my grandmother's embodied presence; here is evidence of the cooking, and brushing, and turning of earth scratched into the band; and here is my own material touchstone that links me with the thousand times I saw, heard, and touched this same watch in her presence. Unlike memory's images which, I have argued in previous chapters, fail to evoke the textured experience of embodiment, our multisensory experience of the objects our loved ones leave behind constructs a *form* for embodied loss. As I discussed in Chapter 4, Freud's focus on the memory work of grief emphasizes the need to test memory against reality in order to gradually sever attachment, on the assumption that, through memory's images, "the existence of the lost object is psychically prolonged" (Freud 1957, 244–245). If, however, memory's images have no bodies—or have bodies that are disembodied by virtue of their smoothness, their shallowness, their untouchability—memory speaks the body's past presence only by highlighting its sensory absence; images of the lost body blur the very dynamics of absent presence they should, in Freud's model, clarify. Barthes's inability to penetrate the flatness of the image frustrates his attempt to locate the site of his loss; Emerson laments the fact of a grief that "does not touch" him, that denies him "contact," not only with his lost son, but with the embodied experience of that loss (Emerson 1983, 472). An exploration of representations of objects in fictional and nonfictional grief narratives points to the function of objects as supplements to the disembodied images of memory and unveils their role in a revised narrative of embodied grief.

Many memory objects are valued for their association with the embodied presence of lost loved ones. In *Death, Memory, and Material Culture*, Elizabeth Hallam and Jenny Hockey offer an anthropological and cultural historical account of the significance of objects as sites of memory in private as well as public spaces. Citing Deborah Lupton's view that emotionally charged objects are most often those that are worn, those that "enclose" the body, or those with which bodies interact on a daily basis, Hallam and Hockey conclude that the most potent markers of memory are those associated with the body; such objects, they suggest, serve "to bind the living and the dead, to hold a fragile connection across temporal distance and to preserve a material presence in the face of an embodied absence" (2001, 18).

In contrast to what Emerson describes as the "shallow" quality of grief, objects possess a depth that links them to the human bodies that would touch and be touched by them. Whereas memory's images fail to penetrate the circle of the touching and the touched so crucial to chiasmic intertwining, Merleau-Ponty argues that things in the world exist in chiasmic relation with human beings by virtue of their depth: "It is the body and it alone . . . that can bring us to the things themselves, which are themselves not flat beings but beings in depth . . . open to him alone that, if it be possible, would coexist with them in the same world" (1968, 136). Touching objects situates the perceiver in a body that can also be touched; the circulation of sense, in Merleau-Ponty's argument, unites the perceiver and the perceived. Working from the assumption of a continuity between the body and the sensory world in which it exists, Merleau-Ponty observes that "things are the prolongation of my body and my body is the prolongation of the world, through it the world surrounds me" (255). In his controversial extension of this idea, he argues that the chiasm "is not only a me other exchange . . . it is also an exchange between me and the world, between the phenomenal body and the 'objective' body, between the perceiving and the perceived" (215). Insofar as our tactile experiences of our loved one's objects invoke what Merleau-Ponty describes as "the thickness of the body" (135), they place us in a sensory exchange that functions in chiasmic terms, a world of depth that contrasts with the flatness of memory or image. If, as Freud argues, "the existence of the lost object is psychically prolonged" through memory's images, mementos like my grandmother's watch sometimes lend images a depth that registers the corporeal contours of the lost body, providing a *sensory* memory that measures present absence against past presence.

In doing so, however, objects lend grief a form that exposes rather than compensates for bodily absence. Lending texture and dimension to my memory of her body, my grandmother's watch taunts me by withholding one side of what Merleau-Ponty describes as "the two 'sides' of our body, the body as sensible and the body as sentient" (136). Insofar as they are sensible but not sentient, engagement with our loved one's objects recalls the interweaving of body and world that underlies Merleau-Ponty's notion of the chiasm only by invoking the depth of an intercorporeality such engagement can never restore. Distinguishing the shared "flesh" of body and object from human intercorporeality, Merleau-Ponty observes, "The flesh of the world is not *self-sensing* (*se sentir*) as is my flesh—It is sensible and not sentient—I call it flesh, nonetheless . . . in order to say that it is a *pregnancy* of possibles" (250). If Merleau-Ponty invokes "a pregnancy of possibles" to establish the shared flesh of object and body, the object marked by a lost body resonates only with aborted possibility. As I trace the scratched surface of the watch face or slide my fingers across the stretched links of its band, sense memory "prolongs" the existence of my grandmother's embodied presence only long enough to exaggerate the immediacy of her absence. If we think of matter in Merleau-Ponty's eyes as "a sinewed depth of the world's body which we meet within the palpability of our embodiment" (Mazis 1996, 77), the press of objects resituates the survivor within a palpable dynamic of fleshly exchange that recalls an embodied experience it cannot recuperate; objects locate embodied grief by rendering loss in sensory form. The object's function, then, is not to substitute for embodied presence but to invoke its absence, acknowledging the irrecuperable dimension of grief that lurks beneath existing cultural discourses of compensation for loss.

In "The Inheritance of Tools," Scott Russell Sanders charts his reaction to the news of his father's death in a memoir essay that represents grief as a problem of bodily location and material presence:

> For several hours I paced around inside my house, upstairs and downstairs, in and out of every room, looking for the right door to open and knowing there was no such door. . . . Where was the door, the door, the door? I kept wondering. . . . I went down into the basement, opened a drawer in my workbench, and stared at the ranks of chisels and knives. Oiled and sharp, as my father would have kept them, they gleamed at me like teeth. I took up a clasp knife, pried out the longest blade, and tested the edge on the hair of my forearm. A tuft came away cleanly, and I saw my father testing the sharpness of tools on his own skin, the blades of axes and knives and gouges and hoes, saw the red hair shaved off in patches from his arms and the backs of his hands. (2001, 174)

Sanders's pacing registers through the desperate and repetitive motions of the body the incomprehensibility of his father's death and the controlled hysteria of the son's search for a place to locate his grief: "Where was the door, the door, the door?" Finding his way into the workroom where he stores the tools passed on to him by his father, Sanders tests the sharp blade of his father's clasp knife against his skin; in doing so, he not only marks his grief on his body but mingles pieces of his own body with traces of his father's. In reaching out for his father, Sanders finds him—quite literally—in the microscopic remnants of hair and skin still clinging to the tools that once belonged to his father. As he tests the blade of the clasp knife on the hair of his own forearm, Sanders uses the material object to come as close as he can to touching his father's missing body with his own. The sensation of that knife blade along his forearm supplements the visual image he conjures up—"I saw my father testing the sharpness of tools on his own skin, . . . saw the red hair"—by lending the image the power of touch and locating it on the sentient planes of his own body. The object blurs the line between memory and materiality, functioning as a trace of bodily presence that lends the image sensory depth.

Dennis McFarland's recent novel, *Singing Boy*, articulates the challenge that embodied understandings of grief pose to existing psychic models of mourning that legislate a process of letting go. Sarah, the widowed protagonist of McFarland's novel, finds herself pressured to let go of a grief others want her to move through in a healing process that works through a Freudian model of detachment from the lost object: "The message is always the same. Let go, move on, get on with it, get over it, put it behind you" (2000, 83). The novel images her failure to progress through the psychic process of mourning in terms that emphasize the spatial, material, and embodied form of her resistance to emotional healing: "Her grief will be too large somehow, larger than it ought to be, and she'll feel indicted by others as inhumane for keeping such a large animal indoors. At every turn, everyone will encourage her to set it free, let it go, and to allow her feelings to change" (19). The cultural gaze that transforms Sarah's resistant grief into a recalcitrant force that occupies too much space simultaneously reduces her (embodied) subjectivity to unwieldy animal form. Refusing the consolation of cultural or religious narratives that would ask her to set that animal free, Sarah remains mired in the fact of "Malcolm's death viewed as plain loss. . . . Viewed this way, it didn't evolve—it began and ended in precisely the same moment" (67). If cultural assumptions about grief frame mourning as a psychic narrative the survivor must propel herself through, Sarah's resistance to that symbolic form of "moving on" surfaces in a series of literal motions that locate grief on the body. In opposition to public discourses of loss and consolation that encourage psychological transformation, the language of bodily grief remains secretive and closeted:

Objects of Grief 181

> Secrets, and more secrets.
> Three times over the last month or so, she has awakened in the middle of the night, climbed out of bed . . . glided down the hallway, and quietly closed Harry's door. Back in her room, she closes her own door, moves to Malcolm's dresser, and opens the top drawer; she gathers in her hands a basketball-size clump of his T-shirts and boxer shorts, which she lifts to her face, pressing the fabrics hard against her eyes and nose and mouth as if she means to obliterate her senses; after a few seconds of this, she moves to his closet, steps all the way inside, and closes the door behind her, where the darkness is absolute and she can smell him, mostly in a favorite parka, which she gropes for in the dark and then clutches in her arms, allowing herself to explore the depth of its emptiness. (184)

While public discourse formulates her "failure to move through her grief quickly enough" (109) as stalled psychic motion, the narrative here breaks down the widow's apparent motionlessness in a litany of verbs that focus painstaking attention on the muscular, embodied motion of her actions. This short passage breaks down her movement through space in excruciating detail that denaturalizes the simplest bodily acts as it recounts her climbing, gliding, moving, opening, gathering, pressing, smelling, groping, clutching. As the narrative forces its attention back onto the subtle complexities of Sarah's body, interrupting the illusion of psychic stalling with the revelation of corporeal complexity, it also highlights the absence of the embodied presence that she struggles not merely to recover but to locate. Faced with the unraveling of a chiasmic intercorporeality that memory cannot hold, Sarah balls up a wad of clothes—"T-shirts and boxer shorts"—notable for the closeness of their contact with her husband's body and shapes them into a "basketball-size clump," a mass of substance and solidity that would allow her to situate grief in space, texture, and dimension in order to experience the fact of bodily loss. Echoes of Emerson's desperate desire to be touched by the loss of his son emerge here in the widow's attempt to lend grief material presence; as she presses her husband's underwear against the sites of sensory deprivation on her own face, Sarah's failure to "get [grief] nearer," render it "penetrative," is marked by the violence required to mimic chiasmic exchange. Just as the narrative focus on the intricacies of her motion highlights the stillness and darkness of the space that surrounds her, the force she exerts in the act of "Pressing the fabrics hard against her eyes and nose and mouth" testifies to the absence of an external force pressing back against her body. Sarah's struggle to locate her loss in corporeal terms reflects a grief dynamic that Christopher Noel's memoir, *In the Unlikely Event of a Water Landing: A Geography of*

Grief, describes as the struggle to develop a new language that marks bodily presence in the face of sensory absence: "Feeling rain and wind on my skin is a storm-walking cliché, but 'feeling' Brigid in me nonvisibly, non-audibly, even nonsensously . . . that's so far from a cliché that a whole new language will be needed, one that can match, nuance for nuance, the small movements of someone who is kept in a black sack inside a black chamber" (1996, 105). As Sarah "moves to [her husband's] closet, steps all the way inside, and closes the door behind her, where the darkness is absolute," her voluntary entrance into the equivalent of Noel's "black sack inside a black chamber" can be read as an attempt to depressurize the intensity of nonsensuous feeling that marks the disequilibrium of grief.

In "Flesh and Verb in the Philosophy of Merleau-Ponty," Henri Maldiney observes that, "before being corporeal, my body is flesh holding onto the flesh of the world with which it can participate" (2000, 70). Maldiney's image of the embrace—the human body "holding onto the flesh of the world"—emphasizes the multisensory, tactile quality of perception. Reaching out for her husband's body and touching only "the flesh of the world," the widow is locked in an object embrace that invokes the form of her relationship with him but holds only absence as its content; "grop[ing]" for the parka that holds his smell, she "clutches [it] in her arms, allowing herself to explore the depth of its emptiness." The "depth" that Merleau-Ponty defines as the shared quality of bodies and objects lends the parka the ability to register absence in "the depth of its emptiness." Whereas Freud claims that, in memory, "the existence of the lost object is psychically prolonged" (Freud 1957, 45), Sarah's exploration of her husband's clothing points to the possibility that embodied existence may be materially recalled through a dynamic of object memory. Although Freud describes melancholia as an unwillingness to acknowledge loss, the character's acts here do not represent an attempt to sustain an intercorporeal relationship. The terrible "secret" that Sarah struggles to hide involves not an imaginative fantasy of coupling with her husband but an embodied opportunity to acknowledge the fact of his loss. If grief contains an embodied dimension that complicates existing understandings of loss, the labor that Freud describes as the "work of mourning" here extends into the forms of the material world, allowing for a type of embodied memory that measures past chiasmic intercorporeality not in order to sustain it but in order to release its hold.

A Sensory Semiotics

The tendency in psychoanalytic theories of grief to render materiality merely symbolic also surfaces in theories of objects that move past the sensuous palpability of things to focus primarily on their functions as signs. In *The System of Objects,* Jean Baudrillard examines the way objects handed down through families serve as family portraits; the antique, he claims, functions as "the immemorialization, in the concrete form of an object, of a former being" (1996, 75). Claiming that objects help us cope with "the irreversible movement from birth toward death" (96), Baudrillard concludes, "What man gets from objects is not a guarantee of life after death but *the possibility, from the present moment onwards, of continually experiencing the unfolding of his existence in a controlled, cyclical mode, symbolically transcending a real existence the irreversibility of whose progression he is powerless to affect*" (96). Baudrillard's semiotic approach to objects, his interest in their function as one means of affecting a symbolic transcendence of "real existence," focuses on the ability of objects to pull subjects out of the limitations of mortality imposed upon them by embodiment. Such a vision contrasts markedly with Merleau-Ponty's interest in the pull of objects; his phenomenology of the body defines objects not as symbolic vehicles for transcending the limitations of corporeal experience but as extensions of the body that engage chiasmically in the exchange of flesh: claiming that "the things are the prolongation of my body and my body is the prolongation of the world" (1968, 255), Merleau-Ponty observes, "The thickness of the body, far from rivaling that of the world, is on the contrary the sole means I have to go unto the heart of the things, by making myself a world and by making them flesh" (135). At stake in these competing visions of the object are also competing definitions of the subject and its relationship to knowledge/experience. In defining what it means to "go unto the heart of . . . things," Merleau-Ponty emphasizes the body's role in perception, its status as a thing among things. If Baudrillard charts the existence of "a material world of use values which grounds the symbolic world of sign values in the system of objects" (Gottdiener 1995, 48), Merleau-Ponty's epistemology of the body encourages us not merely to push past or move through the object to its status as an "expressive symbol" (Gottdiener, 48), but to linger long enough to attend to its material presence, its embodied use, its status as a thing worn, made, touched by an embodied subject.

In *How Societies Remember,* Paul Connerton explores forms of embodied memory neglected or ignored by language-based models of social theory. In certain recent conceptions of social theory, he observes, "the object domain for social theory has been defined in terms of what is taken to be the distinctive feature of the human species, language: language itself being conceptualized by the Wittgensteinian, structuralist and poststructuralist schools as a set of social rules, or a system of signs, or a powerful discourse. The human body can be included in an object domain thus defined only as the carrier of linguistic meanings or of meanings structured like a language. It can be included, in other words, only in an etherealized form" (Connerton 1989, 104). In *A Sense of Things: The Object Matter of American Literature,* Bill Brown traces the powerful history of a similar sign-based understanding of material objects. He describes the modernist understanding of things as caught between two ways of reading objects, dichotomous interpretive modes resulting from objects' "vertiginous capacity to be both things and signs (symbols, metonyms, or metaphors) of something else" (Brown 2003, 11). Brown traces the way that the attempt of modernists such as William Carlos Williams to embrace the thing-ness of things, to treat objects without reducing them to signs of the human subjects that interact with them, breaks down, marking the limits of "modernism's effort to accept opacity, to satisfy itself with mere surfaces.... What first reads like the effort to accept things in their physical quiddity becomes the effort to penetrate them, to see through them, and to find ... within an object ... the subject" (12). In part, of course, the failure of the attempt to "accept things in their physical quiddity" emerges from the impossibility of defining objects—or bodies—outside the parameters of linguistic and cultural forms that shape as they name. What Brown points to, however, is the way such forms construct the language of objects in American culture as a system of signs that returns us again and again to the subject that allows those objects to signify. Rather than implying the possibility or the desirability of accessing bodies and objects *only* as physical phenomena, I would like to reinstitute the pressure of materiality on a dialogue shaped by linguistic and cultural forms that privilege the subject over the object, pushing the body outside the margins of psychic discourse and rendering objects mere signs of subjective presence.

In arguing for the need to supplement a discussion of the body as bearer of social and political meanings with a less "etherealized" analysis of actual bodily practices and behaviors, Connerton distinguishes between incorporating and inscribing practices of memory. Incorporated actions "are all messages that a sender or senders impart by means of their own current bodily activity," whereas inscribing practices involve "storing and retrieving information, print, encyclopedias, indexes, photographs, sound tapes, computers, all require that we do something that traps and holds information" (Connerton 1989, 72, 73). My interest in objects as material markers of grief lies in their capacity to negotiate between incorporated and inscribing practices. Functioning both as signs and as material markers of grief, objects hold onto the body's past presence as subject *and* object, resisting metaphorization yet still articulating embodied loss. In "Some of My Mother's Things," Laurie Sieverts Snyder introduces a series of photographs of objects from her deceased parents' household. Her assessment of the objects' value continually urges the reader to push past inscribing practices to consider material presence as a marker of memory. Although many of the things Snyder photographs and retains are stripped of their original function or narrative value, they retain a value that stems from the fact that they were touched, worn, used by her parents and grandparents. Her mother's tablecloths, "dozens of them, are mended and stained"; as Snyder "set[s] the table on tablecloths that [her grandmother] embroidered," those marks, rather than decreasing the artifacts' value, remember the body's use and point to the body's work (1998, 82). Snyder adapts those items from their original use to bring them as close as possible to her own body; in addition to touching them and eating on them, she literally wraps her body in them each night: "I use a large square damask tablecloth as a bed sheet" (82). Snyder's comments on the collection of her mother's letters that she saves make explicit the criterion for her selection of memoried things. She carefully stores the onionskin copies of her mother's laboriously handwritten letters, despite the fact that they are written in a language Snyder is unable to read or speak. Valuing those letters for their material rather than their linguistic inscriptions, Snyder preserves them as the kind of trace that Anthony Bond describes in terms of bodily memory: "Semiotic analysis is another critical tool that has provided a means for excavating the text embedded in the image. Because of its literary origins, however, it has little to say about the sensory effect of materials that engage bodily memory" (1999). Broadening our analysis of signifying function to read objects through the lens of the body requires attending to the way meaning is not only constructed through but located in material form; in valuing the palpable, sensual presence of objects, Bond points to a form of analysis that would convey the sense of Snyder's mother's letters in the familiar curves and dips of the handwriting and the textured surface of the onionskin paper her mother handled as well as in the sense of her mother's words.

Bodies and Objects in Mark Doty's "The Wings"

"The Wings" (1993, 39–51) marks Mark Doty's attempt to negotiate between his role as poet and his function as caretaker, to bring the room where he sits writing closer to the room next door where his lover lies dying. Although the poem's first-person-singular voice moves fluidly into and out of the communal "we" throughout, only in the final section of this long poem does Doty acknowledge that the poem's meditation on art and experience derives its urgency from the inevitability of loss that threatens to dissolve the speaker's communal identity. In that last section, issues of mortality and aesthetics settle uneasily in the space above the bed that Doty shares with a partner slowly dying of AIDS. Doty's poem, I will argue, is best understood as a meditation on his lover's dying, a response to the immediacy of his partner's vulnerable living presence and the threat of his imagined absence. The largely unspoken presence of his lover's dying body not only exerts pressure on the images of the poem, but troubles the poet's very relationship to metaphor and language. Throughout "The Wings," Doty meditates on the limits and possibilities of art, laboring to construct a vision of poetry that holds up to the pressures of embodiment. Even as Doty manipulates imagery and metaphor to shape the particular into the forms of the universal, his careful control is threatened by his embodied relationship with a partner whose familiar form resists containment within the structures of the poem. Although his partner's body emerges only briefly and in mediated form in the poem, its representational absence by no means reflects its critical insignificance. The bodies in the poem that do appear emerge through the mediated process of a type of reconstruction governed by Doty's anticipation of loss; anticipating a death over which his art has no control, Doty uses his poem to render visible absent and missing bodies, rescuing in imaginative terms signs of material presence that threaten to disappear along with the body in death. Imaging the art he strives for as something living and dynamic, Doty looks for a way to make an art that holds onto the body. In doing so, he turns to objects, raising questions not only about the narratives that they invoke, but about how their materiality renders them oddly capable of marking the presence of bodies now absent or invisible.

The poem opens with an auction scene in which material objects take center stage, each one slowly and carefully revealed before a gathered crowd, the attentiveness of which is echoed in the speaker's careful rendering of the artifact's presence:

> things that were owned once, in place,
> now must be cared for, carried
>
> to the block. A coast of cloud
> becomes enormous, above the wet field,
> while the auctioneer holds up
>
> now the glass lily severed
> from its epergne, now the mother of pearl
> lorgnette. (Doty 1993, 39)

The poem's lingering attention to the delicate physical presence of each individual object transported to the auction block is heightened by the way each object is outlined against the backdrop of an enormous "coast of cloud" that exaggerates the vacant context of the object's present with the suppressed history of its domestic past. Stripped of human ownership, which provided a literal and symbolic means of keeping them "in place," these objects are broken, fragmented not only by accident or wear but by their displacement from a coherent story that would subsume their object status within a meaningful context. "Severed" from semiotic as well as material structures, these things refuse to function as expressive symbols (Baudrillard 1996) or carriers of linguistic meaning (Connerton 1989).

If the foglike "coast of cloud" that engulfs these objects renders them unstable and impenetrable, the poem exploits what Brown describes as the human tendency to "penetrate" things, "to see through them, and to find . . . within an object . . . the subject" (2004, 12) by raising questions about the objects' past owners. Even as the poem invokes the presence of the missing human subjects that once rendered these severed and displaced objects semiotically transparent, however, it leads us not to the stories that would subsume these things but to the bodies that once interacted with them:

> I've bought a dark-varnished painting
> of irises, a dead painter's bouquet
>
> penciled, precisely, Laura M.
> 1890. The woman in front of us has bid
> for a dead woman's plates, iridescent flocks
>
> of blue birds under glaze. (40)

The jarring, repetitive intrusion of the word "dead" sets up an echo in these lines that reverberates around these items at auction, transforming them from artwork to artifacts created by hands now gone. The poem refuses the reader entrance into the transcendent beauty of art—the painting of irises, the representations of birds on china—by disrupting the construction of aesthetic meaning to force the reader's gaze on the material construction of these art objects: the "dark-varnished painting," the "glaze" that preserves the blue birds. Restoring the art object to its status as thing, the passage also heightens the reader's awareness of the physical act of inscription—"penciled, precisely, Laura M./ 1890"—and the past embodied status of the "dead painter" who once held a pencil to form these words. The poem's meditation on these artifacts penetrates the "glaze" that immortalizes the birds and flowers; in the cracks and fissures that erupt, the poem offers glimpses of the embodied subjects that made or used the objects now for sale.

The poem's attention to the missing contexts of these auctioned objects calls attention to what Doty describes elsewhere as the "deep paradox" of objects: "things placed right next to us, in absolute intimacy, yet unknowable. Full of history, but their history is mute" (2001, 66) In his reflections on still life paintings, Doty considers this disconnection of the thing and its human context, the object and the subject, as a fundamental tension existing in the attempt to interpret the object as a sign; still lifes, he argues, reflect the fact that "the things of the world go on without us, that the meaning with which we invest them may not persist, may be visible to no one else, that even that which seems to us most profoundly saturated in passion and feeling may be swept away" (29). In the opening of "The Wings," Doty focuses not only on that which is swept away but on the material remains that survive the erasure of "the meaning with which we invest" objects. Stripped of their human stories, objects persist in sensory, perceptible terms that invoke the bodies as well as the imaginations of those who would touch, use, or wear them. Whereas his focus on the legibility of the object as sign reflects what Connerton describes as the linguistic bias of contemporary constructions of the object domain, "The Wings" also suggests that the relationship between subjects and objects may be constituted in what Connerton would describe as a less "etherealized" form.

That less etherealized form appears in the figure of the angel that Doty introduces in the poem's opening section. As a bored little boy immerses himself in a book until he falls asleep, he becomes, the poem suggests, a thing among things: "Shiny rubber boots, a book forgotten / In one hand, a tired reader's face pressed / Against damp green. He's the newest thing here" (40). As "a being of two leaves, from one side a thing among things and otherwise what sees and touches them" (Merleau-Ponty 1968, 137), the body is marked by what Merleau-Ponty describes as its "double belongingness to the order of the 'object' and to the order of the 'subject.'" Doty's interest in objects as bearers of human stories—signs of subjective presence that may or may not be read by others—is complicated by the "double belongingness" that renders embodied subjects things among things. The continuity between the object body and the world's body that Merleau-Ponty describes manifests itself in a dynamic intertwining that Peter Pels describes as follows: "Not only are humans as material as the material they mold, but humans themselves are molded, through their sensuousness, by the 'dead' matter with which they are surrounded" (Pels 1998, 101). Doty constructs the figure of the angel from a young boy who straps a pair of snowshoes recently purchased at auction to his shoulders; as the objects he dons extend the form of his young body, the speaker's perception of the boy as "winged" generates a strikingly embodied image of the ethereal.

> [H]is father's bought a pair of snowshoes
> Nearly as tall as the boy, who slings them both
> Over his back and thus is suddenly winged.
> His face fills with purpose;
>
> The legendary heroes put away in his satchel,
> He's become useful again, he's moved
> Back into the world of things
>
> To be accomplished: an angel
> To carry home the narrative of our storied,
> Scattering things. (40)

The literal parity of child and object—the snowshoes "nearly as tall as the boy"—prefigures their equal weight in the observer's eye as the pause of the third stanza break perpetuates the illusion of the way in which the child is "moved / Back into the world of things." Although the correction provided in the enjambed opening of the fourth stanza—the child is not a thing himself but has things to accomplish—restores the child to subjectivity, awareness of his object/body lingers in the poem's margins. The final figure of the boy as an angel depends upon the speaker's perception of the boundary between body and object as blurred; the material base of the image disrupts its ethereality and complicates the reader's perception of the signifying function of objects. Although the section ends with the figure of the angel bearing the narrative of storied things, its import is to disrupt what Connerton describes as "the etherealized form" in which the human body enters contemporary social theory. Asserting its material form even as it assumes its function as a sign, the body of the boy/angel simultaneously participates in and resists narrative, becoming one of our "storied, scattering things." If, in Connerton's words, "the human body can be included in an object domain thus defined only as the carrier of linguistic meanings or meanings structured like a language" (1989, 104), the narrative that the boy "carr[ies] home" on his body in Doty's poem is surprisingly weighty; even as the poem constructs its symbolic rendering of the boy as angel, its emphasis on the way in which he hoists the unwieldy snowshoes and "slings them both / over his back" demetaphorizes the reader's perception of both objects and bodies to shift attention toward what Connerton describes as the body's "actual practices and behaviour" (104). Connerton argues that "inscribing practices have always formed the privileged story, incorporating practices the neglected story, in the history of hermeneutics" (100–101). The "storied" things that Doty describes in "The Wings" gesture toward a hermeneutics of the body that entangles "storied" things with the bodies that carry them.

The tension between the way objects and language signify embodied experience reemerges in the AIDS Quilt section of "The Wings." As the speaker watches the quilt unfurled, the "unthinkable catalog of the names" collapses into an endless blur of words too formless for him to grasp. The poet, then, turns from the words embroidered on the panels to the specificity of artifacts:

> . . . It's the clothing I can't get past,
> the way a favorite pair of jeans,
> a striped shirt's sewn onto the cloth;
>
> the fading, the pulls in the fabric
> demonstrate how these relics formed around
> one essential, missing body.
>
> An empty pair of pants
> is mortality's severest evidence.
> Embroidered mottoes blend
>
> into something elegaic but removed;
> a shirt can't be remote. (45)

In this section, Doty embraces the way in which the quilt shatters the glazed surfaces of art to rescue the materiality and specificity of the absent body. The shirt's presence invokes what Brown describes as the interpretive tendency to penetrate an object to find the subject "within"; in this case, however, the object's subject is a lost body: "the fading, the pulls in the fabric / demonstrate how these relics formed around / one essential, missing body." If the function of objects as signs demands the replacement of the thing with its larger meaning, the clothing Doty describes here resists semiotic appropriation as a mere sign of subjective presence. Hovering stubbornly in its palpable, material form, the shirt locates the subject within the object primarily as a body, figuring the lost object as a thing among things. Rather than tidying up the ragged borders of ripped jeans and frayed collars to call up a larger interpretive construct or a coherent rendering of subjectivity, the quilt invites the viewer to move closer to its contents, to apprehend in sensory terms the ragged palpability of signs that refuse an exclusively intellectual manipulation. In "Worn Worlds: Clothes and Mourning," Peter Stallybrass considers the limitations of a disembodied semiotics; frustrated with his inability to remember his recently deceased friend in abstract terms, he locates his loss through the sensory reclamation of his friend's favorite clothing:

> It is only, I believe, in a Cartesian and post-Cartesian paradigm that the life of matter is relegated to the trash can of the "merely," the bad fetish that the adult will leave behind as a childish thing so as to pursue the life of the mind. As if consciousness and memory were about minds rather than things. As if the real could only reside in the purity of ideas rather than in the permeated impurity of the material. . . . I cannot recall Allon White as an idea, but only as the habits through which I inhabit him, through which he inhabits and wears me. I know Allon through the smell of his jacket. (1999, 39, 42)

As the immediate presence of clothing on the AIDS Quilt expands linguistic or imagistic representation into the realm of sensory reclamation, it speaks to an embodied experience of grief that demands a material location for ideas and images. Although it remains an object of interpretation that must be intellectually processed and imaginatively linked to his embodied presence, Allon White's jacket also exists in a sensory realm that locates memory in space, texture, and smell. Its object form lends the body a place in memory.[1]

Whereas Stallybrass and Brown document the cultural resistance to "accept[ing] things in their physical quiddity," clothing on the quilt frustrates the tendency to "penetrate [objects], to see through them" by stalling the semiotic gaze in the realm of the material:

> One can't look past
> the sleeve where two arms
> were, where a shoulder pushed
> against a seam, and someone knew exactly
>
> how the stitches pressed against skin
> that can't be generalized but was,
> irretrievably, you, or yours. (Doty 1993, 45)

Doty's representation of the cultural work of the quilt provide a lens through which to complicate Baudrillard's notion of the object's symbolic transcendence of "real existence." The shirt's function as an expressive symbol rubs up against the palpable presence of a body that has marked the material form of representation. The sign, in Umberto Eco's words, functions as "an instruction for interpretation, a mechanism which starts from an initial stimulus and leads to all its illative consequences" (Eco 1984, 26). If signification pushes outward, the shirt directs us inward to the shoulder that pushed against its seams and the skin that registered the impress of its stitches. Although that body remains an imaginative construction, it is the agent as well as the object of the shirt's meaning; as the shirt's presence on the AIDS Quilt invokes what Brown terms the tendency to "see through" objects, it simultaneously constructs a subject whose object body is impossible to "look past." The gaze that lingers on the textured thing long enough to turn the sign into a material trace invokes the desire to reach out and touch the object; the quilt not only embodies the viewer's gaze but turns it toward the specific "real existence" that the object, in Baudrillard's terms, would symbolically transcend.

Although the language-based form of poetry makes it impossible for Doty to escape a sign-based hermeneutics, his poem gestures toward that which it cannot contain in its consistent representation of and interrogation of objects. In "The Wings," it is the artifact's ability not only to receive but to remember the weight of the body's presence that distinguishes it from its purely aesthetic counterpart. As Doty anticipates the erasure of his partner's embodied presence, he takes comfort in objects that mark the embodied interactions of the individuals that once used, created, or animated them. In her essay "Work and the Body in Hardy," Elaine Scarry observes, "The material record of the interaction between man and world often survives the interaction itself. . . . [W]hile it seems most appropriate to Hardy that man and world should get permanently woven to one another, given that they do not . . . a record at least means that a small piece of one . . . has broken off onto the other, that they have not disengaged from one another as though that engagement had never occurred" (1983, 92–94). The language that Scarry uses in her description of objects as "material records" of embodied interaction suggests a means of complicating the dichotomy that Connerton establishes between inscribing and incorporating memory practices. Arguing for the need to think outside frameworks that consider inscription as the privileged form for the transmission of memory, Connerton suggests that memory is also passed on in nontextual and noncognitive ways (1989, 102–103); because they transmit memory through current bodily activity, however, incorporated memories, in Connerton's words, are "largely traceless" (102).

The idea of the object as a "material record" of the body's interaction with the world suggests that it may hold the traces of embodied experience even in the face of bodily absence. In *Death, Memory and Material Culture,* Elizabeth Hallam and Jenny Hockey explore such a possibility in sociological terms, focusing on "the constitution of memory in the relationships between embodied action and material objects" (2001, 13). Hallam and Hockey make a useful distinction between objects produced for the purpose of ritualizing death and "those material objects that *become* vehicles of memories by virtue of their entanglement or association with persons deceased" (211). It is this second type of object—and the process of *becoming* that transforms an ordinary thing into a material record of embodied experience—that Doty's poem explores.

The last section of the poem opens with a description of the speaker and his partner moving among objects, shopping for antiques. Baudrillard describes the antique as "the immemorialization, in the concrete form of an object, of a former being—a procedure equivalent, in the register of the imaginary, to a suppression of time" (1996, 75). Although Baudrillard does not elaborate on the significance of the antique's "concrete form," Doty's poem suggests that that form functions in the register of the sensory as the correlative to the antique's symbolic function in the register of the imaginary. Underlying the speaker's casual drive through backroads with his partner at his side lies his desperate anticipation of an embodied loss to which the poet's words, images, or ideas cannot speak. Doty's awareness of what Baudrillard describes as the "irreversible movement from birth toward death" leads him to objects; for Doty, however, the pull of things issues not only from their symbolic power to *transcend* "real existence" (Baudrillard 1996, 96), but from their concrete location in its material realm. Accompanied by his partner, Doty searches for objects that will serve not only to memorialize their day together but to carry his partner's body forward in time and space:

> We've been out again on the backroads,
> buying things. Here's a permanent harvest:
> an apple and four cherries
> stenciled on a chair-back,
>
> the arm-wood glowing, so human,
> from within, where the red paint's
> been worn away by how many arms
> at rest. Polished and placed
> by the blue table and the windows

that frame the back garden,
it's a true consolation,
necessary, become *this*

through its own wearing away
by use, festive with its once-bright
fruit. Anything lived into long enough
becomes an orchard. (48)

The value of the chair Doty discovers lies in the way its worn paint bears the imprint of arms that have not, in Scarry's terms, fully "disengaged" themselves from the object (Scarry 1983, 94). In the interaction between person and thing, the chair is animated by human presence, transformed into something that "glow[s] . . . from within" (Doty 1993, 48). In the face of the constant loss that threatens Doty's poem—from the apples that fall off the snapped bough to the dying man who sits at his side—the chair offers "a true consolation." Because it not only holds but holds onto the bodies that interact with it, the chair lends object form, a kind of material permanence, to the transitory, living bodies that inhabit it, functioning as a continued material "witness" to humans' embodied interaction with the world.

Whereas an object created for ritualizing death is conceived of and created as a sign, the second set of objects Hallam and Hockey describe move from casual contact with the body to a symbolic significance that remains antimetaphorical. The metaphorical process relies upon the use of a vehicle subordinated to the tenor that it stands in for; Hallam and Hockey's language points to the way material signification destabilizes such a metaphorical process. As material objects, in their words, "*become* vehicles of memories," they continue to persist in their own terms, as things that take up space, invite use, bear weight (13). As vehicles of bodily memory, such things rely upon, rather than obscure, the object's sensory particularity. In reading the object for the body, Doty acknowledges the chair's double-edged status as bearer of meaning. As the stenciled details of fruit on the chair-back wear off along with its red paint, those carefully constructed images of warmth and bounty gradually lose their power to communicate as signs. Although its "message" is worn away by the friction of the body rubbing against wood, however, the chair comes to communicate a history of use, bodily engagement, touch. Hallam and Hockey's description of object memory as proceeding from a process of "entanglement" suggests that material memory passes osmotically, as a tactile seepage of identity, from body to thing. Literally marked by its interactions with the body, the memoried object emerges out of neither inscribing nor incorporating practices; it marks the body's presence with a material trace "written" out of the body's habitual actions and gestures. The loss of the veneer of shiny red paint that's "been worn away by how many arms / at rest" results in the chair's "arm-wood glowing, so human, / from within." The pressure of the body on what Doty describes elsewhere as "the object's body" wears away one form of signification but yields another; the glowing "arm-wood" records the interface of body and object as a harvest of pressure points that sustains material presence as an antidote to loss: "Anything lived into long enough / becomes an orchard." If the chair functions as a form of material memory, its object immediacy invokes an embodied perceiver whose hands-on access to its grooves and textures implicates the realm of the sensory in what Baudrillard describes as "the register of the imaginary." Tactile but not transparent, the object persists as both a sign and a thing. Offering a material form for memory, the chair refuses to disembody the subject that would occupy it even in symbolic or imaginative terms.

∞

"The Wings" presents a dynamic of textured rematerialization it can thematize but not enact. The objects Doty accumulates representationally speak to his desire to hold onto the human body; the linguistic form of the poem, however, remains incapable of touching or registering the touch of its corporeal counterpart. Having turned to objects to stake out a middle ground between incorporation and inscription, the poet, who must construct his memorials out of words, tries to materialize language in object form. If incorporation, in Abraham and Torok's terms, centers around the literalizing fantasy of taking into the body the object whose loss cannot be spoken, Doty's poem can be read as a metaphorizing fantasy that attempts to forestall bodily loss through language. Writing in the room adjacent to the space where his dying partner sleeps, Doty struggles to find an art that can hold onto the embodied presence of a partner whose projected loss he now experiences only in imaginative terms. Doty's fantasy involves materializing representation to hold onto the familiar body he need only reach out to touch. Collecting signs as if they were things that could build a structure to house the body he fears losing, Doty's poem presses the figurative shapes of representation against the material body threatened by loss.

In a paradoxical attempt to confront language's immaterial bias through its own forms, Doty symbolically manipulates images of his art to construct a poetic language that might bear the weight of the body. Adapting the image of the well-ordered garden as a symbol of his art, the speaker interrogates the possibilities of poetry through a figure that lends symbolic *object* presence to his art. In the fifth section of the poem, Doty introduces his carefully crafted garden, "this ordered enactment of desire," as an aesthetic creation in which living things emerge as malleable and invulnerable objects of the gardener's fancy: "the too-shaded lavender / transplanted to a brighter bed, / a lilac standard bought / and planted in a spot / requiring height, strong form" (46). In the garden, Doty optimistically figures his artistic creation as "an angel, / like those Arcimboldos where the human profile / is all berry and leaf, / the specific character of bloom / assembled into an overriding form." This perfect garden masks the matter of the dying body with living matter that symbolically stands in for Doty's immaterial art. Pulled into the garden, the reader who would interpretively establish a symbolic correspondence between that object domain and Doty's art implicitly lends his poetry a material form that it conspicuously lacks. Just as Arcimboldo's paintings operate by moving the eye between the objects making up the body and the body itself, rather than between the material form and its symbolic implications, Doty hopes to use metaphor that operates by moving us between levels of embodied experience, anchoring the "figurative shape" of representation in the material forms of things.

If the garden in its seemingly effortless beauty "says / any mistake can be rectified" (46) through art, however, the manipulation of its sensory forms still leaves the vulnerable body of Doty's partner untouched. The poem exposes the gap between the garden's flowers, which are constituted metaphorically as bodies ("blooms / supple and sheened as skin" [47]) and the embodied form of the poet's partner; whereas the garden's ailing lavender can be healed simply by transplanting it "to a brighter bed," the partner who lies slowly dying in the next room exists beyond the reach of metaphorical manipulation. Symbolically lending his own art a material form, Doty cannot extend its reach far enough to negotiate the space between the poem and the world in which his partner lies dying. Offering a critique of his own metaphorizing fantasy, Doty admits his lover's dying body into the representational realm he has constructed. The embodied form that forces its way into the garden's ordered space, however, itself exists in a highly symbolic, densely mediated form:

> . . . I dreamed,
> the night after the fall planting,
> that a bird who loved me

Objects of Grief

```
      had been long neglected, and when
      I took it from the closet and gave it water
      its tongue began to move again,

      and it began to beat the lush green music
      of its wings, and wrapped the brilliant risk
      of leaves all around my face. (47)
```

In the midst of creation, the weakened body of Doty's partner forces its way into the gardener's dreams in the form of a neglected bird expelled from the garden. As the dream reveals, the creation of this ordered garden not only results in but depends upon the banishment of the vulnerable body that the speaker finally rescues from the closet. Time spent in the garden represents for Doty a turning away from the dynamics of embodied relationship. Even the symbolically materialized form of Doty's immaterial art falters beneath the weight of the body that intrudes upon the gardener's careful arrangement of living things. Lurking beneath the poem's careful inventory of aesthetic possibility is a sense of all that art cannot control, accomplish, or preserve.

When the speaker figuratively steps out of aesthetic space to minister to the imperiled body of the bird, he sacrifices his voice so that "its tongue [might begin] to move again." The image of the bird's wings beating together as "lush green music" highlights the poet's plunge from the aesthetic control of the ordered garden into an experiential aesthetic where music is composed out of the body's motion. The speaker's entanglement with the bird's moving body strips him of aesthetic distance as well as control; where he once stood back from his own garden to survey the flowers and plants, "setting them in place," he now finds himself plunged into the living forms he used to manipulate, blind to everything but the "brilliant risk / of leaves" wrapped around his face. Imagining himself literally immersed in and surrounded by the body of the other, Doty here sacrifices perspective and control to surrender to the fleeting beat of wings that propel him away from the static aesthetics of the garden toward a "brilliant risk," the vulnerable form of a living body in flux.

Imaginatively anticipating his partner's embodied loss, Doty turns to art to hold onto the corporeal form he need only reach out to touch. Tellingly, however, the body that Doty embraces perpetuates the very metaphorizing dynamic that its presence appears to disrupt. The speaker accesses the beloved body that the poet struggles to hold onto only through layers of mediation that emphasize its purely representational status. The intercorporeal encounter that disrupts Doty's metaphorizing fantasy is notable primarily for its fantastical qualities; positioning himself poetically as the gardener, Doty describes his interaction with his lover as an encounter with a symbolic body that emerges only in a dream. Trapped by metaphorization, the body that haunts Doty's garden is inaccessible except through symbols and dreams that recast its familiar topography; as such, it foreshadows rather than forestalls the embodied partner's collapse into forms of language and images of memory that deny intercorporeality.[2]

In the last section of the poem, Doty's concern with locatedness and embodiment—a concern that erupts as he finally acknowledges not just the proximity but the centrality of his partner's beloved body in the next room—culminates in the attempt to destabilize etherealized forms that privilege sign systems over bodily practices. In this final section, Doty represents his aesthetic manipulation of the poem's most etherealized image—the angel—through a highly materialized language that would locate the poet's image in the world of things. In the attempt to embody his necessarily abstract art, Doty returns the act of image-making to its origin in the poet's physical perception of bodies in space. Claiming that he makes the angel from the bodies of children—the boy "with snowshoe wings slung across his shoulders," the child "sprawled on the marble floor / of the post office yesterday"—he appropriates from those bodies a claim to material presence that lends spatial and material force to the poet's aesthetic construction (49, 50). As he represents himself pulling the angel out of the children's bodies and letting it bend over his own desk, Doty physicalizes the act of image-making to render himself a body among bodies rather than a mere manipulator of words. The poem's repetition of the fact of making—"I make the angel," "I make him again," "I make him lean," "I'm making the rain / part of the angel"—simultaneously contributes to and exposes the illusion of its materiality (50). The more Doty physicalizes his angel, making him bend over objects and lean over people, the more he highlights his own role as artificer, creator of an image that cannot bear the weight of embodiment. Writing only feet from the bed in which his dying partner sleeps, the poet must create an art that works against the ethereally signifying tendencies of metaphorical forms even as he works through and with them.

In the conclusion of "The Wings," the poem allows the reader a glimpse into the intimate and protected space of the "next room" that has always been maintained just outside the perimeters of the poem. In that room, the poem's addressee, the "you" that has been assumed but never identified or embodied throughout the poem's first five sections, lies sleeping:

> I let the light-glazed angel
> in the children's bodies, the angel
> with his face flushed in the heat
> of recognizing any birth,
>
> I let him bend over my desk and speak
> in a voice so assured you wouldn't know
> that anyone was dying. . . .
>
> I make the angel lean over our bed
>
> in the next room, where you're sleeping
> the sturdy, uncompromised sleep
> of someone going to work early tomorrow.
> I am willing around you, hard,
>
> the encompassing wings of the one called
> *unharmed*. (50)

The bodies and objects that circulate throughout the poem settle here not above the desk where Doty writes but above the bed in the room next door where his lover lies dying of AIDS. The angel's words—written and rewritten by the desperate speaker—seem ultimately less important than his immersion in the world of bodies and objects; as Doty lets him "bend over my desk" and makes him "lean over our bed," the intensity of the speaker's longing to hold onto his lover registers in an embodied desire that would render the angel's embrace a means of holding onto the dying body: "I am willing around you, hard, / the encompassing wings of the one called / *unharmed*." The poet not only materializes the abstraction of language— "unharmed"—in the surprisingly weighty image of the angel's "encompassing wings," but directs the angel's protective embrace through a desire that the speaker would regulate in sensory terms. Doty's emphasis on the adverb "hard"—enforced by a pause in the line that drops the reader heavily onto the single-syllable word—locates the act of willing in the speaker's body, lending his abstract desire a corporeal form.[3]

If, as the angel concludes, "The rule / of earth is attachment," the centrality of the body as the site of attachment emerges in the next lines' reference to holding and being held: "here what can't be held / is." On the one hand, the vulnerability of the object body renders existence itself— the "is" of the second line—fragile and impermanent, something that can't be held. At the same time that it renders us susceptible to mortality, however, that object body emerges as the very form through which we sustain chiasmic intercorporeality; what can't be held temporally (the mortal, embodied subject) *can* be held physically. The latter reading locates the paradox of earthly attachment in embodied desire, the tendency to reach out to the very body that renders the subject vulnerable to mortality, to embrace that which can't be held. The poem concludes with the angel's words:

> *You die by dying*
> *into what matters, which will kill you,*
> *but first it'll be enough. Or more than that:*
> *your story, which you have worn away*
> *as you shaped it,*
> *which has become itself*
> *as it has disappeared.* (51)

In attempting to respond to mortality not as an abstract issue but as the very real, very immediate threat of embodied loss, Doty refuses the consolation of mind over matter as he collapses the dichotomy between the material object/body and its story. The angel offers a vision located rather than abstract, spatial in form; as he directs the speaker to be "certain / . . . *where* you're looking," the angel's stress on locatedness returns us not only to earth, but to the sight/site of the bed in which the speaker's lover lies. In claiming that "You die by dying / into what matters, which will kill you, / but first it'll be enough," Doty plays on the idea that "what matters" is what matter is, not the transcendence of materiality but the embrace of embodied subjectivity. The phrase "You die by dying / into what matters" also reminds us that someone *is* physically dying, that what Doty's students describe as poetry's inexplicable "insisten[ce]" on mortality can here be traced to the anticipated absence of "one essential, missing body," the embodied loss of a particular, loved, person who shares the poet's bed.

In the poem's last stanza, then, Doty reverses the tendency to read objects only for their stories—an interpretive act that renders the material a mere sign of subjective presence—by rendering stories susceptible to the body's material powers. In this rendering, words, like chairs, are "worn away" as they are "shaped" by embodied existence; in order to "become itself," the story must disappear, its veil of words swept away to reveal its thingness, its material form, its body. Doty's reference to the story becoming "itself" recalls an earlier moment in the poem when the speaker, overwhelmed by the beauty of his surroundings, describes the inadequacy of words. Responding to a field in bloom as "more than I can say," he redefines representation as a nod in the direction of the thing: "There were geese. *There were.* / the day's narration is simple assertion." The poem, like the story the angel describes, would wear itself away to evoke the body around which it revolves. As the poem moves, in Umberto Eco's terms, from an act of signification to an act of reference, it erases the signs it manipulates in the hope of restoring the stability of the body language cannot hold.

In invoking a material basis for his metaphorizing fantasy, Doty hopes to construct an artistic edifice that has some power to shape the material world and intervene in the possibility of embodied loss. He succeeds only to the extent that the words he manipulates appear rooted in materiality. If the literalizing fantasy of the cryptophore works to obscure the fact of loss by actively destroying representation, reducing words to collections of mere objects, Doty's attempt to make words into things serves the opposite purpose. Nicholas Rand's description of cryptonymy's "manipulation of verbal entities" bears striking similarity to Doty's image of the garden and the Arcimboldo paintings: "In fine, words are manipulated by cryptonymy as dried flowers in a herbarium. Divested of metaphorical reach and the power to institute or depose an extralinguistic event or action, cryptonyms create a collection of words, a verbarium, with no apparent aim to carry any form of knowledge or conviction" (Abraham and Torok 1986, lviii). Whereas the cryptophore's "verbarium" consists of accumulations of seemingly nonreferential words—a "collection" of broken signifiers reduced to meaningless things—Doty's discussion of worn language reveals his attempt to recast the object quality of words as the very source of their referentiality. Choosing to embrace rather than "cure" his own antimetaphorical tendencies, Doty uses language to thematize a process of symbolic materialization his poetry cannot enact.

The AIDS Memorial Quilt

Critics responding to the AIDS Quilt have focused on the symbolic significance of its origins in cloth as they consistently describe its intimacy, citing the quilt's connection to the private space of the bedroom and the way in which "private identity is held up as monumental; the intimate stretches as far as the eye can see" (Hawkins 1996, 176). Although critics have suggested that the viewer's desire to touch as well as see the quilt's panels reflects that intimacy, their focus on the object status of the quilt—and the objects literally sewn onto it—remains largely symbolic. As Judy Elsey describes the quilt's invitation to tactility, for example, she compares it to the novel: "Like the novel, the quilt brings us into 'a zone of direct and even crude contact . . . where one can finger it familiarly on all sides, turn it upside down, inside out . . .'" (Elsey 1992, 195). Her invocation of Bahktin's work on the novel elides crucial differences in sensory/material access to the two forms. What is obscured through Elsey's parallel of the quilt form with the novel is exactly what my children reacted to during a recent AIDS Quilt exhibition when they had to be reminded, again and again, *not to touch*: the tactile specificity of each quilt panel, the physical presence of objects that exist not merely or even primarily as vehicles through which ideas are accessed but as objects that mark and incite bodily contact, exerting the force of "the tangible upon the touching body" (Merleau-Ponty 1968, 146). If objects on the quilt function as expressive symbols, their function is not limited to symbolic status. The spatial and material dimensions of objects on the quilt complicate the process of their signification by continually returning us from the realm of the symbolic to an understanding of the way in which things mark and are marked by embodied use.

Elsey's argument about the quilt's intimacy, like her comparison of the quilt to the novel, works through a logic that invokes embodiment only to metaphorize it. A quilt, Elsey observes, "lies on a bed, which is the most intimate place in the home. The NAMES Project, *by analogy*, brings this disease . . . into the most intimate parts of our lives" (1992, 189, emphasis mine). The tensions associated with the quilt's object engagement with the body emerge when the symbolic intimacy of the form is pressured by the threat of a physical intimacy that demetaphorizes the notion of contact. In *The Quilt: Stories from the NAMES Project*, Cindy Ruskin shares a moving narrative about a quilt panel which bears witness to a mother's love for her son and her willingness to care for him right up until the moment of his death. In constructing her son's panel from the bed sheets on which he slept in the final days of his life, the mother not only symbolically but literally records her intimacy with her son's embodied experience. As she describes the form of that panel, Ruskin invokes the sentimental power of the quilt while trying to contain the perceived threat posed by the viewer's literal contact with the quilt form: "All the materials Ann used for Anthony's quilt panel came from his bed. *After a thorough washing of the linens*, she stitched Anthony's name onto his red, white and blue pillow cases" (1988, 50, emphasis mine). In prefacing the second sentence with a qualifying clause, Ruskin reveals how one mother's literalization of the quilt metaphor—her choice to construct her son's panel out of his actual bedding—denaturalizes the welcomed symbolic intimacy of the form. The panel's signifying power—its patriotic and emotional content—is temporarily disrupted by the revelation of the object's doubled status; a bearer of meaning, the object also bears the body's marks and holds the body's traces.

"Quilt for an Unknown Child" (Storey 1996), the quilt panel designed by fashion designer Helen Storey, points toward some of the tensions between reading objects as signs and reading objects as material markers of past bodily presence. Storey's quilt panel clearly invokes the viewer's body through its invitation to tactile as well as visual engagement. The backdrop of the panel is constructed from two woven cotton infant blankets sewn together, one white and one natural. A series of baby garments designed by Storey are stitched onto the blankets themselves. The cloth-on-cloth contact of baby clothes and blankets exaggerates the panel's textured softness; the clothes themselves are sewn on the panel with arms outstretched and positioned at unusual angles—sideways, diagonally, upside down—in a way that denaturalizes their commodity/garment status and invites the viewer to consider the absences toward which the panel gestures. Those absences are figured as embodied through the intimacy of the bedding and clothes stitched to the panel, but emerge primarily as symbolic absences. There is no attempt here to allow space for where individual bodies might have protruded from the garments; the diaper snaps of the onesie in the lower right corner hug the margin of the panel, while a pair of disproportionately large socks sewn in on the lower left occupy the space where a torso and legs would have extended below the baby T-shirt sewn in just above. While the red AIDS ribbon sewn onto the lapel of a jumpsuit on the upper left functions most obviously as a symbol, the crimson-colored thread that anchors several of the garments to the panel invokes a wounded body through its crude, bright red stitches. Whereas the mass-produced commodity objects of some of the quilt's other panels are individualized through wear, this panel is marked by the proliferation of Storey's distinctive and exclusive designer label on a multitude of garments defined by a pristine, uniform whiteness exaggerated rather than disrupted by the occasional image of Mickey Mouse or "Mr. Bounce." Although Storey's panel invokes bodily absence through texture, symbolism, and content, the unknown child that it figures remains an idea.

In contrast, a quilt panel constructed for Megan Jewel Ashley Brown[4] evokes the two-year-old's specific, embodied presence not only through the careful embroidery of her full name and the central placement of a photographic image of the little girl, but through objects that supplement that image. The viewer's access to a picture of Megan is mediated through the plastic screen that protects the image; while that layer of plastic exaggerates the little girl's inaccessibility through gathers of material that reflect back light, its shimmering presence forces the viewer to squint and draw closer in order to catch a glimpse of the engaging two year old pictured there. The depth and inviting texture of the puffy, pink satin frame contrast with the flatness and the tactile inaccessibility of the visual image the frame surrounds. If the photograph seems picture-perfect but inaccessible—a beautiful, unknown toddler carefully posed in a frilly white dress and little white booties—the worn objects that surround it are accessible not only because they can easily be touched but because, in bearing the traces of the toddler's touch, they become what Merleau-Ponty describes as a "fold," a textured surface that marks the intertwining of the touching and the touched. The yellowish formula stain on a T-shirt in the panel's lower right corner marks the garment as lived into; its value lies not in its heirloom quality as an antique that transcends the "absolute singularity" that Baudrillard associates with mortality, but in its presence as an artifact that bears the traces of Megan's embodied experience. The materiality of cloth renders it capable of recording the body's presence; the depth and texture of objects afford them what Doty describes in *Still Life with Oysters and Lemon* as an object body that, instead of transcending temporality, bears "the individuating marks of time's passage" (2001, 40): "These marks and wearings-down mark the evidence of time, the acclimation of the object's body to human bodies" (30). In the same way that the frayed, lace-edged baby bib that bears her name also bears the signs of her body's use, the T-shirt supplements the image and the word by testifying to its encounters with the body of the little girl who wore it, ate in it, dribbled on it, slept in it.

Marks of dirt and signs of wear also register the toddler's bodily interaction with the stuffed animal sewn into the quilt panel next to Megan's photograph. The stuffed rabbit's posture and placement symbolically exaggerate its embodied connection to the image it supplements; if the rabbit's head initiates a vertical line that parallels the vertical lines of the photograph frame, its body gradually leans into that frame, appearing almost to sidle closer to the image of the little girl pictured there. The stuffed animal not only records the trace of Megan's touch in the unevenness of its color and wear—one arm dirtier than the other, its plush face flattened in spots—but extends a tactile invitation to the viewer exaggerated by its placement on the quilt panel; its "hands" clasped together, its left leg bent so that one foot caresses the other, the posture of the loved animal enacts the solipsistic frustration of chiasmic touch. In marking the shared flesh of the body and the world, Merleau-Ponty is also careful to distinguish between them: "The flesh of the world is not self-sensing (se sentir) as is my flesh—It is sensible and not sentient—I call it flesh, nonetheless . . . in order to say that it is a *pregnancy* of possibles" (Merleau-Ponty 1968, 250). If the inanimate object, unlike the human body, is flesh only insofar as it represents a "pregnancy of possibles," signs of intimate, individualized wear on the textured surface of this stuffed animal materialize the exchange of flesh even as the object's fixed position on the quilt attests to the disruption of chiasmic possibility.

Whereas the sheer number and variety of things sewn into the quilt—toys, stuffed animals, boxer shorts, keys, glasses, computer diskettes, sweatshirts, jeans, candy, drivers' licenses, uniforms, medals, ornaments—testify to the significance of objects as conduits for memory, the number of things that had clearly been used, owned, worn, presumably by the deceased, points to the relationship of object memory to embodiment. Although many of the quilt's panels include representations of a loved one's experiences or interests—signified either in writing or through symbolic objects such as charms, miniatures, or patches—many more include actual objects visibly marked by use or wear. In one panel, a series of objects including an AIDS ribbon, a cork, a pair of miniature porcelain clogs, rainbow ribbons, two keys, and a sequined parrot ornament are displayed; whereas the public significance of the AIDS ribbon and the rainbow array of colors renders those objects symbolically legible, the significance of the other items remains veiled without knowledge of their context.

In contrast, the surface on which the objects are displayed—a white hotel towel imprinted with the words "The Inn, Del-Mar"—shifts from ambiguity into intelligibility because of its status as not only a symbol or a sign but a material record of bodily encounter. Although the source of a brownish stain on the towel's lower corner is unknown to the viewer—Is it dirt? Makeup? Sweat?—the towel's testimony to its interaction with a specific body complicates its anonymous status. In recording its tactile encounter with an individual, the towel bears the literal traces of bodily intimacy; the stain on the mass-produced and institutionally identified towel resignifies this most generic of objects through a process that Deborah Lupton describes as appropriation: "In the process of appropriation, mass-produced artifacts may be reshaped through embodied use. They may take on the imprint of human traces or be deliberately manipulated and changed (within limits) by their owners. In doing so, these objects become autobiographical in bearing the marks of an individual's use, or acting as signifiers and mnemonics of personal events" (Lupton 1988, 144). In an age of brand names, mass-produced objects and internationally marketed cartoon characters, many of the things attached to individual quilt panels emerge as shockingly generic. In some ways, moving through the rows of panels resembles strolling through a contemporary mall to view Gap jeans, Star Trek key rings, Pluto sweatshirts. What renders these mass-produced commodities intelligible expressions of individual lives rather than generic signs of anonymous existence are the marks of the way in which, through use and wear, an individual body encroached upon, disrupted, reshaped the familiar contours of a mass-produced object. Jennifer Gonzalez's designation of objects that bear the marks of use as "prosthetics" of the self suggests a way of reading objects left behind after an individual's death not just as autobiographical signifiers but as extensions of a missing body. Gonzalez's list of "prosthetic" objects points to the crucial ways the human body rubs off on the world's body: "Clothing and cloth with all of its scents and residues; furniture with all of its bodily imprints, shapes and sags from years of use; worn silverware and shoes. All of these serviceable objects receive the imprint of a human trace as the autonomy of their purely functional status is worn away by time" (Gonzalez 1995, 133). The fact that the "human trace" which Gonzalez locates on objects is specifically a bodily trace points to the unique way in which objects hold onto a corporeality elided not only by the physical loss of the body but by a discourse of grief that revolves around the consolations of imagery and language. Embodied use disrupts the signifying function of the towel that bears the name and the crest of The Inn at Del-Mar to gesture toward this anonymous object's function as a prosthetic extension of an embodied subject unknown by the viewer and inaccessible to the panel maker.

Similar acts of appropriation through embodied use can be traced throughout the quilt. Affixed to the shiny exterior of a one-pound bag of Peanut M&Ms on one quilt panel is half of a single candy cane in a fragile cellophane wrapper taped shut, apparently after its initial use. Whereas the M&M wrapper signifies an individual's snacking tastes, the half-eaten candy cane testifies to the fact that it was literally tasted; the shift from taste to tasting renders the generic specific and the subject embodied. That shift also occurs in many pieces of clothing affixed to the quilt: a Garfield cap stained brown where it would have touched the forehead of its wearer, Levis jeans ripped at the knees, children's shoes worn unevenly at the soles. Although these objects remain susceptible to analysis and generate multiple meanings, they resist appropriation as *mere* symbols insofar as they insist upon continually returning the viewer who would trace their semiotic effects to their origin in an individual body.

In gesturing toward embodiment, many of these objects invoke the absence of subjects who once wore, used, or inhabited them. Frequently, panel makers sew the garments of loved ones onto their quilt panels in a way that animates the surface of cloth. Layers of clothing lend the illusion of dimensionality as a sweater or jacket reveals not the body but the cloth beneath. One arm bent at the elbow and the other extended, a shiny baseball jacket sewn on with a T-shirt visible in the space beneath its gaping snaps suggests a belly that no longer strains against the cloth. In another panel, a flannel shirt primly buttoned at the top reveals its unwillingness to return to pure commodity status as it gapes open at the bottom to reveal the inner surface of cloth that would have touched its wearer. Sewn onto the panel with arms outstretched, the shirt sleeves' irregular folds and gathers testify to the absence of the arms that would have filled those sleeves. A cuff unbuttoned and spread open on one side reveals a quilted hand sewn onto the panel, while the other sleeve dangles empty, its disequilibrium pointing to a body that cannot be restored representationally.

As the motion of gesturing toward embodiment slides into the act of acknowledging absence, many quilt panels enact the disappearance of the embodied subjects they represent. Although the panel of Brian Ortiz, a five-year-old boy, makes no attempt to represent the embodied form of the little boy that inhabited the sleeveless jersey and athletic shorts sewn onto the panel, the placement of two action figures to the right and left of the waistline created by the clothing highlights the absence of the little hands that once clutched those figures. On the left side of the panel, colored handprints and footprints mark the way the panel creators have pressed their own bodies against the cloth of the quilt, and exaggerate the stark absence of the little boy once clothed in the outfit stitched onto the panel.

The friction generated by the press of the body upon cloth becomes one means of holding onto the *absent* body's presence as well. The preponderance of jeans on the quilt may reflect their popularity as leisure wear, but may also be due to their ability to mark past bodily presence. Very few of the jeans that I saw looked new; instead, most were unevenly worn, with patches of faded color, frayed seams, rips, tears, and holes where the body rubbing against them had broken through. On the quilt, those holes reveal what they cannot reveal as they both gesture toward the body that pressed against fabric and reveal the holes left in the body's absence. The panel created for Randy Jon Mills, for example, features a pair of frayed, bleached jeans shorts most notable for the large hole next to the base of the zipper. Even this most intimate of apertures, which would threaten to expose the body at a site heavily guarded by the demands of privacy, reveals only another layer of cloth. The patch sewn onto the skin-side surface of the fabric no longer screens the body that threatens to emerge but fills the hole the body leaves behind. On this panel, wads of cotton that press through and out of the shorts pocket supplement bodily absence; as the ripped fabric reveals only more fabric, cascading balls of cotton invoke the missing material stuff of the lost body.

Although clothing cannot hold onto the lost body, it can suggest what is missing, calling the viewer's attention to shared materiality in order to invoke that which can no longer be held. The texture and dimensionality of objects construct the viewer's desire to touch or the fear of being touched as the objects themselves mediate intimate encounters with unknown subjects. The panels of the AIDS Quilt often reflect the panel makers' vacillation between the desire to celebrate the lost subject publicly and the desire to reserve and protect the intimacy of an embodied relationship that the viewer has not shared. The tension between the public signification and the private references of the panels' contents often emerges in the viewer's struggle to contextualize and access worn, used, or made objects on the quilt. The lack of clear context disrupts the symbolic value of objects which, for the viewer, function neither as signs that can be decoded and narrativized nor as "mere" things that can be recognized for their use value or dismissed with acknowledgment of their commodity status. Intimately marked by a specific, real body that remains unknown and inaccessible to the viewer, objects such as used towels, well-loved teddy bears, or worn shoes invoke an embodied presence that the quilt viewer cannot access. The object as bodily trace suggests the possibility of a material interface with the dead but does not return the pressure of contact for a viewer unable to supplement the dynamic of solipsistic touch with the memory of past intercorporeality.

To some degree, then, the panel maker's deployment of appropriated objects on the quilt represents not only an attempt to mark specific, embodied loss but an opportunity to exercise some degree of control over a missing body that cannot, under any circumstances, be restored. In simultaneously invoking and frustrating the viewer's access to the lost body, the panel maker withholds what he or she can no longer hold; gaining representational control over the presence of a body that remains literally inaccessible affords the mourner the opportunity to preserve as private what could not be made public. Keys—one category of object found in surprising numbers on the quilt's panels—enact a parallel dynamic of tangible inaccessibility. Without a location or reference for use, these objects—designed, presumably, to give access to something of value—tantalize the viewer whose unanchored speculation about their past function leads only to an exaggerated awareness of their present uselessness. Taunting the viewer with the possibility of an unrealizable access, the keys—scratched, worn, and discolored by use—flaunt the suggestion of the valuables they once unlocked but open up nothing. In gesturing toward the bodies that once interacted with them, many objects on the quilt mark an embodied presence that is equally inaccessible to the viewer. In several cases, the panels' assertion of a body *representationally* withheld obscures with the claim of privacy the fact of the lost body's universal inaccessibility. If the central placement of objects without stories pulls the reader into a tactile, sensory apprehension of things worn or used by unknown and inaccessible bodies, *hidden* objects on the quilt suggest the panel makers' deliberate exclusion of the viewer from the dynamics of anonymous contact. Many panels contain things hidden within other things, most of them only partially visible to the viewer. In one case, a pants pocket is literally sewn shut at the top, the bulging object contained within not only existing in the place where the body should be but flaunting the panel maker's ability to render public a claim to what is private. What can no longer be held is withheld; in showing us what can't be shown, the panel maker controls the viewer's access to an object/body inaccessible to the mourner.

Objects on the quilt serve many functions as they point toward the subjects whose lives and experiences they invoke. In the desire to analyze the signifying function of the quilt, however, many critics police their own desire to stretch past literal or symbolic barriers that block tactile access to the quilt's contents. Thinking about the way we know objects on the quilt in and through the body allows us to resist the pressure of immaterialization that would exclude palpable, multisensory experience not only from the realm of knowledge in general but from our understanding of grief in particular.

∽

The cultural force of disembodied theories of loss is apparent in the pressure to read even those objects stained by blood and marked with sweat of a lost loved one as signs of *subjective* presence. In her essay "What Remains," Kathryn Harrison describes a cultural fascination with relics of the dead, exploring how objects—particularly objects used, worn, bloodied, or sweated into by bodies now absent—achieve a personal and cultural significance proportionately linked to the way they have been marked by use. In moving from the blood-stained scarf worn by her grandmother and retained, unlaundered, by Harrison after her grandmother's death to public auctions of objects associated with famous people—John Lennon's washbasin, Elvis's razor—Harrison examines the value (personal/cultural/financial) attributed to object use. Reflecting on the fact that at a recent auction at a New York City auction house, a stained, frayed shirt worn by Elvis was valued at $25,000 more than a pristine white cardigan sweater owned by the performer, Harrison traces the value of worn artifacts to their contact with the lost body. Even as she describes the value of bodily traces on artifacts of the dead, however, Harrison's theoretical explanation of value covers over those traces of blood, sweat, and skin by subsuming the category of embodiment within the culturally sanctioned framework of the "spirit" of the dead: "All of us persist against reason in believing that some manifestation of the dead's personality or spirit remains in his or her corpse, and our faith extends to include the dead's possessions, especially those objects that routinely come into direct contact with the body: clothing and tools used for eating or for grooming" (2003, 137). Although Harrison's essay is marked by the refusal to back away from the body even in its most abject forms—she describes opening the urn to taste her grandmother's ashes, cradling the dirty, blood-stained scarf her grandmother left behind—her narrative of her own grief, as well as her discussion of larger cultural trends about how we deal with "What Remains" after death, finds no theoretical place to locate an understanding of grief in the body; ultimately, the body becomes a mere "manifestation" of the "personality or spirit" and the object a manifestation of that manifestation.

Such a formulation recasts the urgency of embodied loss that the essay would seem to uncover. In argumentative terms, Harrison dons her grandmother's blood-stained scarf only to veil the immediacy of her own embodied loss. Insisting on the material object's status as a sign of lost spiritual presence, she resignifies the abject as the subject, leaving her own desire to embrace bodily traces unexplained and unresolved. While recognizing the difficulty (indeed, the impossibility) of reading things only as things, my consideration of objects in the context of embodied grief suggests the possibility of literalizing Bill Brown's words to think about finding—in the sense of locating or materializing—the subject in the object. Reading the object for the body entails thinking about things neither as simple objects nor as mere signs of human subjectivity, but as things marked—both literally *and* figuratively—by their chiasmic interactions with human bodies.

POSTSCRIPT

❧

Laying the Body to Rest

The literary and photographic texts that I have discussed in this book thematize and theorize loss, raising questions about how the fact and the experience of embodiment shape our apprehension of death and grief. By calling attention to the fact of the body's marginalization in discourses of illness and grief that render embodiment a tool of subjectivity or reduce the body to object status, I have tried to show what is at stake in constituting presence at the expense of the body. Some might argue, however, that my argument overemphasizes the body's marginalization, especially in the context of the dead body's increasing visibility in popular culture domains. Recently, the proliferation of images of the dead in television, advertising, and popular fiction has led cultural historians such as Gary Laderman to declare that an American culture of denial marked by the fear of or disavowal of death has given way to a "cult of the dead" that "unabashedly brings the dead to life for public consumption" (Laderman 2003, 206, 175). The popularity of death as a subject of contemporary mass cultural inquiry—a popularity that Laderman documents persuasively—clearly reflects contemporary America's engagement with issues of mortality. As I will explore here, however, images of the dead in contemporary American mass culture often direct our attention to death by engaging in representational processes that obscure the embodied dynamics of loss in the very process of depicting the lost body. In "bring[ing] the dead to life," popular culture often appropriates the body as a mechanism rather than a subject of representation. Contemporary popular cultural forms may disembody the dynamics of loss not only by reducing the lost body to object form but by lending death a body animated by the conventions of representation. Insofar as embodiment is subsumed within a series of representational conventions which a mass audience is encouraged to bypass in the meaning-making process, the reader or viewer naturalizes the body's continuing presence in the imagistic rendering of death.

Bringing the Dead to Life in Popular Culture

In the days following my father's death, sympathy cards flooded in from friends and family. In retrospect, those cards provide a simple index of the cultural consolations we circulate in response to death, and of the way we reconstruct absence as presence. Not surprisingly, many of the cards we received were religious in nature, offering comfort in the idea of a loved one passing on to a better place in the embrace of God. Others, though not specifically religious, focused on the continuing existence of a beloved's spirit. Many invoked the consolation of memory as an antidote to loss; while one announced, "Those we hold most dear never truly leave us," another observed, "Within our hearts, the ones we love are never really gone—In spirit and in memory, their legacy lives on." The messages these cards transmitted are so naturalized in our culture that they blurred in the face of familiarity and grief. Ripping open envelope after envelope, my sister and I scanned quickly through the sentiments of the cards to focus on the signatures below.

One card, however, broke through the glaze of my exhaustion even in those early, raw days of loss. Its cover pictured a brightly colored sketch of a smiling middle-aged man looking over his shoulder and tipping his hat at the viewer as he embarked on an excursion down a winding tree-lined road. The card's sentiment was a familiar one, as was its text: a few lines from "Away," a well-known poem by James Whitcomb Riley often quoted in sympathy cards, obituaries, and funeral ceremonies:

> I cannot say, and I will not say
> That he is dead. He is just away.
> With a cheery smile, and a wave of the hand,
> He has wandered into an unknown land
> And left us dreaming how very fair
> It needs must be since he lingers there.
> And you—O you, who the wildest yearn
> For the old-time step and the glad return—
> Think of him faring on, as dear

In the love of there as the love of here;
Think of him still as the same, I say;
He is not dead—he is just away! (Riley 1982)

Whereas my sister found herself comforted by the text of Riley's poem and its greeting card illustration, my response to the card—which she tacked on the kitchen wall not far from my father's place at the table—was to recoil from its glossy literalization of the idea of memory's recuperative power. Virtually all of the sympathy cards my family received after my father's death lacked acknowledgment of the immediacy of grief and the irrecuperable dimensions of loss; their marginalization by omission operated by rendering invisible and unspoken embodied dimensions of loss outside the boundaries of cultural articulation. By extending a dynamics of compensation circulating throughout the culture and the sympathy card industry into the domain of the ordinary and the corporeal, however, this card denaturalized the process of recuperation it sought to enact.

The mistake of the card's combined textual and visual message, I might argue in retrospect, lay not in its disavowal of the embodied dynamics of grief but in its acknowledgment of the mourner's "yearning" for the restoration of tangibility and its realistic rendering of a specific body in a material world. Listening and longing for "the old-time step" renders the addressee of this verse embodied and the mourner's grief "wild" in its resistance to the very containment the card would enact. I found the rhyming text's upbeat celebration of denial an affront, its facile manipulation of language an absurdly inadequate response to the aching immediacy of my father's absence. In its literalization of the recuperation of loss as a spatial relocation of embodied presence, the card's brilliantly colored image of a smiling, waving man would not hold my gaze, a gaze which slipped again and again to the empty chair at my parents' kitchen table.

In situating both loss and longing in the domain of the corporeal, then, this sympathy card exposes the implications of its sentimental project for an embodied understanding of grief. The recuperation of absence as presence—the central project of a continuing impulse toward memorialization in American culture—involves an appeal to the sustaining power of memory that implicitly glosses over the distinction between image and embodiment I analyzed in chapter 4. The card's evocation of a familiar spatial and corporeal world pressures its consolatory message; the card simultaneously creates and deconstructs its own material landscape. Riley's verse highlights the role of language in perpetuating the illusion of presence—"I cannot say, and I will not say / That he is dead"—even as it entreats the addressee to ignore the purely rhetorical nature of the compensation it supplies: "Think of him still as the same, I say; / He is not dead—he is just away!" The card's injunction to "Think of [the lost loved one] still as the same" demands a literalized rendering of absence and presence manifested in its illustration of a smiling, cheery (dead) man blithely waving as he strolls down a winding road. In explicitly embodying and spatializing the process of cultural consolation, the poem pushes us toward a textured vision of presence that it labors to sustain. Its vibrantly detailed rendering of the lost loved one's presence exposed, for me, not the possibility of my father's return but the specificity and inaccessibility of his embodied presence.

The widespread use of Riley's poem in a discourse of grief spanning from obituaries of the 1920s and '30s to greeting cards and funeral service programs at the beginning of the twenty-first century points to a surprising continuity in sentimental articulations of loss in American culture. Of the many current forums for memorialization that include Riley's poem, one is the *Women's Army Corp Veterans' Association Chaplain's Handbook*. Side by side with the text of Riley's poem—a suggested resource for contemporary memorial services—the Handbook offers a prayer that articulates in both religious and psychological terms the necessity of rewriting the fact of embodied absence as a form of presence: "Dear God, we are especially aware today of that precious verse which says, that to be absent from the world is to be present with Thee. For recently one whom we have loved has gone from our midst, giving us a new perspective on the meaning of the words absent and present" (*Women's Army Corps*, 5). Like the Riley poem, which replaces the articulation of death with the spatial deferral of absence—"He is not dead—he is just away!"—this prayer invokes the "precious" consolation of religious doctrine while simultaneously acknowledging the move from absence to presence as a semantic shift; the new perspective necessitated by loss focuses on "*the meaning of the words* absent and present" (emphasis mine). This prayer renders visible a process of resignification often naturalized in a culture where the articulation of loss seldom emerges unbracketed by religious, psychological, or cultural discourses that deflect attention away from the outlines of absence.

My uneasy reaction to a card that my sister found mildly uplifting can't be explained by any claim about the literal dangers of accepting linguistic and cultural resignifications of loss. Surely, my sister recognized that the smiling man in the card before her was not and never could be her father, that her father was and never could not be dead. In asserting the power of signification over the reality of death, however, the card's self-conscious recasting of absence as presence not only denied the immediacy of embodied loss but appropriated the empty space of grief as a representational location. In his memoir about the death of his son, Nicholas Wolterstorff employs spatial metaphors to opposite effect as he argues that cultural consolations for loss often not only ignore but deny the experiential immediacy of grief: "If you think your task as comforter is to tell me that really, all things considered, it's not so bad, you do not sit with me in my grief but place yourself off in the distance away from me. Over there, you are of no help. . . . To comfort me, you have to come close. Come sit beside me on my mourning bench. I know: people do sometimes think things are more awful than they really are. Such people need to be corrected—gently, eventually. But no one thinks death is more awful than it is. It's those who think it's not so bad that need correcting" (Wolterstorff 1987, 34–35). Claiming to make a space for the lost body, the card, like the consolations Wolterstorff describes, effectively displaces its reader's claim to embodied loss. Its image-based recuperation performs a series of visual and textual sleights-of-hand which afford consolation at the expense of rendering the sensory immediacy of grief mere illusion. These illusory operations are culturally accepted, even embraced by many who take momentary comfort in them without taking them to heart. In absorbing and even naturalizing such cultural messages in times of crisis, however, we take what we can get without recognizing how much we are giving up. With the power of repetition, the gentle entreaty that coaxes us into a posture of denial—"Think of him still as the same"—gradually stiffens into a cultural injunction that makes it harder and harder to articulate the immediacy with which we experience embodied absence. Patricia Hentz's study of the body's role in grieving exposes a gap between cultural articulations of mourning and its experiential dynamics. Noting again and again that "their experiences did not fit into existing paradigms," participants in her study "spoke of feeling that they were not heard" (Hentz 2002, 171). In imaginatively stepping out of the desolate location of loss into the colorful landscape of compensation, we participate in a cycle of cultural silencing that may pathologize our own experience of embodied grief. If that grief circles around the empty space of a lost body, the ease with which popular representations of death effectively bring the dead to life may imaginatively dispossess the mourner's claim to a material landscape of loss.

∽

Published in 2002 and occupying a top-ten slot on the *New York Times* Best-seller list for 66 weeks, Alice Sebold's wildly popular debut novel, *The Lovely Bones,* testifies to our cultural fascination with the dead and to our collective need to recuperate the lost body even in the process of giving voice to loss. The novel presents as its first-person narrator a dead girl who tells the story of her own sexual assault and murder, as well as her family's response to her death. In Sebold's attempt to explain the shocking popular success of her novel, she traces its appeal to a widespread audience to the simple fact that "almost everybody has had some kind of loss. And so it keys into that somehow." Arguably a cultural phenomenon as much as a financial success, the book generated not only record sales but water cooler conversations, book club meetings, and overwhelming critical acclaim. Echoing Sebold's assessment of the novel's contribution to a literature of loss, American reviewers described the book as "an elegy" (Kakutani 2002), "a story about the energy that emerges from the void left behind" (Caldwell 2002), and "a stunning meditation on grief" (Heltzel 2002). Tapping into cultural fears not just about death but about violence, the novel opens by graphically detailing from Susie's own perspective the horror of her rape and murder in an underground cave designed by her tormentor. The novel's subject matter and its widespread popularity speak to Laderman's claims about the American public's increasing willingness to consume death.

In bringing the dead to life, however, Sebold resituates loss as deftly as she relocates her protagonist from earth to heaven. Given what critics have described as the novel's elegiac status, Sebold's construction of a young narrator whose voice sparkles with wit and personality might have served to emphasize the horror of the violent interruption of Susie's life. In the novelistic world that we enter, however, that life is sustained rather than interrupted, not just by virtue of the distinctive voice that shapes the narrative, but by Sebold's decision to lend her dead narrator an embodied form and locate her in a heaven that assumes aesthetic equivalence with the novel's "real world" landscape. The details of Susie's heaven are less surprising than the textured, sensory immediacy of the language that Sebold uses to construct it. Neither a pale imitation of earth nor a transcendently ethereal revision of it, Susie's heaven contains not just the idea of a swing set but a specific version of it, with "bucket seats made out of hard black rubber that cradled you and that you could bounce in a bit before swinging" (2002, 17). The textured materiality of this language emphasizes color, shape, and density, as well as the way the rubber swing cradles and resists a young body that emerges paragraphs later as Susie's own: "I sat down on the swing next to her and twisted my body around and around to tie up the chains. Then I let go and spun until I stopped" (18). Sebold represents Susie as fully embodied in heaven both by emphasizing her vulnerable material presence—she shivers with fear, touches other bodies, feels faint, and is knocked down by her dog when he joins her—and by consistently positing a corporeal connection between Susie and her friends and family on earth through parallel sentences and clauses: "I noticed Ruth's lip curl in disgust. Mine was curling up in heaven" (39). "Lindsey's face flushed; mine was flushed up in heaven" (71).

If the novel describes the line between the living and the dead as "murky and blurred," (48) its representations consistently depict *and* enact such ontological ambiguity. Even as the narrative remains preoccupied with the Salmon family's search to locate Susie's body in the attempt to achieve closure about her life or death, the novel sustains Susie's presence in representational terms that blur the categories of living and dead. In *The Dominion of the Dead,* Robert Pogue Harrison establishes the way in which the corpse functions to detach the dead from their remains "so that their images may find their place in the afterlife of the imagination" (2003, 148). Because all literary characters—living or dead—come to us as images, however, Harrison argues that all such "characters, as well as their voices, belong to the order of the posthumous image. . . . Between the living and the dead in literature the difference is strictly 'fictional.' Be they invented or historical, contemporary or bygone, dead or alive, the persons who speak in and through the literary work belong to the afterlife" (150). If the nature of representation dictates that all fictional characters exist for the reader as "posthumous image[s]," Sebold's decision to situate her dead narrator not only through voice but through space and embodiment contributes to the blurring of the distinction between embodied presence and disembodied image. Susie attains a representational presence that asserts her ontological equivalence with the novel's other characters and thus belies the embodied absence at the very heart of her family's grief.

If *The Lovely Bones* is an elegy, then, or a "stunning meditation on grief," its representations work to collapse the distinction between absence and presence, image and reality, central to the embodied dynamics of loss. The novel's simultaneous attempt to uncover and fill the space of absence results in the odd juxtaposition of its representations. Even as it unflinchingly reveals the facts of her murder, the novel conspires with the family's denial of her death through representational processes that not only compensate for but obscure absence. Critical responses to the novel's dark subject matter, however, offer a key to understanding how the novel renders contact with death oddly appealing. "It's hard to imagine," Melinda Bargreen of the *Seattle Times* observes, "but this novel that begins with a rape and murder is oddly comforting. It is drenched with blood and tears, but it's never morose" (Bargreen 2002). Maria Russo in the *Chicago Sun-Times* attributes Sebold's "unusual flair for both owning and transforming dark material" to the novel's ability to "make its readers inhabit a seamless, oddly comfortable loop between life and death, the living and the dead, with all the casually assertive finesse of an Emily Dickinson poem.... It's perhaps Sebold's biggest achievement that Susie's story is, in the end, even more consoling than it is disturbing" (Russo 2002). Given these and other claims that the novel "carves out a new space and a new understanding about surviving the death of someone you love" (Heltzel 2002), it's interesting to juxtapose *The Lovely Bones* with Riley's nineteenth-century sentiment and its contemporary greeting card illustration.

The recurring spatial metaphors used by critics of the novel suggest that the "oddly comfortable loop between life and death" that Sebold asks her readers to inhabit rests upon the relocation of the lost body in a space adjacent to life. Riley's contention that the lost loved one is not dead but is "just away" in an "unknown land" is paralleled by the relocation of Susie to a place where she continues to exist in a fully embodied form. Although the novel on some level traces the pathos of a grieving family's denial, it simultaneously denies the force of Susie's embodied absence. Susie's relocation to an adjacent (and imaginatively comparable) landscape renders the illusion of her absence explicable even as Sebold's representation of heaven renders the "unknown land" of Riley's poem "comfortably" habitable. Indeed, the novel's appropriation of representational strategies to literalize religious and cultural compensations for grief functions to obscure, rather than illuminate, the psychological and experiential dimensions of embodied loss. In a voice of opposition to the many glowing American reviews of *The Lovely Bones*, one British reviewer concludes, "But the worst and most sickening mistake, which ultimately kills the book stone dead, is that it hardly seems, towards the end, as if Susie has disappeared at all. She starts putting in appearances so regularly, in the lives of pretty well every living character, that you start to wonder when any of them are going to tell her to push off and leave them alone. Everyone feels her presence, and keeps saying so—her mother, her father, her brother, her sister, her high-school sweetheart, her high-school sweetheart's new boyfriend . . . What, you start to ask, are they all grieving for?" (Hensher 2002). Although I suggest that the novel's contrived plot represents only the most obvious means through which it denies the impact of Susie's death, this reviewer's blunt comment highlights the tension between embodied absence and representational presence in *The Lovely Bones*. If this novel about grief begins with the complex challenge of articulating the impact of loss, its representational maneuvers encourage the reader to dissolve the space between the image and the body and to rewrite the gap of representation as a habitable space.

The novel's continued assertion of Susie's embodied presence authorizes not only the family's denial of Susie's absence but the reader's interpretive allegorization of her loss. By the narrative's conclusion, the body—attended to with such care in the novel's opening chapter and sustained through the power of representation—has subtly disappeared until the only bones in view are metaphorical: "These were the lovely bones that had grown around my absence: the connections—sometimes tenuous, sometimes made at great cost, but often magnificent—that happened after I was gone. And I began to see things in a way that let me hold the world without me in it. The events that my death wrought were merely the bones of a body that would become whole at some unpredictable time in the future. The price of what I came to see as this miraculous body had been my life" (2002, 320). This passage unveils the symbolic and imagistic means through which the novel has representationally enacted compensation for the embodied loss it would expose. *The Lovely Bones* subtly but forcefully moves us from the details of Susie's rape and the gruesome image of a dog discovering her elbow three days after her disappearance to the miraculous restoration of a body that exists not in spite of but only because of death. Whereas the novel's representations of its dead protagonist rewrite the literal dynamics of loss by artificially sustaining Susie's body through representation, Sebold's final image of the "body that would become whole" exists only at the expense of abandoning the experiential body to the realm of the immaterial. If all characters, in Harrison's terms, belong to the world of the posthumous image, Sebold appropriates literature's necessary dissolution of ontological distinctions between the living and the dead to authorize the collapse of embodied presence into image. In locating the "real" meaning of bones in a space beyond the corporeal, the novel deauthorizes as literal an embodied experience of loss, rendering the perception of absence misperception and the grieving subject merely a faulty reader.

∞

The centrality of the dead body in the popular HBO television series *Six Feet Under* would seem to render it, in opposition to *The Lovely Bones*, a forum for unveiling the complex dynamics of embodied grief in the context of contemporary cultural attitudes about death. Laderman points to the existence of shows like *Six Feet Under* as evidence of American culture's increasing willingness to come to terms with the realities of death and dying. As it focuses on the lives of a family supported by the funeral home business they own and operate, *Six Feet Under* renders grief personal and immediate for the characters involved by initiating the first season's opener with the death of Nathaniel Fisher, the husband and father of the family. Scenes of grieving families devastated by loss enter into every episode. In addition, each show acknowledges the immediacy of the dead body through graphic depictions of embalming procedures and camera angles that locate the viewer in uncomfortable proximity to the dead body. If the experience of embodied grief testifies to the inextricability of the psychical and the corporeal dimensions of loss, however, *Six Feet Under* acknowledges the dead body as object only to naturalize the embodied status of the lost subject.

The series responds to a cultural lineage that constructs death in sentimental terms through its irreverent representations of the dead body and its self-conscious attention to the workings of the grief industry. Each episode of the first season of *Six Feet Under* contains a scene about prepping the dead body—almost always comic—that centers on the mechanics of the embalmers' attempts to restore the illusion of corporeal integrity. The series' humorous focus on cosmetic work testifies both to the power of technological and medical advances and to the necessarily illusory status of the "wholeness" of the reconstituted body. In "The Foot," one of the early episodes, for example, a client whose body parts are severed by a large mixing machine represents an aesthetic and technological challenge to the undertaker who must reconstruct a familiar form for the mourners to bid farewell to. When the client's severed foot goes missing—turning up later in an unsuspecting student's locker and finally in a happy dog's mouth—the show's humor revolves around the tension between the integrity of a beloved's familiar form and the necessary objectification of the body worker who uses technology in the service of cosmetic reconstruction. In this case, the deceased's family is duped by a prosthetic foot constructed with a leg of lamb. By positioning the viewer in a close-up relationship to the logistics of the embalming process and flaunting the viability of the well-crafted material construct as a replacement for the loved one's body, *Six Feet Under* quickly translates the living subject into a comic object, fragmented and/or in need of various kinds of cosmetic work.[1]

Whereas the requisite mortuary scene involving prepping the dead body for show humorously undercuts the illusion of reassembling the dead to figure the body as object, later fantasy sequences in each show dictate that the person who has died and been reassembled is put back together in an organic form—as themselves—through the fantasy or wish-fulfillment of a survivor. Although Nathaniel Fisher is killed in the first season opener in a collision with a bus, the show obscures the import of his bodily absence by figuring his continued presence in embodied form. As the actor who plays his part continues to pop up in scene after scene, the father's continuing presence is remarkable in its corporeal unremarkability. Neither angelic, ghostlike, nor wounded, the father intermittently and offhandedly materializes in each show, thus speaking to the impossibility of extricating his presence from the family landscape even after death. While the father's casual postures and informal clothing resist an ethereal vision of the supernatural, extending the show's anti-romantic critique of death culture, his quotidian presence and familiar bodily form stop short of interrogating the irrecuperable dimensions of embodied loss. Television conventions render the father's imaginative or remembered presence visually indistinguishable from its embodied counterpart.

The dead body as object thus gives way to the sustained fantasy presence of the lost subject naturalized in an embodied form. For the television viewer, *Six Feet Under* renders the lost body continually accessible through its polarization into subject or object status. The show stages the survivor's *embodied* grief only within a materialistic dynamic that renders intercorporeal loss as a naïve longing for an inaccessible body sustained through the illusion of material reconstitution. As the undertakers in "The Foot" episode position themselves watchfully over the reconstituted corpse with its leg of lamb prosthesis, Federico identifies the threat posed by the dead man's weeping widow, observing that Mrs. Romano looks like a "casket climber." His humor sets up a scene in which the grieving widow races to her husband's casket to hurl herself on his dead body, rolling her overweight form from side to side in an exaggerated parody of the wailing mourner overcome by spasms of grief that comically invokes the rollicking postures of sex. The scene's humor derives from the absurdity and cultural unspeakability of the notion of having sex with a corpse. Even as it constantly asserts the dead body's presence, then, the show either eclipses the significance of bodily loss by naturalizing the embodied presence of the lost loved one in its fantasy sequences or reducing the longing for a lost body to literal terms that parody the attempt to sustain intercorporeality.

If, as Gary Laderman (2003) argues persuasively, the twenty-first century has ushered in a fascination with death that is beginning to replace a culture of denial, the words and forms through which we speak the dead and the dying often suspend us between competing discourses of objectification and transcendence. In the space of death literalized in the viewing room of *Six Feet Under,* the return to the body represents not just an impossible but an inappropriate desire. If policing that desire—a process made manifest in Agee's agonizing depictions of a young boy's effort to renounce his longing to touch his dead father's hand—results in social acceptability, articulating such a longing culminates in accusations of impropriety occasioned by Sharon Olds's poems about her dying father or implicitly leveled by *Six Feet Under*'s parodic rendering of "casket climbing."

In displacing gendered theories of the phallus with a focus on the scar of the navel, Elisabeth Bronfen asserts not sexual difference but mortality as the forbidden threat we refuse to acknowledge in order to rescue ourselves from our shared disempowerment before death (Bronfen 1992, 35). If the taboo against death continues to erode, our postmodern embrace of postmortem fragmentation contributes to the disavowal of that discomfort by casting embodied grief as a literalization of loss. In naturalizing the body as a sign of subjective presence or defining it as an infinitely malleable object, *Six Feet Under* speaks for and to a prosthetic culture which, in revealing the constructedness of presence, implicitly denies the legitimacy of absence. The show's radical unveiling of the mechanics of the undertaking industry licenses its romanticized excursions into the compensation of fantasy, leaving the urgency of embodied loss largely unrepresented.

September 11 and Beyond

Although my focus throughout this work has been on the individual's embodied experience of death, dying, and loss in contemporary American culture, it seems almost impossible to conclude a book entitled *Lost Bodies* without thinking about the thousands of bodies literally lost on September 11, 2001. Implicit in my arguments throughout is the assumption that individual and cultural attitudes toward loss are theoretically inextricable; our experiences of dying and grief reflect engagement not just with our physical environments but with the psychic landscapes of American culture that construct the parameters of embodiment and draw the boundaries between life and death. My commitment to theorizing embodiment through the category of the experiential, however, has made me hesitant to attempt to characterize the enormity of loss associated with the events of September 11. Is it possible, as a cultural critic of such an event, to speak in a language that addresses the significance of September 11 without abstracting the materiality and specificity of overwhelming loss? How, in other words, might we investigate the cultural trauma associated with September 11 without appropriating the embodied grief of specific individuals as symbolic capital? Exploring the personal and collective responses of Americans to the events of September 11, I found my own hesitations about the unauthorized articulation of loss echoed in individual testimonies and in academic essays, in the confessions of newspaper reporters, psychiatrists' patients, and ground zero volunteers. In the shadow of an overwhelming grief experienced so intimately by so many, how might those of us at a critical remove from the lost bodies of September 11 speak to the dynamics of personal and collective loss?

The terrorists' appropriation of the power of the image has often been cited as a contributing factor in the horrific impact of the events of September 11. Targeting not merely a series of buildings and an outrageous number of citizens but a carefully chosen group of icons, the terrorists used America's image culture to attack not just Americans but America. Eye-witness descriptions of the attacks often express the shock of watching the first plane hit the World Trade Center only to focus in more depth on the horrific reiteration of the second strike and the difficulty of distinguishing reality from image or representation. The uncanny parallel between this highly visible attack and its filmic predecessors led many individuals to compare the experience of watching the destruction of the World Trade Center to the experience of watching a film. As Claire Kahane observes, "But even in real time, knowing that we were watching a unique act of devastation, the scenes before our eyes seemed familiar and unreal" (Kahane 2003, 107). In what Alessia Ricciardi describes as a postmodern culture beyond mourning, the Lacanian idea of the continuous "performance of loss" promotes a "postmodern politics of transience and detachment" that dulls us to the perception of historical instances of cataclysmic loss, rendering them mere simulacra (Ricciardi 2003, 46). One after another, writers responding to September 11 describe their difficulty distinguishing the original from the copy, the real from the image. Kahane concludes, "Thus the actual reality before our eyes was almost immediately transformed into and by the virtual reality of Hollywood and made familiar, déjà vu. . . . [A]s we turned to the movies to orient us to the real disaster, the historical was confused with the fictional, and the event of 9/11 itself—familiar and unfamiliar, real and unreal—took on an uncanny ambiguity" (107). "Once the event happened as lived experience," E. Ann Kaplan echoes, "it still felt 'unimaginable'" (Kaplan 2003, 100).

The representational conventions of literature and film conspire, in both *The Lovely Bones* and *Six Feet Under,* to elide distinctions between the living and the dead, the real and the unreal; insofar as Susie Salmon and Nathaniel Fischer are present to us as readers and viewers, their inclusion in what Harrison describes as "the order of the posthumous image" renders their embodied presence virtual and their virtual presence embodied. In contrast, the unreal images of September 11 captured explosions and collapsing skyscrapers that literally contained the bodies of thousands of ordinary people hidden from our view. Kaplan's description of September 11 simultaneously distinguishes and dissolves the boundaries between the real and the imagined, raising the question of how we might define our "lived experience" of 9/11 in a postmodern world of images. What does it mean to have "lived" 9/11? Is the fact of living its experience shared by those who watched the towers fall on television as well as by those who escaped the buildings through smoky stairwells moments before they fell? What of the couple in midtown Manhattan who saw the planes hit from their balcony? The young West Coast widow whose husband died in those towers? The people in Brooklyn who choked on the ash of incinerated flesh? Tracing Americans' ability to "move on" after September 11 to the absorption of its images by our information culture, Thomas De Zengotita argues, "what counts is the code. Silicon- or carbon-based. Artifact or animate. The difference between them is disappearing. . . . Someday, it will be obvious that all the content on our information platforms converges on this theme: there is no important difference between fabrication and reality, between . . . expressing and existing. And that is why we moved on after September 11, after an event that seemed so enormous, so horrific, so stark, that even the great blob of virtuality that is our public culture would be unable to absorb it. But it could. It has"(De Zengotita 2002, 34). In De Zengotita's compelling argument, the "virtuality" of contemporary American culture ultimately erodes the distinction between reality and representation to such a degree that we not only apprehend the images of September 11 within a filmic context but process them as representations: "Conditioned thus relentlessly to move from representation to representation, we got past the thing itself as well; or rather, the thing itself was transformed into a sea of signs and upon it we were borne away"(40). If we accept the critical argument that the terrorists conceptualized the events of September 11 primarily in terms of their imagistic and symbolic impact, their manipulation of representation emerges as primary and the loss of life as secondary. Similarly, if we process the events of September 11 as images absorbed within the virtual landscape of an information culture, the distance of representation mediates our apprehension of the human costs of the terrorists' attacks. In both scenarios, "the thing itself" disappears except as sign.

Countering the emphasis on images and the invisible appropriation of the thing within its representation, however, are the many newspaper articles and essays after September 11 which focus on the literal absence of bodily remains for the thousands of victims who died that day. Story after story—including those in a *New York Times* series entitled "A Nation Challenged: The Remains"—documents the continued search for bodies at the World Trade Center, the work of volunteers combing through landfills piled with rubble and body parts, the lack of closure for the grieving survivors that accompanies the absence of a corpse.[2] Countering a collective agreement not to photograph recovered remains of the victims was what might be characterized as popular media's obsessive attention to the tragic absence of bodies and the massive energy directed toward uncovering them. Although some cultural critics have argued that the press's coverage of the (often failed) search for lost bodies functions as a form of sensationalism that echoes the public's voyeuristic desire to visit the gaping hole of ground zero, the media's continued attention to the topic creates a representational space for the lost body that dwarfs its occasional depiction of the objects unearthed—a piece of bone, a remnant of clothing, a woman's purse, a tooth—through a painstakingly slow recovery process. The reflection that follows responds to September 11 by thinking about the role of lost bodies in a cultural event of large-scale devastation experienced by most Americans only at a distance, through images, representations, and words. Even as individual mourners struggle to comprehend the enormity of loss without the closure of a loved one's body, what role do lost bodies play in constructing and articulating the collective grief of Americans whose connection to the events of September 11 is mediated through physical distance and the space of representation?

For the families and friends of victims of the World Trade Center attacks, the absence of any bodily remains of their loved ones rendered closure difficult and the mourning process unusually complex. Almost all the popular media stories focusing on the process of recovering bodies after 9/11 frame that recovery process in terms of the survivors' ability to apprehend loss and achieve closure.[3] Although the public's interest in the grief of victims' families and friends might be described as explicable if not ghoulish, the sustained media attention to a narrative of recovery inevitably doomed to failure can't fully be explained by fascination with the suffering of others or even, I would argue, by sensationalism. In story after story, reportage of the painstakingly slow process of sifting through truckloads of debris includes few details of dramatic recovery. Instead, headlines and narratives emphasize the frustration of the desire for recovery, the virtual impossibility of locating the bodies of most of the victims.[4] At some level, then, the news that almost all the stories of this genre report is the absence of news, the failure to locate and identify bodies, the endlessly elusive process of seeking "the thing itself."

If the absence of a loved one's dead body frustrates what Robert Pogue Harrison describes as the living's need to detach the dead from their remains "so that their images may find their place in the afterlife of the imagination" (2003, 148), the absence of the bodies of the dead after September 11 contributes to a different dilemma for Americans whose connection to the events was mediated through representation. Whereas mourners of the lost struggle to relegate their loved ones to "the afterlife of the imagination," Americans in general struggle to bring those lost out of the realm of the image to render their past presence real. For most Americans, the difficulty of locating loss defines an experience of psychic trauma—described by one critic as "secondary trauma" (Greenberg 2003, 23)—that struggles to penetrate past images to an objective correlative for loss. Although the cultural narrative of mourning after September 11 focuses—and rightly so—on the impossibility of coming to terms with a loved one's inexplicable death and absent body, the continued news reporting on the endless search for bodies also speaks to the public's impossible attempt to access the object of a deeply felt but anonymous loss. One journalist, after months of contacting families of the dead to write profiles of their lost loved ones, describes her inability to free herself of "the phantom ache I felt in sympathy for the relatives of the people I had written about" (Smith 2002, 400). Her representation of her emotion as "phantom" grief raises the question of how we, as a culture, name and understand a loss the "lived experience" of which most of us can claim but cannot embody. James Krasner's (2004) persuasive invocation of phantom limb experience as a figure for embodied grief points to the way individual loss revolves around corporeal absence, an absence largely unrecognized, I argue, in cultural terms. In the case of September 11, however, the knowledge of thousands of American lives lost creates a space—literal, cultural, and psychic—for a bodily absence which implies a presence once known or accessed. If the embodied dynamics of grief contribute to the illusion of sustained material presence, the knowledge of devastating absence after September 11 generates a "phantom grief" that implies the severing of a connection generated only through "the afterlife of the imagination." Suspended between the image and the thing itself, the phantom griever struggles to apprehend as lived experience a loss that both is and is not virtual.

For many not directly connected to the victims of September 11, the gap between the felt experience of grief and dislocation from a specific object of loss generates questions not only about how to name such an experience but also about the implications of claiming ownership of loss in a situation where "real" grief exists. Judith Greenberg asks, "How do those of us whose grief is harder to specify address our encounter with violence and death? . . . For some, there was even a shame of claiming a relationship to the events, as if such recognition could usurp the trauma of the victims and their loved ones" (Greenberg 2003, 23). In his powerful essay "Reflections on Trauma, Absence, and Loss," Dominick LaCapra critiques theories of trauma that level the distinction between ontological and historical loss.

Citing the need to attend to the material and political consequences of particular events, LaCapra formulates the dangers of collapsing the distinction between the lived experience of historical trauma and an understanding of loss as constitutive of existence: "By contrast to absence, loss is situated on a historical level and is the consequence of particular events. . . . Furthermore, the conflation of absence and loss would facilitate the appropriation of particular traumas by those who did not experience them, typically in a movement of identity formation that makes invidious and ideological use of traumatic series of events in foundational ways or as symbolic capital" (2000, 186). September 11 raises questions about the way LaCapra's important distinction between absence and historical loss might be finetuned to account for an increasingly complex definition of "experience" in an age of images. The "secondary" trauma of September 11 is, in Greenberg's words, "harder to specify" insofar as its subjects are caught between an experience of loss that is neither purely ontological nor experientially immediate. One New York psychiatrist marks the confusion of patients who experienced the trauma of 9/11 without being able to lay claim to a location for their loss: "Many of my patients who had not lost family or close friends in the September 11 attacks expressed, with shame, their envy of the families who had, because those victims, they felt, had legitimate reasons to grieve and an external environment in ruins that mirrored the interior world of a mourner. These patients struggled with what they experienced as more invisible and 'objectionable' losses, such as the loss of security and the illusion of immortality" (Bassin 2003, 196). Donna Bassin's patients wrestle not only with their psychic fragility but with the labor to legitimize an experience of loss rendered "objectionable" in the context of an embodied grief they might be seen to appropriate. Neither specific nor symbolic, the "phantom" grief of 9/11 is constituted in the shadows of overwhelming material and specific loss.

In many cases, the disjunction between an intensity of feeling and the absence of a specific relationship to loss results in the emotional attempt to cultivate intimacy with the dead. When September 11 accounts cannot establish the writer's relationship to the event by charting connectedness to specific individuals who died, authors of firsthand accounts often attach themselves to such losses through co-workers, neighbors, or relatives of the dead. For those without a connection to those connected to the victims, the *New York Times*'s "Portraits of Grief" often functioned to personalize loss. For many Americans, reading these portraits became a daily ritual of mourning that allowed them imaginative access to the intimate details of lives lost. The daily process of reading the "Portraits" became, for many, a means of legitimizing feeling by directing preexisting emotions toward individual victims constituted as presence only to be acknowledged as absence. In the words of Paul Auster, "We weren't mourning an anonymous mass of people, we were mourning thousands of individuals. And the more we knew about them, the more we could wrestle with our own grief" (Scott 2001). Beginning with the experience of grief, survivors without a direct connection to loss struggled not with memory's taunting presence but with its absence as they sought in the "Portraits" a means of intimacy with the anonymous that would render their phantom grief real. The "Portraits of Grief," in Orly Lubin's terms, "converted short obituaries of the victims into personal memories as much as images of the collective memory" (Lubin 2003, 125).

If these "Portraits" represented an opportunity for the reader to draw close to loss, however, the most faithful of readers—and writers—sometimes found themselves frustrated in the attempt to penetrate past linguistic platitudes to access the person behind the "portrait." Jennifer Smith, author of many of the individual portraits in *Newsday*'s series of tributes to September 11 victims, exposes the difficulty of using language to assert the specificity and individuality of the lost: "The only problem was, I hadn't anticipated how hard it would be to pinpoint what made one person different from the next. After two weeks on the job, I found myself wanting to outlaw a handful of phrases" (Smith 2002, 391). The more profiles she wrote, "the more difficult finding new ways to say the same old things became" (394). Smith's heartfelt effort to capture the immediacy and specificity of embodied existence brought home to her the limits of language and the generalizing conventions of discourse. Her attempt to resuscitate the victims of 9/11 through interviews with their loved ones collapses into an accumulation of words impossible to animate: "All the correct details are there, but the overall effect is two-dimensional, lifeless. When you know someone, when you have loved someone deeply, and perhaps changed their diapers and watched them grow up to adulthood, summing up that life as a combination of adjectives, or a list of favorite hobbies, tends to ring a bit hollow" (398). Readers of the "Portraits," as well, echo Smith's frustration with the collapse of specific presence into platitude and cliché. After describing her obsessive need not only to read but to collect all of the portraits of the lost in the *New York Times,* Nancy K. Miller acknowledges the portraits' failure to lend her a personal connection to the dead: "I can't say I cried reading the portraits. On the contrary, I experienced a powerful sense of disbelief. . . . Was it possible that no one who ever died in the attack on the World Trade center was ever depressed . . . self-centered . . . without a passion . . . or sometimes found life not worth living . . . ? . . . I could not perform the translation, identify with these lives from which all traces of unhappiness were banished" (Miller 2003, 46). For the postmodern reader, self-conscious consumer of words and images, language's failure to embody absence renders even the specific portraits of the lost failed attempts to supplement the unreal images of September 11.

For Miller, however, her daily return to the portraits of the victims assumes a structural equivalence with the mourner's painful and constant encounter with memories of the dead. Having acknowledged the failure of the portraits to render the lost in specific terms, Miller stresses the way temporal and spatial reiteration make up for the sacrifice of individuality to representational convention. Her obsessive collection of the portraits testifies, she asserts, to her connection to the accumulated lives they represent: "But the fact that I can't stop collecting, that I know I will buy the book, that I can't stop reading about these interrupted lives and the people left behind, means that, having lost no one close to me on September 11, I'm no less located on the map of loss it produced—a map of trauma whose borders are still missing" (46). Miller negotiates the tensions of phantom grief—along with the gap between the virtual and the real—by insisting upon the locatedness of her grief on "the map of loss." Her image of the map materializes loss without removing it from the realm of the representational, just as her insistence on the significance of her embodied encounter with the portraits renders her grief somehow more real: "Stacks of newspaper clippings from the *New York Times* clutter my study. . . . Of course, for a while now the portraits have been available on the Web, and I could jettison my dusty piles. But since I read the *New York Times* 'on paper' (not on-line, as a student recently characterized my retrograde tendencies), I felt that I had to stare at the newsprint, spread it out like the morning news, and dirty my hands in order to figure out the place the portraits occupied both in the newspaper . . . and in my mind" (45–46). Miller's insistence on the spatial and material dimensions of the reading process allows her to locate the place the portraits occupy not just in her mind but in her lived experience. Her assertion that the stacks of newspapers she collects have overwhelmed her study with dust and forced her to dirty her hands implicitly constructs her relationship to the losses at ground zero in embodied terms, appropriating the gap of representation to accomplish what the portraits cannot. Miller's commentary figures the effort to become intimate with the specifics of loss after September 11 as a material encounter between the body and the image; like the rescue worker sifting through the rubble of ground zero for traces of bodies, Miller breathes the dust and wears the dirt associated with her struggle to locate the victims of September 11.

In an information age that continually manipulates perception, the fractured experience of loss renders representation inseparable from the thing itself. Not surprisingly, then, attempts to confront the urgency and specificity of loss after 9/11 sometimes abandon the idea of contact with the thing itself by figuring representation as a form of wounding. In her essay "I Took Pictures: September 2001 and Beyond," Marianne Hirsch uses Barthes's *Camera Lucida* to make the argument that photography "can communicate the bodily wounding that is trauma and the sense memory of it" (Hirsch 2003, 81). Her central example is a photograph of an individual being tattooed with a detailed drawing of the collapsing Twin Towers. The tattoo, Hirsch argues, "emblematizes the profound bodily effect of . . . September 11 and the ways in which—for this artist and subject— the nation has been materially wounded by it, has had its memory carved onto its skin, as it were. . . . The drawing on the skin shows the citizen's defiant appropriation and flaunting of the attack displayed for all to see, and more importantly, to feel. . . . The visceral display of the very act of wounding elicits spectatorial identification on a physical, bodily level" (79). Although Hirsch's reading of the photograph stresses the function of the image as an emblem of the "profound bodily effect" of September 11, her continued reiteration of the visceral immediacy of the material wounding suffered by both the individual photographed and the nation glosses over the significance of the fact that the man in the picture is literally wounded not by an act of terrorism but by an act of representation. Here, as in Miller's essay, the observer's attempt to penetrate the images of September 11 by drawing closer to the reality of corporeal loss is limited to an embodied encounter with the mechanisms of representation. If, as Bassin observes, "Mourning requires a confrontation with the emptiness occasioned by loss. It requires a body and a place" (Bassin 2003, 202), phantom grief displaces the solipsism of intercorporeal loss onto a mourning body intact in all but representational terms.

Although the tattooed body Kaplan analyzes remains relatively unique, the attempt to bring the body to an experience of trauma mediated through representation is apparent in the reactions of American citizens who flocked to their local hospitals and blood banks after September 11 to donate blood for victims whose anticipated rescue never occurred. The patience with which individuals across America queued up in endless lines—some more than twelve hours long—and eagerly presented their arms to have their blood drawn suggests not only the importance of any measure of response or control in the face of catastrophe but the power of an imagined embodied connection to the victims of 9/11. One donor supervisor at Florida Blood Services traced the overwhelming turnout of first-time donors (a group which constituted 40 percent of the people who gave blood after September 11) to donors' willingness to put aside their own fear of needles in the knowledge of how much the victims must have suffered (Thurston 2001).[5] The desire to heal the wounded or access the dead also inspired record donations to September 11 victims, rescuers, and charities. Within five days of the attack, leaders of national nonprofit groups delivered a statement to the press urging Americans not to send any more clothing, food, or stuffed animals to ground zero, where rescuers, literally overwhelmed by donations, had to dump uneaten food and truck clothing and teddy bears to warehouses as far as ninety miles away (Mollison 2001). While aid organizations pleaded with Americans to send checks—and if need be, to auction off the personal items they had purchased and offer the proceeds to charity—underwear, socks, blankets, and stuffed animals continued to pour in, establishing the possibility of a material link between givers and the rescuers who wore those pieces of clothing at the site or the orphaned children whom they imagined comforted by a teddy bear.

The testimonies of many New Yorkers after 9/11 extend such symbolic connections to trauma into the realm of the phenomenological by establishing their proximity to loss in spatial and sensory terms. For New Yorkers, the search for what Bassin describes as "an external environment in ruins that mirrored the interior world of a mourner" (196) logically focused on the ruined environment of ground zero, which emerges in testimonials as an absent presence that could be claimed by any survivor said to exist in corporeal relation to it. In attempting to locate themselves on the map of trauma, New Yorkers routinely authorize their narratives with sensory references to ground zero that connect their bodies to the site through their geographical proximity at the time of the attacks (measured most often in number of blocks or walkable minutes), their sensory experience (what they could smell, see, breathe on September 11 and in the days after), or their habitual proximity to the location (a daily commute that took them past the towers, a weekly visit to the playground at the site). Judith Greenberg asserts, "In my neighborhood, the aftermath could be felt viscerally. I encountered seemingly familiar faces on missing person fliers posted on streetlight posts and shop windows. For days (or was it weeks?) I could see a huge gray cloud hovering over the southern end of the city, and when the winds shifted and blew uptown I inhaled the death-infused air" (Greenberg 2003, 22). Greenberg's assertion of her ability to feel viscerally what otherwise might only be felt psychically serves to render her grief experiential rather than imagined, just as the seeming familiarity of the faces posted on missing person flyers establishes her location in the space of real loss.

Lacking an obvious connection to the lost bodies of September 11, Greenberg establishes a posthumous intimacy with the victims whose remains she inhales. Ann Kaplan reveals what is at stake in such a shift from symbolic to phenomenological apprehensions of loss in her assertion that many New Yorkers experienced the devastating losses of September 11 with an immediacy and a specificity denied to others who did not lose loved ones on that day: "Looking at the event from a distant intellectual perspective, Žižek in his article overstated the political/psychic symbolism of the attacks.... [His] thesis does not exhaust or actually get close to the specificity of the event for those of us living close by. It is possible that the Twin Towers represented to the terrorists ... postmodernity, technology, the city.... But for those nearby, the towers functioned phenomenologically as part of people's spatial universe, in and of themselves, not standing in particularly for American capitalism or American might" (2003, 99–100). To some extent, Kaplan's objection to the reduction of historical loss to symbolic terms echoes LaCapra's objection to the conflation of absence and loss in the definition of trauma. In contrast to absence, which he describes as an ontological category transhistorical in nature, LaCapra observes that "losses are specific and involve particular events, such as the death of loved ones on a personal level" (2000, 179). Echoing LaCapra's emphasis on what he terms "the problem of specificity" (199), Kaplan attempts to rescue the events of September 11 from Žižek's "distant intellectual perspective." Her assertion of the need to "get close to the specificity of the event," however, eschews the abstraction of symbolism to focus not on the embodied loss of a loved one but on the violent destruction of a spatial reference point around which her body oriented itself. Barthes's meditation on photography in *Camera Lucida* represents an impossible attempt to recuperate the dynamics of embodied loss after his mother's death. In appropriating Barthes's argument about the photograph to address her own experience of September 11, however, Kaplan imagines *the towers* as the missing body that photography can restore: "The photographs of the towers are touched by the towers, and looking at them enables viewers to be touched by that touch" (83). By metaphorically translating the lost touch of the absent body onto the material site of September 11, Kaplan resituates her own body in relation to the body of loss.

Eric Darton's history of the World Trade Center buildings reveals the labor of Kaplan's effort to embody an architectural site designed to disguise rather than reveal the human forms within. Constructed in a way that obscures both the function of the buildings as office centers and the presence of the workers within, the trade towers, he observed, "disappeared as sites of human habitation" (Darton 1999, 119). Nilufer Gole parallels the design characteristics of the World Trade Center with the terrorist attacks on September 11, which "made the bodies disappear both materially and visually" (Gole 2002, 339). If mourning requires a body and a place, the anthropomorphic rendering of the collapsed Twin Towers after 9/11 testifies to the impossible struggle to constitute an object of loss to anchor the phantom experience of grief. The Towers, Gole observes, "were crumpling under our gaze, but the death of so many thousands was not visible to the eye, remaining just an abstract figure. . . . We still had to realize that bodies had simply vanished and incinerated under steel, glass, and fire" (339). In the quest of many to authorize the immediacy of a grief with no accessible human object, lending corporeal dimension to the vanished World Trade Center becomes a way of anchoring the "abstract figure" of loss.

If the body, in Merleau-Ponty's terms, functions as "the pivot of the world," many New Yorkers sought to anchor their phantom grief in the absent presence of a building referred to by Rick Burns on a PBS documentary as "our phantom limb," an extension of the body both imagined and real: "You feel it but it's not there; you look to where you feel it should be" (Hirsch 2003, 83). As the focus of grief shifts from the individual's embodied connection with a specific victim to his or her sensory participation in the collective body of the Manhattan landscape, the missing structures of lower Manhattan constitute not merely the site of loss but the object of mourning. Describing the impact of the gaping hole in a familiar landscape as "a profound dislocation," Greenberg asserts, "New York has a wound" (Greenberg 2003, 25). After September 11, as Jill Bennett observes, memorials to the World Trade Center victims in the parks of lower Manhattan included "RIP notices to the anthropomorphized 'twins'" (Bennett 2003, 136). New Yorkers grieved not only over the losses of family, friends, and neighbors, but also "mourned the loss of the World Trade Center itself" (136). Critics have often viewed Americans' willingness to travel to ground zero from all across the country in voyeuristic terms that stress the commodification of a devastating loss. If the families of September 11 victims were, in one journalist's words, "robbed of the intimacy of the deathbed" (Sengupta 2001), Americans' pilgrimage to a site that Bassin describes provocatively as "the body of the traumatized group" (Bassin 2003, 201) may represent not a voyeuristic desire to witness the suffering of others but a longing to become intimate with what has been lost, to penetrate steel, glass, and image by bringing the body into the psychic experience of grief. In his response to September 11, Don DeLillo suggests that the psychological proximity to loss manifests itself in an embodied apprehension of grief not limited to those who can claim a direct relationship to either the victims of September 11 or the World Trade Center landscape: "What has already happened is sufficient to affect the air around us, *psychologically*. We are all breathing the fumes of lower Manhattan, where traces of the dead are everywhere, in the soft breeze off the river, on rooftops and windows, in our hair and on our clothes" (DeLillo 2001b, 39, emphasis mine).

The shocking events of 9/11 interrupt American culture's tendency to gloss over the absent presence that underlies the embodied experience of grief by exposing and attending to the significance of the lost body. The inaccessibility of that body in its object status after September 11 not only exaggerates the difficulty of achieving closure for grieving families but functions as a means of articulating the gap at the center of Americans' phantom grief. Popular media's attention to the thousands of bodies obliterated on September 11 thus speaks not only to the abrupt and unintelligible experience of embodied loss for families and friends of victims, but to the dislocated grief of those many Americans who lacked the means to embody an overwhelming absence the urgency of which they seemed to experience but could not claim. In the aftermath of 9/11, over 5,000 of us a day purchased tickets to stand patiently in an endless, winding line which culminated in the chance to bring our bodies to the edge of loss and see for ourselves what was not there. New Yorkers' graphic, reiterated descriptions of being coated with ash and breathing in the dead, I would argue, testify to a response many of us share as we push our bodies closer and closer to the material site of a loss we struggle simultaneously to escape and to absorb.

After September 11, Olu Oguibe, artist-in-residence in Tower One of the World Trade Center in 2000, created an art installation that speaks to the problem of the lost body. Whereas the *New York Times*'s "Portraits of Grief" attempted to forge a connection between the reader and individual victims of September 11 rescued from the realm of the anonymous, Oguibe's "Ashes" renders the experience of phantom grief by representing the embodied specificity of an anonymous loss accessible only retrospectively. The installation locates the losses of September 11 in the modest space of an uninhabited bedroom, the contents of which are blanketed in gray ash. The body in Oguibe's piece is everywhere and nowhere, overwhelmingly present in the reiterated assertion of its inaccessibility. An unmade bed at the center of the room, its sheets exposed and covers rumpled, captures in its folds and bunchings of cloth the physical imprint of the lost body. A suit jacket and pants laid out on the bed not only stand in for but take the measurement of that absent form; their arms and legs drape over the side of the bed to hang empty in the space above the wooden floor. Two shoes arranged side by side extend the scope of disembodied space to the place where feet would slip into the worn leather of slightly buckled oxfords. In the words of Koan Jeff Baysa, exhibit curator, "an assemblage of clothing is laid out like a cast of its owner, one which will wait interminably for investment by its owner" (Baysa). The textured traces of embodiment in Oguibe's installation testify to the immediacy of a past presence the viewer experiences only as absence. The dark liquid in a partially filled water glass on the bed stand and the uneven collection of ash on its rim mark the past presence of lips against glass and testify to the murky borders of the material and the organic. Like the sheets scraped by debris, the ash-coated water glass on the bed stand both insists on the embodied immediacy of past presence and rebuffs the viewer's facile attempt to reverse the trajectory of loss by imaginatively occupying this impossibly ruined landscape.

Although the specific imprints of bodily contact on matter support Baysa's description of "Ashes" as "a mental snapshot for forensics," the force of the installation depends upon its ability simultaneously to invoke and frustrate the viewer's quest to identify (or identify with) the room's past inhabitant. Even as the intimate traces of sleeping, drinking, and dressing render past presence in specific and embodied terms, the installation enforces an anonymity that parallels the constant, mediating presence of the ashes that disrupt the viewer's access to its details. The open book on the bed stand waiting to be picked up lends the viewer no access to the interrupted life toward which it gestures; the contents of that book, including its title, are completely obscured by ash. Although the suit laid out on the bed and the briefcase standing amidst the rubble seem to identify the room's former inhabitant as a businessman, this middle-class equivalent of a uniform discloses little about its wearer's personality, habits, or identity. Similarly, the generic status of the room's furnishings (a simple twin bed, standard-issue dark dresser and bed stand) and what Baysa describes as the "nondescript framed prints on the wall" lend the room's missing body no distinctive subjectivity. If "Ashes" functions as a version of a forensics scene, the clues it offers assert the intimacy and the specificity of past presence only to deauthorize the viewer's claim to knowledge or connection by withholding any marks of individual identity. Oguibe's installation exaggerates the viewer's frustration by reiterating the immediacy of embodied presence even as it enacts the impossibility of unmediated access to those lost on September 11. In its simultaneous assertion of the specificity and anonymity of the lost body, "Ashes" stages the impossibility of recuperating a presence the absence of which we experience in textured, sensory terms.

After September 11, at least temporarily, the psychic space of grief assumed the form of a lost body inaccessible for many Americans as both presence and absence. In his response to September 11, Don DeLillo observes, "For the next fifty years, people who were not in the area when the attacks occurred will claim to have been there. In time, some of them will believe it. Others will claim to have lost friends or relatives, although they did not. This is also the counternarrative, a shadow history of false memories and imagined loss" (2001b, 35). In exposing the dynamics of a phantom grief that would culminate in the false claim to an embodied experience of trauma, DeLillo also raises the question of what it means to define our experience of September 11 in terms of "imagined loss." After September 11, the *New York Times*'s "Portraits of Grief" lent us "personal memories" of the victims that were merely illusory, echoing the forced if not "false" claims made by many of their spatial and embodied proximity to loss. Insofar as the false claims DeLillo predicts are evidence of the appropriation of the trauma of 9/11 by those whose did not experience it, the dynamics he sketches emerge as deeply troubling. I wonder, however, if there might be another way to read the "shadow history" DeLillo describes by seeing it as a reflection of our ultimate failure to transform the loss of "the thing itself" into "a sea of signs." If, as Thomas De Zengotita claims, "we inevitably moved on after September 11" (De Zengotita 2002, 34), our continuing—though necessarily failed—attempts to embody our "imagined loss" may mark the possibility that our experience of September 11, like our phantom grief, creates the possibility of experiencing as absence something we as a culture naturalize as presence: the force of embodiment and, consequently, the power of its loss. If America finds itself, as Alessia Ricciardi posits, in an age beyond mourning, Ann Kaplan suggests that as a result of September 11 "America has learned to mourn and to respect mourning" (Kaplan 2003, 102). Insofar as it creates a space for the lost bodies that are the objects of our phantom grief, the struggle to embody our imaginings might be a first step toward acknowledging, rather than appropriating, the materiality and specificity of loss.

Notes

Introduction

1. In *Heaven's Coast*, Mark Doty describes a literally paralyzing form of this response. After months of caring for his partner, Doty was left after his partner's death with back problems so severe he could barely move: "I had no idea then . . . what it means to 'let go' of a person. How can we, when someone is bonded to us, welded into the mesh of ourselves? The dead live on in our bodies, in the timeless flux of memory, inseparable from ourselves" (1996, 118). For a powerful analysis of Doty's grief, see James Krasner, "Doubtful Arms and Phantom Limbs: Literary Portrayals of Embodied Grief" (2004).

2. For a fuller discussion of Foucault's idea of the medical gaze and its application to the terminal body, see chapter 1.

3. For a powerful analysis of the "abrogation of autonomy" in a different context, see Kevin Ohi, "'The Author of "Beltraffio"': The Exquisite Boy and Henry James's Equivocal Aestheticism" (2005).

4. For a classic cultural history of death, see Philippe Ariès's *Hour of Our Death* (1981). Although not yet published, Sandra M. Gilbert's *Death's Door: Modern Dying and the Ways We Grieve* promises to offer a new cultural history of death and grief in modern Western culture.

5. See, for example, Kathleen Woodward's *Aging and Its Discontents (1991)* and *Figuring Age: Women, Bodies, Generations* (1999), Lennard J. Davis's *Enforcing Normalcy: Disability, Deafness, and the Body* (1995), and Rosemarie Garland Thomson's *Extraordinary Bodies: Figuring Physical Disability in American Culture and Literature* (1997).

6. See *The Body in Pain* (1985), especially chapter 1.

7. Alessia Ricciardi develops the idea of a culture beyond mourning in *The Ends of Mourning: Literature, Psychoanalysis, Film* (2003). Dominick LaCapra anticipates some aspects of Ricciardi's critique in his important essay "Reflections on Trauma, Absence, and Loss," in which he observes, "I think it is misguided to situate loss on an ontological and transhistorical level, something that happens when it is conflated with absence and conceived as constitutive of existence" (2000, 179).

Terminal Illness and the Gaze

1. Although it does not address issues of death and disease specifically, Kaja Silverman's *The Threshold of the Visible World* offers one of the few psychoanalytic models for exploring what I describe here as the "uncomfortable" gaze. Silverman calls for visual texts which activate in the viewer the capacity to idealize non-normative bodies, exploring "how we might put ourselves in a positive identificatory relation to bodies which we have been taught to abhor and repudiate" (1996, 79). Silverman's model relies upon a narrativization of the gaze; she describes a process of looking and relooking that enables us as viewers to "painstakingly reverse the processes through which we have arrogated to ourselves what does not belong to us, or displaced onto another what we do not want to recognize in ourselves" (3). Although the emotional dynamics of an existing father/daughter relationship in *The Father* complicate Silverman's formulation of the way in which "the eye can confer the active gift of love upon bodies which have long been accustomed to neglect and disdain" (227), her theorization of productive looking represents an important model for an ethical critique of the gaze.

2. In *Fragments on the Deathwatch*, Louise Harmon describes the way in which, after her father's diagnosis with terminal illness, her personal conversations with her family become subsumed by a medicalized discourse which, like the gaze Foucault describes, would place her father "in parenthesis" and represent him as an accumulation of physiological symptoms: "But when my father was sick, there was a new and horrible dimension to our conversations. I had to ask, and she had to answer, 'How is Daddy?' There were only two responses: 'Just the same' or 'Worse.' Then there were the words of elaboration. They were not words about my father. They were not words about the man who gave his children a sense of belonging in the world, a love of music, travel, and history. They were words about my father's body. About his broken, infected skin. About his bladder and his bowels. About what came out and what went in. About how his hands had frozen into the shape of a garden trowel. About how he moaned all the time like some miserable animal, beyond names, beyond faces, beyond recognition. And yet not beyond pain" (1998, 34).

3. The very term "death-watch" has largely disappeared from contemporary American speech, due in part to the growth of medical technology and the hospital industry in general. Despite a growing number of hospices, those dying of terminal illness are more likely to die in a hospital attended to by professionals than in their own bed, surrounded by family or friends. One function of the growing industry of medicine, then, has been to diminish the visibility of people dying of terminal illness for the general public. Whereas the letters of Emily Dickinson are filled with page after page recounting her vigilance at the bedside of dying friends, neighbors, and family members, her witness to the moment of death itself, the process of dying remains for many contemporary Americans a mystery that they will encounter firsthand only with their own deaths. For an in-depth discussion of this phenomenon, see Sherwin Nuland's *How We Die* (1994).

4. In *Body Work*, Peter Brooks uses Freud's theories to suggest "that the visual inspection of reality, as the core component of the epistemophilic project, is doomed never to grasp its 'real' object, since that object is imaginary, impossible.... Thus it may be that looking at the body is inherently unsatisfactory; sight finally gives no access to that which would satisfy its demands by offering some version of 'truth'" (1993, 100). Brooks's analysis raises the question of where truth resides, and how accessible it is to vision. The questions he asks about the epistemophilic project are especially relevant to the issue of viewing the body with disease. The body that presents itself to be known visually never announces its identity so absolutely as when it is marked by illness.

5. The body often provides the healthy subject an illusion of stability, of imperme-

ability; the physical borders of the body that render the subject susceptible to objectification also provide useful boundaries that allow the subject to construct borders of identity, to separate self from world. The experience of terminal illness, however, may hurl a person further and further inside the confines of the body even as it ruptures any illusion of the body as protective boundary.

The experience of terminal illness renders Olds's father vulnerable to a gaze that accesses the subject through the body precisely because his illness has pushed him to acknowledge the urgency of his own materiality. Olds's depiction of her father's final days unveils with frightening immediacy the body's transgression of its own boundaries and its simultaneous failure to protect the subject from external violation. The person with terminal illness may experience the body's materiality as an extended violable surface that commands the subject with an agency of its own. In "His Terror," Olds explores the way in which her father's body is literally and symbolically taken from him by disease. As surgeons enter it, leaving gaping holes sutured with wire, and tumors grow out of it to transform its familiar planes and angles, the subject is unhoused and finds himself searching for verification of existence: "The lumps of the cancer are everywhere now, / he can lay his palm where they swell his skin, he can / finger the holes where the surgeon has been in him. / He asks me to touch them" (ll. 13–15). The "them" that Olds's father asks her to touch may be lumps or holes, two sides of a boundary rendered permeable by a disease that leaves father as well as daughter probing the surfaces of the body as a way of mapping the unintelligible flux of illness.

6. Olds's look here bears some resemblance to what Kaja Silverman describes as the "productive" look: "The ethical becomes operative not at the moment when unconscious desire and phobias assume possession of our look, but in a subsequent moment, when we take stock of what we have just 'seen,' and attempt . . . to look again, differently" (Silverman 1996, 173). The "productive looking" that Silverman describes, however, requires "a constant conscious reworking of the terms under which we unconsciously look at the objects that people our visual landscape" (184). Insofar as the speaker of Olds's poem immediately identifies with her father's body—"Right away / I saw how much his hips are like mine"—the dynamics of looking she displays diverge from the conscious acts of relooking Silverman describes.

7. In "Reflections on Trauma, Absence, and Loss," Dominick LaCapra marks an important distinction between empathy and full identification with the trauma victim that is relevant here: "empathy that resists full identification with, and appropriation of, the experience of the other would depend both on one's own potential for traumatization (related to absence and structural trauma) and on one's recognition that another's loss is not identical with one's own loss" (LaCapra 2000, 196).

Haunted Images

1. See, for example, Douglas Crimp's "Portraits of People with AIDS" (2002). Crimp includes Nixon's photographs among media images portraying people with AIDS as "ravaged, disfigured, and debilitated" victims of their own immorality (86). The sympathy elicited by these portrayals, he contends, contributes to the Othering process. Crimp argues that such images mainly express "the terror at imagining the person with AIDS is still sexual" (106), and singles out Stashu Kybartas's documentary, *Danny,* as a non-exploitative portrayal because of it formulates "the relationship between artist and subject not as one of empathy or identification, but as one of explicit sexual desire" (100).

2. The focus that I adopt here marginalizes other equally important approaches to

the photographs that I discuss. Perhaps the most significant omission in my argument is the absence of any discussion of the cultural construction of AIDS as a disease associated with gay men. Although not all the photographs I discuss here are representations of gay men, issues of sexuality and desire connected with these images frequently return the viewer to political issues connected with homosexuality. For discussions of the sexual politics of representations of people with AIDS, see, for example, Thomas Yingling and Robyn Wegman (1997), John-Manuel Andriote (1999), Douglas Crimp (2002), and Sarah Brophy (2004).

3. For a useful overview of photographic representations of people with AIDS, see Michael Bronski, "Picturing Aids" (2000).

4. Describing the "bulk of photography" as "naturalizing in its effect," Michael J. Shapiro observes, "This is primarily because of the historically forged link between photography and evidence or truth, a link which presents a greater barrier against critique or demystification than other forms of writing in which it is more difficult for the writer or the writing to be distanced from the production of meaning and in which the interpretive codes of readers are more diverse and contentious" (*The Politics of Representation,* 1988, 135).

5. The communicability of AIDS, of course, raises issues of literal and symbolic contagion often inseparable from questions of sexual identity. Although AIDS shares many of the properties of other terminal illnesses, it also functions culturally and politically in unique ways. For a discussion of cultural responses to AIDS as opposed to other terminal illnesses, see Susan Sontag, *AIDS and Its Metaphors* (1989).

6. I will purposefully limit my analysis to the photographs in these two collections; a critical exploration of how the written texts of these works signify with and against their visual images remains to be undertaken.

7. Monika Gagnon has charted the significance of the photograph in producing knowledge of AIDS: "The imperative to visualize, confirm, and fix AIDS on the body solves the 'problem' of how to know the disease—how to understand what is in fact an invisible cellular disorder within the body—yet again, situating the confirmation of knowledge in the visual field, a visuality that is itself a discursive production. Knowledge, then, can be produced visually, and knowledge of HIV infection and AIDS is produced, in many ways invented, by the photograph" (Gagnon 1992, 61). I have chosen to focus on Billy Howard's *Epitaphs for the Living* and Nicholas Nixon's *People with AIDS* in part because the contrast between them reveals the extent to which their photographs not only produce but invent knowledge.

8. Shapiro provides a very helpful discussion of this issue in *The Politics of Representation* (1988).

9. See *The Body in Pain* (1985), especially pp. 27–59.

10. For a fuller discussion of the way the visual codes of AIDS signify, see Sontag's *AIDS and Its Metaphors.*

11. See Sigmund Freud, "Fetishism" (1953–74).

12. The question of how the subject's sexual orientation may or may not be coded visually is an issue that my analysis doesn't tackle here. On the one hand, homosexuality sets the subject apart from the culturally normative status that his looks might otherwise imply. On the other hand, it could be argued that advertising, film, and popular culture are happy to exploit the beauty of the (gay) male body as long as sexual orientation is not coded in a manner disruptive to the (straight) gaze.

13. This imagining is fueled both by the viewer's knowledge of the content of the book and the caption that accompanies the photograph, which begins, "We are all born terminal."

14. The marginalized gloss that in many ways overshadows the portrait of Howard's subject parallels the advent of new methods for detecting HIV infection; in the context

of such knowledge, Jan Zita Grover observes, "the threat of AIDS was no longer embodied only in people with visible lesions: it might also be your neighbour (who looked a little effeminate), your boss or your secretary. . . . The invisibility of infection threw into question the comfortable categories that had kept anxieties manageable for many 'low-risk' people and reinforced the need to shore them up" (Grover 1992, 35).

15. The gritty medical "realism" of these photographs is only part of their story; Shapiro's discussion of realist images from painting to photography provides another way into Nixon's reiterative visual narratives of dying: "Our resistance or possible distancing from the re-presenting of a particular reality is overcome to the extent that we fail to recognize we are created as a subject/viewer as the objects are rendered in a particular way. . . . [W]e fail to see that the painting's reality *for us* is an enactment, reflecting a reality-making process in which we are implicated as users of visual codes" (Shapiro 1988, 136).

16. Bethany Ogdon offers a detailed description of how Nixon's photographic procedures also disrupt the conventional assumption that the photographic subject is looking at the viewer. Nixon's use of a large 8 x 10 camera, she observes, dictates the appearance that the subject focuses the gaze on something closer than the camera. "Because the photographic subject's gaze doesn't meet the viewer's," Ogdon argues, "the viewer may feel placed in the uncomfortable position of voyeur" (Ogdon 2001, 81).

17. The parallels between Nixon's photographs and photographs of holocaust victims are clear here, although I would argue that the experience of dying from AIDS, in which the assault on the body is launched by the body's own immune system, has important consequences for its unique representation.

18. Focusing on Nixon's signature camera work in *People with AIDS,* Bethany Ogdon argues that Nixon's terminally ill subjects are no more inanimate or objectified than the healthy subjects in his other photographic series. Nixon's use of close-up on bodily detail, she claims, uniformly transforms and effaces his subjects: "The grotesqueness of Nixon's People with AIDS photographs, then, results not from the photograph's presenting in such sharp detail the lesions of Kaposi's sarcoma or even the more generally symptomatic wasting away associated with many AIDS-related illnesses. It results from the photographs' rendering the subjects devoid of animation, and in this way forcing them to undergo an 'absolute change'" (Ogdon 2001, 87). Although I applaud Ogdon's focus on the technical elements of Nixon's photographs, it seems fabulous to suggest that the viewer makes no distinction between a body made grotesque when its hairs and pores are rendered visible and the body of a person with AIDS made grotesque by the symptoms of that illness coming into closer view. Although Ogdon goes to great pains to divorce the power dynamics of viewership from the terminally ill body's presentation of the narrative of illness (88), the existence of social conventions defining the visual appearance of AIDS at the time that Nixon's photographs were published makes it impossible, I would argue, to separate Nixon's use of close-up from culturally sanctioned visual paradigms which intensify the viewer's tendency to perceive people with AIDS as emaciated, lesioned Others; the "absolute change" of the close-up body marks, I would argue, the absolute physical, social, and personal change effected by AIDS.

19. Irving Kenneth Zola explores the idea of patient "responsibility" for illness in his analysis of medicine as an institution of social control (Zola 2001).

The Body in the Waiting Room

1. In recent cultural and philosophical analysis, theories of the body have become increasingly entwined with questions about space. Although Maurice Merleau-Ponty's

Phenomenology of Perception (1962) charts the way in which body and space are interconnected and Henri Lefebvre's *The Production of Space* (1991) suggests the impossibility of abstracting the body and our understanding of it from its relationship to space, recent works have begun to probe the relationship between bodies and space in great detail. Works in this area range from Richard Sennett's *Flesh and Stone: The Body and the City in Western Civilization* (1994), a history of the city told through bodily experience, to psychoanalytic studies that explore the ways in which embodied subjects can be understood through a "psychoanalysis of space" (Steve Pile, *The Body and the City: Psychoanalysis, Space, and Subjectivity,* 1996; see also Elizabeth Grosz, *Space, Time, and Perversion: Essays on the Politics of Bodies,* 1995, and Radhika Mohanram's *Black Body: Women, Colonialism, and Space,* 1999).

2. These ideas are central to the arguments of both Lennard Davis's *Enforcing Normalcy: Disability, Deafness, and the Body* (1995) and Rosemarie Garland Thomson's *Extraordinary Bodies: Figuring Physical Disability in American Culture and Literature* (1997).

3. In *Heaven's Coast,* Doty links the dying person's entrapment in and as the body of the patient to the spatial configuration of a waiting room that announces "that there's no place else to go" (1996, 86). Hamilton's literal representation of a hospital in which "nothing was rooted to the floor" is echoed in Doty's more abstract discussion of the way patients' severed attachments to the familiar contexts of their lives are reflected in the anonymous spaces in which they are immobilized, spaces that "have in common the absence of context" (1996, 86).

4. If the healthy body can be rendered symbolically ill due to its immobilization and lack of productivity in the medical waiting room, the opposite is also true; as Davis observes in *Enforcing Normalcy,* "Value is tied to the ability to earn money. If one's body is productive, it is not disabled" (131). Although I don't explore it here, capitalism's role in the cultural equation between health, normality, and productivity is clearly a significant one.

5. The medical waiting room, it could be argued, functions to express in spatial terms an experience of time associated with critical illness. Literary representations of life-threatening illness often echo the theme of expulsion from the narrative world of the present. Paul Zweig's memoir, *Departures,* recounts his response to diagnosis with lymphoma as sudden immersion in a world "where there was no time": "Time had been cut off from before my face. The world was unchanged. The streets were full of cars and pedestrians; the sun still caught in the windows of buildings. The radio reported worldwide events. Everything was the same, but time had been removed. And without time, everything was unreal, but I was horribly real, oversized, bursting as a body bursts in a vacuum" (1986, 203). In "The Ship Pounding," a poem about his wife's battle with cancer, Donald Hall figures her oncology ward as a ship that seemed to promise return to "a harbor / of breakfast, work, and love" to all who board; by poem's end, the trope of the voyage dissolves into an image of a docked ship that locks its passengers in an experience of motionless, undifferentiated time, a huge "vessel that heaves water month / after month, without leaving / port, without moving a knot, / without arrival or destination, / its great engines pounding" (1998, ll. 30–34).

6. Although I invoke disability theory throughout my argument, what I see as useful parallels between the disabled body and the body threatened by illness or death in the waiting room should not obscure differences between the categories of "illness" and "disability" and the ways in which they are deployed in our culture.

7. Attention to the power dynamics of the gaze in this situation shouldn't push aside the immediacy of concerns of contagion and exposure for AIDS patients with suppressed immune systems in the waiting rooms they share.

The Contours of Grief

1. In spite of the fact that I address theories of mourning at various points in this book, I define my interest in loss largely in terms of grief rather than mourning. Although the colloquial and theoretical definitions of grief and mourning vary, I agree with Tammy Clewell's assertion that "mourning names an experience of grief and a process of working through during which the mourner relinquishes emotional ties to the lost object" (Clewell 2002, 44). An embodied theory of loss, I will argue, problematizes prevailing models of mourning as emotional relinquishment. The term "grief" seems to me less laden with cultural and theoretical assumptions that implicitly endorse existing disembodied models of loss.

2. In his fascinating essay "Doubtful Arms and Phantom Limbs: Literary Portrayals of Embodied Grief" (2004), James Krasner uses the theory of embodied loss I develop here as a stepping stone to explore the way that the lost body registers its continuing presence in the survivor's experience of embodiment as a kind of phantom limb registered in posture, habit, and perception.

3. Gail Weiss explores this idea in more depth in *Body Images: Embodiment as Intercorporeality* (1998).

4. Merleau-Ponty's application of this concept to objects raises a series of questions about the role of the inanimate body in chiasmic perception. For the purposes of this chapter, I will not engage in debate about whether or not our relationships with objects can be fruitfully understood within Merleau-Ponty's model of chiasm. Instead, I will concentrate on the chiasmic relationship between human bodies; this relationship most clearly and most literally expresses the dynamic of reversibility that Merleau-Ponty describes.

5. Despite a number of important critiques, Freud's work on mourning continues to provide a frame of reference for cultural and psychoanalytic definitions of loss. In *The Ends of Mourning*, Alessia Ricciardi traces a twentieth-century genealogy of mourning that begins with Freud and encompasses Butler, Derrida, Kristeva, and Lacan. She argues provocatively, "The passage from a Freudian vision of loss as a contingent, historical event to the Lacanian view of lack as an a priori, ontological condition of psychic life marks a decisive shift in the way that psychoanalysis as a discipline conceptualizes the relationship between subject and object" (2003, 27). In her persuasive critique of the way Lacanian theories of loss obscure the historical location of the object, Ricciardi analyzes how contemporary understandings of the aesthetic, especially in cinema, establish "the space of an encounter with the Real, a confrontation that advances beyond nostalgia to open a new way of thinking and remembrance. . . . cinema is proposed as the performance of remembrance, not the glorification of simulacra" (205). Rather than pursue the psychoanalytic genealogy of dehistoricization that Ricciardi traces, a genealogy that aligns Freud with acknowledgment of loss as a contingent, historical event, my argument would read her critique of a postmodernism politics of detachment back onto Freud's "Mourning and Melancholia" to explore the way Freud's text implicitly dematerializes the subject. Such dematerialization, I would argue, paves the way for the shift that Ricciardi describes. Attending to the lived body, on the other hand, demands acknowledging its placement both in time and in space; whereas contemporary theories of loss strip mourning of its historicity, the need to reconstruct "the specificity and ethical urgency of loss" (47) demands the critique of a disembodied dynamic of mourning that originates with Freud. I engage with Ricciardi's argument in more depth in chapter 5. For a relevant discussion of how academic discourses thrive by consuming the very traumas they would expose, see Patricia Yaeger's "Consuming Trauma; or, The Pleasures of Merely Circulating" (2002).

6. In "Mourning beyond Melancholia: Freud's Psychoanalysis of Loss," Tammy Clewell critiques Woodward's "otherwise insightful" analysis of Freud's theory of mourning by pointing out that the theory of loss Woodward posits as Freud's represents his early views on mourning and "neglects the substantially revised theory Freud proposes in *The Ego and the Id*" (Clewell 2002, 47). Clewell's contextualization of "Mourning and Melancholia" within the body of Freud's writings is significant, especially in the context of psychoanalytic dialogues about loss. I would suggest, however, that the continuing cultural currency of Freud's early work renders justifiable its primacy in Woodward's argument—and in my argument as well.

7. Although I do not look at the concept of embodied grief in gendered terms, Sandra M. Gilbert suggests a basis for doing so in her provocative essay, "Widow."

8. Although she doesn't address this passage, Christine Caver calls attention to what she describes as Ruth's repeated "rhetorical strategy of affirmation through denial" in *Housekeeping* (132).

9. In "Sighs Too Deep for Words," George Toles makes the argument that "privation or lack ultimately *does* accommodate those in the world of *Housekeeping* who put their faith in it" (1991, 138). Although I agree with Toles's insistence that Robinson's metaphor needs to "find ways to engage us at the level of lived experience" (138), his conclusion locates that experience in a model of subjectivity which posits a disembodied psyche: "So whatever we may lose, very craving gives it back again. It is out of lack, perhaps, that the psyche always renews its images" (155). Karen Kaviola convincingly critiques Toles's affirmation of the compensations of loss in the novel by calling attention to the tensions in Ruth's narrative: "Ruth would have us believe that in the present narrative moment she is beyond loss.... But given the way Ruth tells her story, she's not entirely convincing, for her narrative is filled with deprivation, pain, and longing" (Kaviola 1993, 682). Instead, Kaviola concludes, "the text suggests that there can be no adequate compensation in Ruth's present for the acute deprivations of her past" (689).

10. In writing to a friend whose child had recently died, Freud acknowledges the partiality of his own recuperation after the death of his daughter. He observes, "Although we know that after such a loss the acute state of mourning will subside, we also know we shall remain inconsolable and will never find a substitute. No matter what may fill the gap, even if it be filled completely, it nonetheless remains something else" (Freud 1960, 386).

11. Tsu-Chung Su frames the text's relationship to grief in slightly different terms: "The grief inflicted by the affective punctum of the Winter Garden Photograph is the pure grief which cannot be recuperated by transforming grief into mourning. There is only pure grief, not mourning, not grief transformed nor purified" (Su 1995, 40).

12. In describing rather than reproducing the photograph of his mother, Barthes retains control of its interpretation, as Joann Blais observes: "By declining to represent himself, by refusing to produce his mother's photograph, the subject circumvents the process of figuration, thus protecting his own freedom to invent himself" (Blais 1994, 236). Erin C. Mitchell also offers an extended analysis of this phenomenon in three texts, including *Camera Lucida*.

13. Mary Bittner Wiseman emphasizes the significance of the child's corporeality in terms that support my argument: "the photograph of the never-seen body is, then, neither mechanical substitute memory nor an aid to memory; it is rather a counter-memory, traversing time, backwards" (Wiseman 1989, 40).

14. In a move that emphasizes the significance of Barthes's reference to the embodied subject, Joann Blais reads this question as a send-up of Descartes.

15. Michael Moriarty observes that in *Camera Lucida* "Barthes reverts to the phenomenological method of taking one's consciousness as the measure of the object, though stressing, as we saw, the bodily dimension of this consciousness" (Moriarty 1991,

202). Joann Blais observes, "The book's subject . . . becomes sensual, reading through the frames of his memories, his desire, his emotions, his unfigured body" (Blais 1994, 231).

16. Joann Blais reads this failure as staged: "*Camera Lucida* is an explicitly staged memory, a staged performance of contradiction and negation, a shifting of ground that slyly mimics the acts of hermeneutic investigation while preparing for the very failure—the negation—of that inquiry" (235).

Teaching the Body to Talk

1. *The Dogs of Babel* locates language in the body as it emphasizes not just the physiology of articulation but the sensory apprehension of words. After painting the kitchen a bright yellow, Lexy informs Paul that she has left him a surprise. Wandering around to touch one object after another—new sponges, a can of chickpeas, heads of garlic—he is unable to "locate" the surprise Lexy leaves for him until the next day, when a secret border of words she painted on the wall suddenly emerges; her message is written in a translucent glaze rendered visible only from a certain angle, when illuminated by the slant of morning light. "Almost transparent," the words Lexy paints are nonetheless material; their message—"I love you"—can't be held like a sponge or stacked like a series of cans, but emerges as apprehensible only when the perceiving body and its physical environment conspire to locate language in space.

2. For a discussion of the language game, see *Philosophical Investigations*, especially pages 2–26.

3. As Lexy's words provide one means of accessing hidden meaning, the novel casually locates its most important secret in her body as Paul discovers the fact of her pregnancy.

4. My critique of Freudian theories of mourning in chapter 4 reflects my assumption of the continued cultural currency of Freud's theories of loss.

5. See Adam Begley (2001), Tim Adams (2001), and Eric Wittmershaus (2001).

6. Despite the easy intimacy of the novel's first chapter, Lauren's knowledge of her husband is also revealed to be limited, partial, constructed; she has no idea he is about to kill himself, doesn't know he owns a gun, cannot access the depths of his inner being: "you lie next to your husband after you've made love and breathe the heat of his merciless dreams and wonder who he is, tenderly ponder the truth you'll never know" (56).

7. See James Krasner (2004).

8. Later, glimpsing for the second time a white-haired Japanese woman whose body she had appropriated as a vehicle for her performance piece on grief, Lauren zeroes in on a perceptual illusion that renders the woman handless, unable to touch or hold: "She wore a padded jacket and had her hands concealed. Her hands were fisted up inside the sleeves of her jacket, for warmth, and she watched the woman, sleeves seemingly empty, and cursed herself for not having thought of this for the piece, because it was fantastic, no hands, it was everything she needed to know about the woman and would have been perfect for the piece, inexplicably missing hands" (117–118). The "inexplicably missing hands" of this woman register through materialized absence the ineffectual reach of a mourner who projects herself "through the intermediary of the body" toward an embodied absence. If the unlimited consciousness that *The Body Artist* explores in chapter 1 implies a disembodied freedom, this image denaturalizes that conception of consciousness to locate grief on the body in and through which consciousness experiences loss.

9. After his death, Rey's existence in Lauren's consciousness assumes a virtual qual-

ity that the novel links with the reflection in a mirror: "When she could not remember what he looked like, she leaned into a mirror and there he was, not really, only hintingly, barely at all, but there in a way, in a manner of thinking, in some mirrors more than others, more than rueful reproduction, depending on the hour and the light and the quality of the glass, the strategies of the glass, with its reversal of left and right, this room or that, because every image in every mirror is only virtual, even when you expect to see yourself" (114–115). Lauren's perception of the image in the mirror parallels her experience of Rey's presence in her consciousness; there but not there, he exists not in embodied form but "in a manner of thinking." Using the mirror as an intermediary vehicle that would reflect back toward a body she can see but not see, Lauren takes comfort in the tenuous continuity between the mediation of the glass and the perceptual fog of memory as she struggles to embody her memory of Rey, rendering it, like the mirror's image, "more than rueful reproduction."

10. Although Philip Nel makes this point as well, he does not connect the form of Mr. Tuttle's speech with Lauren's experience of grief.

11. Philip Nel applies this passage from Garrett Stewart's discussion of *The Waves* to *The Body Artist*.

12. Merleau-Ponty's work on gesture emphasizes the impossibility of isolating thought from embodiment in the act of communication: "What I communicate with primarily is not 'representations' or thought, but a speaking subject, with a certain style of being and with the 'world' at which he directs his aim" (1962, 183).

13. Merleau-Ponty describes the need to renounce "the bifurcation of the 'consciousness of' and the object, by admitting that my synergic body is not an object, that it assembles into a cluster of the 'consciousnesses' adherent to its hands, to its eyes, by an operation that is in relation to them lateral, transversal" (1968, 141).

14. A person's two hands, Elizabeth Grosz observes, "remain irreducible to each other (the left hand feeling the right hand is not the same as the right hand feeling the left), split between touching and being touched, in spite of their potential interchangeability" (1994, 102).

15. Existence, in Merleau-Ponty's terms, "is not a set of facts (like 'psychic facts') capable of being reduced to others or to which they can reduce themselves, but the ambiguous setting of their inter-communication, the point at which their boundaries run into each other, or again their woven fabric" (1962, 166).

16. In its concluding sentences, the novel makes explicit the fact that Lauren's motion into the bedroom is also a reintroduction to space and time: "She threw the window open. She didn't know why she did this. Then she knew. She wanted to feel the sea tang on her face and the flow of time in her body, to tell her who she was" (126).

Objects of Grief

1. Describing his own frustration with his elderly parents' insistence on determining who would inherit the pieces of furniture they treasure after their death, Stallybrass observes, "At first, I found such questions tiresome. To a good post-Cartesian, it all seemed rather grossly material. But, of course, I was wrong, and they were right. For the questions are: Who will remember my grandmother, who will give her a place? What space, and whom, will my father inhabit?" (Stallybrass 1999, 42).

2. Interrogating the very forms of mediation his poem enacts, Doty returns again and again throughout "The Wings" to aesthetic demands that the body bend, recede, transform, or disappear to accommodate itself to the immaterial forms of art. "The Wings" invokes *Wings of Desire,* a film in which the director's representation of angels

emphasizes the tension between the angels' bodilessness and the extreme embodiment of the actors who portray them: "the director pictures them perched / on the balustrades, clustering / on the stairs, bent over / the solitary readers. . . ." In each example mentioned, action and intention point back to the body; as we are returned again and again to the awkward postures of the actors who portray the angels, Doty's representation belies the understanding of their bodies as mere artistic conventions. Because of the obvious ways that filmic representation depends upon distancing conventions—live actors playing fictional characters whose bodies are accessed by the viewing audience only through projected images—film embodies tensions Doty associates with all art. Caught between the inability to "get past" the actors' real bodies and the impossibility of accessing them, the film viewer experiences the story by continually bracketing the distracting fact of the actors' embodiment, closeting that which can neither be expelled from nor accessed through representation.

3. If the poem's first section traces the speaker's ability to transform the physical perception of material objects into the image of an angel, Doty here attempts to reclaim from the poetic figure he has constructed the materiality of the snowshoes/wings. In this case, the return of the image to object status reflects not a process of aesthetic collapse but a desperate attempt to bridge the gap between subject and object, word and body, sign and thing.

4. I viewed Megan Brown's panel and the panels that I describe in the pages that follow at an exhibit of the AIDS Memorial Quilt in Albany, New York, in January 2003.

Postscript

1. My thanks to Anne Fleche for her ideas about the show.
2. See, for example, Powell (2002), Sengupta (2001), Worth (2001), Lipton (2001), Murphy (2001), Gellman and Blumenfeld (2001), Christian (2002), Faber and Eisenberg (2005), and Gittrich (2002).
3. See, for example, Worth, Faber, Gittrich, and Lipton.
4. See, for example, Powell and Murphy.
5. When it became clear that blood supply had quickly outstripped demand, some agencies stopped accepting donations. Others, like the Red Cross, continued to make donor appeals, with officials citing not just the potential need for blood but the fact that blood donation became a way for Americans to respond to their grief (Davis 2001).

Bibliography

Abraham, Nicholas, and Maria Torok. 1986. *The Wolf Man's Magic Word: A Cryptonymy*. Translated by Nicholas Rand. Minneapolis: University of Minnesota Press.
———. 1994. "Mourning or Melancholia: Introjection versus Incorporation." In *The Shell and the Kernel: Renewals of Psychoanalysis*, vol 1., edited and translated by Nicholas T. Rand, 125–138. Chicago: University of Chicago Press.
Adams, Tim. 2001. "The Library in the Body." *Guardian* February 1. http://books.guardian.co.uk/reviews/generalfiction/0,6121,436287,00.html.
Agee, James. 1998. *A Death in the Family*. New York: Vintage Books.
Aldrich, Marcia. 1989. "The Poetics of Transience: Marilynne Robinson's *Housekeeping*." *Essays in Literature* 16, no. 1: 127–140.
Andriote, John-Manuel. 1999. *Victory Deferred: How AIDS Changed Gay Life in America*. Chicago: University of Chicago Press.
Ariès, Philippe. 1981. *The Hour of Our Death*. Translated by Helen Weaver. New York: Knopf.
Bargreen, Melinda. 2002. "'Lovely Bones': Comfort in Wake of Death." *Seattle Times*, July 14, K10.
Barthes, Roland. 1981. *Camera Lucida*. Translated by Richard Howard. New York: Hill and Wang.
Bassin, Donna. 2003. "A Not So Temporary Occupation inside Ground Zero." In *Trauma at Home after 9/11*, edited by Judith Greenberg, 195–203. Lincoln: University of Nebraska Press.
Baudrillard, Jean. 1994. *Simulacra and Simulation*. Translated by Sheila Faria Glaser. Ann Arbor: University of Michigan Press.
———. 1996. *The System of Objects*. Translated by James Benedict. London: Verso.
Baysa, Koan Jeff. Review of "Ashes" by Olu Oguibe. http://www.camwood.org/ashespress/html.
Bedient, Calvin. 1993. "Sentencing Eros." *Salmagundi* 97: 169–181.

Begley, Adam. 2001. Review of *The Body Artist*. *New York Times Book Review*. February 4, 106:12.
Bennett, Jill. 2003. "The Limits of Empathy and the Global Politics of Belonging." In *Trauma at Home after 9/11*, edited by Judith Greenberg, 132–138. Lincoln: University of Nebraska Press.
Berger, John. 1982. "Stories." In *Another Way of Telling* by John Berger and Jean Mohr, 277–290. New York: Pantheon Books.
Blais, Joann. 1994. "Negation and the Evil Eye: A Reading of *Camera Lucida*." In *Negation, Critical Theory, and Postmodern Textuality*, edited by D. Fischlin, 227–239. Dordrecht and Boston: Kluwer.
Bloomer, Kent C., and Charles Moore. 1977. *Body, Memory, and Architecture*. New Haven: Yale University Press.
Bond, Anthony. 1999. "TRACE: A Historical Contextualization of the Theme." Trace: 1st Liverpool Biennial of International Contemporary Art. http://www.artgallery.nsw.gov.au/staff/tonybond/lectures/1999/trace.
Bordo, Susan. 1997. "Normalization and Resistance in the Era of the Image." In *Feminisms*, edited by Sandra Kemp and Judith Squires, 451–454. New York: Oxford University Press.
Bronfen, Elisabeth. 1992. *Over Her Dead Body: Death, Femininity, and the Aesthetic*. New York: Routledge.
Bronski, Michael. 2000. "Picturing AIDS." *Artery: The AIDS Arts Forum*. November 30. http://www.artistswithaids.org/artery/.
Brooks, Peter. 1985. *Reading for the Plot: Design and Intention in Narrative*. New York: Random House.
———. 1993. *Body Work: Objects of Desire in Modern Narrative*. Cambridge: Harvard University Press.
Brophy, Sarah. 2004. *Witnessing AIDS: Writing, Testimony, and the Work of Mourning*. Toronto: University of Toronto Press.
Brown, Bill. 2003. *A Sense of Things: The Object Matter of American Literature*. Chicago: University of Chicago Press.
———. 2004. "Thing Theory." In *Things*, edited by Bill Brown, 1–22. Chicago: University of Chicago Press.
Broyard, Anatole. 1992. *Intoxicated by My Illness*. New York: Clarkson Potter.
Broyard, Sandy. 2005. *Standby*. New York: Knopf.
Caldwell, Gail. 2001. "Winter's Tales." *Boston Globe*. December 2, E1.
———. 2002. "Winged Victory: Narrated by a Slain Teenager Turned Guardian Angel, 'The Lovely Bones' Acutely Portrays Heaven and the Here and Now." *Boston Globe*, August 4, D3.
Cameron, Sharon. 1991. "Representing Grief: Emerson's 'Experience.'" In *The New American Studies*, edited by Philip Fisher, 201–227. Berkeley: University of California Press.
Casey, Edward S. 1997. *The Fate of Place: A Philosophical History*. Berkeley: University California Press.
———. 1998. "The Ghost of Embodiment: On Bodily Habitudes and Schemata." In *Body and Flesh: A Philosophical Reader*, edited by Donn Welton, 207–226. Malden, Mass: Blackwell.

Cataldi, Suzanne Laba. 2000. "Embodying Perceptions of Death: Emotional Apprehension and Reversibilities of Flesh." In *Chiasms: Merleau-Ponty's Notion of Flesh,* edited by Fred Evans and Leonard Lawlor, 189–202. Albany: State University of New York Press.

Caver, Christine. 1996. "Nothing Left to Lose: *Housekeeping*'s Strange Freedoms." *American Literature* 68, no. 1: 111–137.

Christian, Nicholas. 2002. "Remains of More Bodies Found at Ground Zero." *Scotsman Publications,* June 9, 18.

Clewell, Tammy. 2002. "Mourning beyond Melancholia: Freud's Psychoanalysis of Loss." *Journal of the American Psychoanalytic Association* 52, no. 1: 43–67.

Connerton, Paul. 1989. *How Societies Remember.* Cambridge: Cambridge University Press.

Corrigan, Maureen. 2001. Review of *The Body Artist. Fresh Air,* January 23. National Public Radio.

Creekmur, Corey K. 1996. "Lost Objects: Photography, Fiction, and Mourning." In *Photo-Textualities,* edited by Marsha Bryant, 73–84. Newark: University of Delaware Press.

Crimp, Douglas. 2002. "Portraits of People with AIDS." In *Melancholia and Moralism: Essays on AIDS and Queer Politics,* 83–108. Cambridge: MIT Press.

Dale, Leigh, and Simon Ryan, editors. 1998. *The Body in the Library.* Atlanta: Rodopi.

Darton, Eric. 1999. *Divided We Stand: A Biography of New York's World Trade Center.* New York: Basic Books.

Davis, Lennard J. 1995. *Enforcing Normalcy: Disability, Deafness, and the Body.* New York: Verso.

Davis, Robert. 2001. "Blood Given after Sept. 11 Going Bad." *USA Today,* October 25, 5A.

Dawes, James. 1995. "Narrating Disease: AIDS, Consent, and the Ethics of Representation." *Social Text* 43: 27–44.

de Certeau, Michel. 1984. *The Practice of Everyday Life.* Translated by Steven F. Rendall. Berkeley: University of California Press.

DeLillo, Don. 2001a. *The Body Artist.* New York: Simon & Schuster.

———. 2001b. "In the Ruins of the Future." *Harper's Magazine,* December, 33–41.

De Zengotita, Thomas. 2002. "The Numbing of the American Mind." *Harper's Magazine,* April, 33–41.

Doane, Mary Ann. 1985. "The Clinical Eye: Medical Discourses in the 'Woman's Film' of the 1940s." In *The Female Body in Western Culture,* edited by Susan R. Suleiman, 152–174. Cambridge: Harvard University Press.

Donnelly, Nora. "Interview with Shellburne Thurber by Nora Donnelly." In *HOME: Photographs of Shellburne Thurber,* 19–20. Boston: Institute of Contemporary Art.

Doty, Mark. 1993. "The Wings." In *My Alexandria.* Urbana: University of Illinois Press.

———. 1996. *Heaven's Coast.* New York: HarperCollins.

———. 2001. *Still Life with Oysters and Lemon.* Boston: Beacon Press.

Douglas, Mary. 1969. *Purity and Danger.* Boston: Routledge.

Eco, Umberto. 1984. *Semiotics and the Philosophy of Language.* Bloomington: Indiana University Press.

Elkins, James. 1996. *The Object Stares Back: On the Nature of Seeing.* San Diego: Harcourt.
Elsey, Judy. 1992. "The Rhetoric of the NAMES Project AIDS Quilt: Reading the Text(ile)." In *AIDS: The Literary Perspective,* edited by Emmanual S. Nelson, 187–196. New York: Twayne.
Emerson, Ralph Waldo. 1983. "Experience." In Ralph Waldo Emerson, *Essays and Lectures,* edited by Joel Porte. New York: The Library of America.
Evans, Fred, and Leonard Lawlor, eds. 2000. *Chiasms: Merleau-Ponty's Notion of Flesh,* 1–22. Albany: State University of New York Press.
"Eyewitness Account from firefighter at 'ground zero.'" 2001. *Trusteesandestates.com* September 17. http://www.trustsandestates.com/ar/estate_eyewitness_acount_firefighter.
Faber, Lindsay, and Carol Eisenberg. 2005. "161 Still Missing; Medical Examiner's Office Says There's Not Enough DNA to Identify the Remains of WTC Victims." *Newsday* (New York), February 23, A07.
Featherstone, Mike. 2001. "The Body in Consumer Culture." In *The American Body in Context,* edited by Jessica R. Johnston, 79–102. Wilmington: Scholarly Resources.
Foucault, Michel. 1973. *The Birth of the Clinic: An Archaeology of Medical Perception.* Translated by A. M. Sheridan Smith. New York: Pantheon.
——. 1977. *Discipline and Punish: The Birth of the Prison.* Translated by Alan Sheridan. New York: Vintage.
Freud, Sigmund. 1953–1974. "Fetishism." *The Standard Edition of the Complete Psychological Works of Sigmund Freud,* vol. 21. Translated by James Strachey, 152–157. London: Hogarth.
——. 1957. "Mourning and Melancholia." *The Standard Edition of the Complete Psychological Works of Sigmund Freud,* volume 14. Translated by James Strachey, 243–258. London: Hogarth.
——. 1960. *Letters of Sigmund Freud.* Edited by Ernest L. Freud. Translated by Tanya Stern and James Stern. New York: Basic Books.
Gagnon, Monika. 1992. "A Convergence of Stakes: Photography, Feminism, and AIDS." In *Fluid Exchanges: Artists and Critics in the AIDS Crisis,* edited by James Miller. Toronto: University of Toronto Press.
Gellman, Barton, and Laura Blumenfeld. 2001. "Sifting, Moving 16 Acres of Rubble; Debris Field Holds Evidence of Crime, Remains of Thousands." *Washington Post,* September 14, A22.
Gilbert, Sandra M. 2001."Widow." *Critical Inquiry* 27, no. 4: 559–579.
——. 2006 (forthcoming). *Death's Door: Modern Dying and the Ways We Grieve.* New York: Norton.
Gilman, Sander. 1988. *Disease and Representation: Images of Illness from Madness to AIDS.* Ithaca: Cornell University Press.
Gittrich Greg. 2002. "3 Bravest Remains Found; Last Rubble Pile Has Yielded 18 Bodies since Tuesday." *Daily News* (New York), March 14, 23.
Gole, Nilufer. 2002. "Close Encounters: Islam, Modernity, and Violence." In *Understanding September 11,* edited by Craig Calhoun, Paul Price, and Ashley Timmer, 332–344. New York: The New Press.

Gonzalez, Jennifer. 1995. "Autotopographies." In *Prosthetic Territories*, edited by Gabriel Brahm Jr. and Mark Driscoll, 133–150. Boulder: Westview Press.

Goodwin, Sarah Webster, and Elisabeth Bronfen, editors. 1993. *Death and Representation*. Baltimore: Johns Hopkins University Press.

Gottdiener, M. 1995. *Postmodern Semiotics: Material Culture and the Forms of Postmodern Life*. Cambridge: Blackwell.

Greenberg, Judith. 2003. "Wounded New York." In *Trauma at Home after 9/11*, edited by Judith Greenberg, 21–38. Lincoln: University of Nebraska Press.

Grosz, Elizabeth. 1994. *Volatile Bodies: Toward a Corporeal Feminism*. Bloomington: Indiana University Press.

———. 1995. *Space, Time and Perversion: Essays on the Politics of Bodies*. New York: Routledge.

Grover, Jan Zita. 1992. "Visible Lesions: Images of the Person with AIDS in America." In *Fluid Exchanges: Artists and Critics in the AIDS Crisis*, edited by James Miller. Toronto: University of Toronto Press.

Grundberg, Andy. 1990. *Crisis of the Real: Writings on Photography, 1974–1989*. New York: Aperture Foundation.

Hall, Donald. 1998. *Without*. Boston: Houghton Mifflin.

———. 2002. *The Painted Bed*. Boston: Houghton Mifflin.

Hallam, Elizabeth, and Jenny Hockey. 2001. *Death, Memory and Material Culture*. New York: Berg.

Hamilton, Jane. 1994. *A Map of the World*. New York: Doubleday.

Harmon, Louise. 1988. *Fragments on the Deathwatch*. Boston: Beacon.

Harrison, Kathryn. 2003. "What Remains." In *Seeking Rapture: Scenes from a Woman's Life*. New York: Random House.

Harrison, Robert Pogue. 2003. *The Dominion of the Dead*. Chicago: University of Chicago Press.

Hatley, James. 2000. "Recursive Incantation and Chiasmic Flesh: Two Readings of Paul Celan's *Chymisch*." In *Chiasms: Merleau-Ponty's Notion of Flesh*, edited by Fred Evans and Leonard Lawlor, 237–250. Albany: State University of New York Press.

Hawkins, Peter S. 1996. "Ars Memoriandi: The NAMES Project AIDS Quilt." In *Facing Death: Where Culture, Religion, and Medicine Meet*, edited by Howard M. Spiro et al., 166–179. New Haven: Yale University Press.

Heltzel, Ellen Emry. 2002. "The Verdict: A Stunning Mediation on Grief." *Atlanta Journal-Constitution*, July 14, 5F.

Hensher, Philip. 2002. "An Eternity of Sweet Nothings: This Heaven-set US Blockbuster Is Cute Going on Mawkish." *Observer* (London), August 11, 6.

Hentz, Patricia. 2002. "The Body Remembers: Grieving and a Circle of Time." *Qualitative Health Research* 12, no. 2: 161–172.

Herzlich, Claudine, and Janine Pierret. 1987. *Illness and Self in Society*. Translated by Elborg Forster. Baltimore: Johns Hopkins University Press.

Hirsch, Marianne. 2003. "I Took Pictures: September 2001 and Beyond." In *Trauma at Home after 9/11*, edited by Judith Greenberg, 69–86. Lincoln: University of Nebraska Press.

Holland, Sharon Patricia. 2000. *Raising the Dead: Readings of Death and (Black) Subjectivity*. Durham: Duke University Press.

Howard, Billy. 1989. *Epitaphs for the Living: Words and Images in the Time of AIDS.* Dallas: Southern Methodist University Press.

Jones, R. S. 1995. *Walking on Air.* Boston: Houghton Mifflin.

Kahane, Claire. 2003. "Uncanny Sights: The Anticipation of the Abomination." In *Trauma at Home after 9/11,* edited by Judith Greenberg, 107–116. Lincoln: University of Nebraska Press.

Kakutani, Michiko. 2002. "Books of the Times: The Power of Love Leaps the Great Divide of Death." *New York Times,* June 18, E1.

Kaplan, E. Ann. 2003. "A Camera and a Catastrophe: Reflections on Trauma and the Twin Towers." In *Trauma at Home after 9/11,* edited by Judith Greenberg, 95–106. Lincoln: University of Nebraska Press.

Kaviola, Karen. 1993. "The Pleasures and Perils of Merging: Female Subjectivity in Marilynne Robinson's *Housekeeping.*" *Contemporary Literature* 34, no. 4: 670–690.

Kenney, Susan. 1989. *Sailing.* New York: Penguin.

King, Kristin. 1996. "Resurfacings of the Deeps: Semiotic Balance in Marilynne Robinson's *Housekeeping.*" *Studies in the Novel* 28, no. 4: 565–580.

Krasner, James. 2004. "Doubtful Arms and Phantom Limbs: Literary Portrayals of Embodied Grief." *PMLA* 119, no. 2: 218–232.

Kristeva, Julia. 1982. *The Powers of Horror: An Essay on Abjection.* New York: Columbia University Press.

LaCapra, Dominick. 2000. "Reflections on Trauma, Absence, and Loss." In *Whose Freud? The Place of Psychoanalysis in Contemporary Culture,* edited by Peter Brooks and Alex Woloch, 178–204. New Haven: Yale University Press.

Laderman, Gary. 2003. *Rest in Peace: A Cultural History of Death and the Funeral Home in Twentieth-Century America.* New York: Oxford University Press.

Lefebvre, Henri. 1991. *The Production of Space.* Translated by Donald Nicholson Smith. Oxford, OX, UK and Cambridge, MA: Blackwell.

Levine, Claire. 1999. "Trying to Do It All." In *Parting Company: Understanding the Loss of a Loved One,* edited by Cynthia Pearson and Margaret L. Stubbs. Seattle: Seal Press.

Lewis, C. S. 1961. *A Grief Observed.* New York: Seabury Press.

Lingis, Alphonso. 1996. "The Body Postured and Dissolute." In *Merleau-Ponty: Difference, Materiality, Painting,* edited by Veronique M. Foti, 60–71. Atlantic Highlands, NJ: Humanities Press.

Lipton, Eric. 2001. "A Nation Challenged: The Remains; In the Ongoing Search For Bodies, Hope Is Derived from Horror." *New York Times,* December 7, B1.

Lubin, Orly. 2003. "Masked Power: An Encounter with the Social Body in the Flesh." In *Trauma at Home after 9/11,* edited by Judith Greenberg, 124–131. Lincoln: University of Nebraska Press.

Luce, Mark. 2001. "DeLillo in Miniature: 'Body Artist' Examines Identity on a Small Scale." *Atlanta Journal-Constitution,* February 4, C3.

Luke, Timothy. 2003. "From Body Politics to Body Shops: Power, Subjectivity, and the Body in an Era of Global Capitalism." In *The Politics of Selfhood: Bodies and Identities in Global Capitalism,* edited by Richard Harvey Brown, 87–108. Minneapolis: University of Minnesota Press.

Lupton, Deborah. 1988. *The Emotional Self.* London: Sage.

Maldiney, Henri. 2000. "Flesh and Verb in the Philosophy of Merleau-Ponty." In

Chiasms: Merleau-Ponty's Notion of Flesh, edited by Fred Evans and Leonard Lawlor, 51–76. Albany: State University of New York Press.

Mazis, Glen. 1996. "Matter, Dream, and the Murmurs among Things." In *Merleau-Ponty: Difference, Materiality, Painting*, edited by Veronique M. Foti. Atlantic Highlands, NJ: Humanities Press.

McElreavy, Timothy. 1999. "Camera Obscuring." In *HOME: Photographs by Shellburne Thurber*, 6–13. Boston: Institute of Contemporary Art.

McFarland, Dennis. 2000. *Singing Boy*. New York: Picador.

Merleau-Ponty, Maurice. 1962. *Phenomenology of Perception*. Translated by Colin Smith. London: Routledge & Kegan Paul.

———. 1968. *The Visible and the Invisible*. Translated by Alphonso Lingis. Edited by Claude Lefort. Evanston: Northwestern University Press.

Metz, Christian. 1985. "Photography and Fetish." *October* 34: 81–90.

Mile, Sian. 1990. "Femme Foetal: The Construction/Destruction of Female Subjectivity in *Housekeeping*, or NOTHING GAINED." *GENDERS* 8: 129–136.

Miller, Nancy K. 2003. "Reporting the Disaster." In *Trauma at Home after 9/11*, edited by Judith Greenberg, 39–47. Lincoln: University of Nebraska Press.

Mitchell, Erin C. 2000. "Writing Photography: The Grandmother in *Remembrance of Things Past*, the Mother in *Camera Lucida*, and Especially, the Mother in *The Lover*." *Studies in Twentieth-Century Literature* 24, no. 2: 325–339.

Mohanram, Radhika. 1999. *Black Body: Women, Colonialism and Space*. Minneapolis: University of Minnesota Press.

Mollison, Andrew. 2001. "Donations: As Goods Pile Up, Agencies Say: Give Money." *Atlanta Journal-Constitution*, September 16, 3A.

Moon, Michael. 1995. "Memorial Rags." In *Professions of Desire: Lesbian and Gay Studies in Literature*, edited by George E. Haggerty and Bonnie Zimmerman, 233–240. New York: Modern Language Association.

Moore, Lorrie. 1998. "People Like That Are the Only People Here: Canonical Babbling in Peed Onk." In *Birds of America*. New York: Picador.

Moriarty, Michael. 1991. *Roland Barthes*. Stanford: Stanford University Press.

Morris, Mary. 1989. *The Waiting Room*. New York: Doubleday.

Mulvey, Laura. 1978. "Visual Pleasure and Narrative Cinema." *Screen* 16, no. 3: 6–18.

Murphy, Dean E. 2001. "A Nation Challenged: The Families; Slowly, Families Accepting Ruins as Burial Ground." *New York Times*, September 29, B1.

Nel, Philip. 2002. "Don DeLillo's Return to Form: The Modernist Poetics of *The Body Artist*." *Contemporary Literature* 43, no. 4: 736–759.

Nixon, Nicholas, and Bebe Nixon. 1991. *People with AIDS*. Boston: David R. Godine.

Noel, Christopher. 1996. *In the Unlikely Event of a Water Landing: A Geography of Grief*. New York: Random House.

Nuland, Sherwin B. 1994. *How We Die*. New York: Knopf.

Nussbaum, Martha C. 2004. *Hiding from Humanity: Disgust, Shame, and the Law*. Princeton: Princeton University Press.

Ogdon, Bethany. 2001. "Through the Image: Nicholas Nixon's 'People with AIDS.'" *Discourse* 23, no. 4: 75–105.

Oguibe, Olu. "Ashes." http://www.camwood.org/ashespress/html.

Ohi, Kevin. 2005. "'The Author of "Beltraffio"': The Exquisite Boy and Henry James's Equivocal Aestheticism." *ELH* 72, no. 3: 747–767.

Olds, Sharon. 1992. *The Father.* New York: Knopf.
Oliver, Kelly. 1993. *Reading Kristeva.* Bloomington: Indiana University Press.
Parkhurst, Carolyn. 2003. *The Dogs of Babel.* Boston: Little, Brown.
Pels, Peter. 1998. "The Spirit of Matter." In *Border Fetishisms: Material Objects in Unstable Spaces,* edited by Patricia Spyer, 91–121. New York: Routledge.
Phillips, Carl. 1998. *From the Devotions.* St. Paul: Graywolf Press.
Pile, Steve. 1996. *The Body and the City: Psychoanalysis, Space, and Subjectivity.* New York: Routledge.
Powell, Michael. 2002. "Landfill Turns into 'Humbling Holy Place'; NYPD Sorts Debris for Remains, Effects." *Washington Post,* January 12, A03.
Punday, Daniel. 2003. *Narrative Bodies: Toward a Corporeal Narratology.* New York: Palgrave Macmillan.
Rand, Nicholas. 1986. "Translator's Introduction: Toward a Cryptonymy of Literature." In *The Wolf Man's Magic Word: A Cryptonymy* by Nicolas Abraham and Maria Torok. Translated by Nicholas Rand. Minneapolis: University of Minnesota Press.
Ricciardi, Alessia. 2003. *The Ends of Mourning: Literature, Psychoanalysis, Film.* Stanford: Stanford University Press.
Richardson, Miles. 2001. "The Gift of Presence: The Act of Leaving Artifacts at Shrines, Memorials, and Other Tragedies." In *Textures of Place: Exploring Humanist Geographies,* edited by Paul C. Adams et al., 257–272. Minneapolis: University of Minnesota Press.
Riley, James Whitcomb. 1982. *The Best of James Whitcomb Riley.* Edited by Donald C. Manlove. Bloomington: Indiana University Press.
Robinson, Marilynne. 1982. *Housekeeping.* New York: Bantam.
Ruskin, Cindy. 1988. *The Quilt: Stories from the NAMES Project.* New York: Simon and Schuster.
Russo, Maria. 2001. Review of *The Body Artist. Salon.com* February 21. http://archivesalon.com/books/review/2001/02/21/delillo.
———. 2002. "Sebold's 'Lovely Bones' Still Sizzles on the Lists." *Chicago Sun-Times,* September 8, Fiction 20.
Sanders, Scott Russell. 2001. "The Inheritance of Tools." In *Sorrow's Company: Great Writers On Loss and Grief,* edited by Dewitt Henry. Boston: Beacon.
Sartre, Jean-Paul. 1948. *The Psychology of Imagination.* New York: Philosophical Library.
Scarry, Elaine. 1983. "Work and the Body in Hardy." *Representations* 3: 90–123.
———. 1985. *The Body in Pain: The Making and Unmaking of the World.* New York: Oxford University Press.
———. 1999. *Dreaming by the Book.* Princeton: Princeton University Press.
Scott, Janny. 2001. "A Nation Challenged: The Portraits; Closing a Scrapbook Full of Life and Sorrow." *New York Times,* December 31, B6.
Sebold, Alice. 2002. *The Lovely Bones.* Boston: Little, Brown.
Sengupta, Somini, with Al Baker. 2001. "A Nation Challenged: The Memorials; Rites Of Grief, without a Body to Cry Over." *New York Times,* September 27, A1.
Sennett, Richard. 1994. *Flesh and Stone: The Body and the City in Western Civilization.* New York: Norton.
Shapiro, Michael. 1988. *The Politics of Representation.* Madison: University of Wisconsin Press.

Silverman, Kaja. 1996. *The Threshold of the Visible World*. New York: Routledge.
Smith, Jennifer. 2002. "The Lost." In *At Ground Zero*, edited by Chris Bull and Sam Erman, 381–401. New York: Thunder's Mouth Press.
Snyder, Laurie Sieverts. 1998. "Some of My Mother's Things." *Diacritics* 28, no. 4: 82–98.
Sontag, Susan. 1977. *On Photography*. New York: Farrar, Straus and Giroux.
———. 1989. *Illness as Metaphor and AIDS and Its Metaphors*. New York: Doubleday.
Stallybrass, Peter. 1999. "Worn Worlds: Clothes and Mourning." In *Culture, Memory, and the Construction of Identity*, edited by Dan Ben-Amos and Liliane Weissberg, 27–44. Detroit: Wayne State University Press.
Stam, Robert. 1989. *Subversive Pleasures: Bakhtin, Cultural Criticism, and Film*. Baltimore: Johns Hopkins University Press.
Storey, Helen. 1996. *Always Remember*. Photography by Paul Margolies. New York: Simon and Schuster.
Studlar, Gaylyn. 1988. *In the Realm of Pleasure: Von Sternberg, Dietrich, and the Masochistic Aesthetic*. Urbana: University of Illinois Press.
Su, Tsu-Chung. 1995. "Violence in the Photographic Image: An Essay on the Punctum in Roland Barthes's *Camera Lucida*." *Selected Papers, 1995 Conference, Society for the Interdisciplinary Study of Social Imagery*: 35–42.
Taussig, Michael. 1993. *Mimesis and Alterity: A Partial History of the Senses*. New York: Routledge.
Thomson, Rosemarie Garland. 1997. *Extraordinary Bodies: Figuring Physical Disability in American Culture and Literature*. New York: Columbia University Press.
Thurber, Shellburne. 1999. *HOME: Photographs of Shellburne Thurber*. Boston: Institute of Contemporary Art.
Thurston, Susan. 2001. "Blood Centers Hope New Donors Return." *St. Petersburg Times*, October 20, 1B.
Toles, George. 1991. "'Sighs Too Deep for Words': Mysteries of Need in Marilynne Robinson's *Housekeeping*." *Arizona Quarterly* 47, no. 4: 137–156.
Trachtenberg, Alan. 1989. *Reading American Photographs*. New York: Hill and Wang.
Weaver, Darlene Fozard. 2004. "Sorrow Unconsoling and Inconsolable Sorrow: Grief as a Moral and Religious Practice." In *Making Sense of Dying and Death*, edited by Andrew Fagan, 31–50. Amsterdam, NY: Rodopi.
Weiss, Gail. 1998. *Body Images: Embodiment as Intercorporeality*. New York: Routledge.
———. 2000. "Ecart: The Space of Corporeal Difference." In *Chiasms: Merleau-Ponty's Notion of Flesh*, edited by Fred Evans and Leonard Lawlor, 203–218. Albany: State University of New York Press.
Welty, Eudora. 1972. *The Optimist's Daughter*. New York: Random House.
Wiseman, Mary Bittner. 1989. *The Ecstasies of Roland Barthes*. London: Routledge.
Wittgenstein, Ludwig. 1968. *Philosophical Investigations*. New York: Macmillan.
Wittmershaus, Eric. 2001. Review of *The Body Artist*. *Flakmagazine*, February 7. http://flakmag.com/books/bodyart.html.
Wolterstorff, Nicholas. 1987. *Lament for a Son*. Grand Rapids: William B. Erdmans.
Women's Army Corps. *Women's Army Corps Veterans' Association Chaplain's Handbook*. http://www.armywomen.org/pdf/ChaplainHB.pdf.

Woodward, Kathleen. 1991. *Aging and Its Discontents: Freud and Other Fictions.* Bloomington: Indiana University Press.

———. 1990–1991. "Freud and Barthes: Theorizing Mourning, Sustaining Grief." *Discourse* 13: 93–110.

———. 1992–1993. "Grief-Work in Contemporary American Cultural Criticism." *Discourse* 15, no. 2: 94–112.

———. 1999. *Figuring Age: Women, Bodies, Generations.* Bloomington: Indiana University Press.

Worth, Robert F. 2001. "A Nation Challenged: The Remains; DNA Matches Surge, Aiding in the Identification of Victims." *New York Times*, December 21, B6.

Yaeger, Patricia. 2002. "Consuming Trauma; or, The Pleasures of Merely Circulating." In *Extremities: Trauma, Testimony, and Community*, edited by Nancy K. Miller and Jason Tougaw, 25–54. Urbana: University of Illinois Press.

Yingling, Thomas E., and Robyn Wegman. 1997. *AIDS and the National Body.* Durham: Duke University Press.

Young, Katharine. 1997. *Presence in the Flesh: The Body in Medicine.* Cambridge: Harvard University Press.

Zola, Irving Kenneth. 2001. "Medicine as an Institution of Social Control." In *The American Body in Context*, edited by Jessica R. Johnston, 201–220. Wilmington: Scholarly Resources.

Zweig, Paul. 1986. *Departures.* New York: Harper & Row.

Index

abjection
  Harmon on, 23–24
  Kristeva on, 9, 24, 43, 65, 78
Abraham, Nicholas
  on incorporation, 135–37, 149, 150, 195
  on mourning, 14, 135–42, 152
  on psychoanalytic listening, 146
Adams, Tim, 155
Agee, James, 84–87, 89
AIDS
  community and, 77–78
  Doty on, 15–16, 185–201
  homosexuality and, 94, 240n2, 240n12
  R. S. Jones on, 77–78
  lesions of, 22
  photography and, 12, 40–63, 239n1
  political visibility and, 9
  visualizing of, 12
AIDS Memorial Quilt, 5, 16, 190–92, 201–9
Aldrich, Marcia, 96
angels, 103, 188–89, 196, 198–201, 221, 246n2
antiques, 183, 193, 195, 204
Arcimboldo, Giuseppe, 196, 201
Ariès, Philippe, 237n4
Auster, Paul, 228

Bahktin, Mikhail, 202
Bargreen, Melinda, 217

Barthes, Roland, 132
  Blais on, 133–34, 245n16
  Hirsch on, 230
  Kaplan on, 232
  Moriarty on, 110, 244n15
  on photography, 5, 14, 43–44, 54–56, 107–16, 127, 177
  on posing, 62
Bassin, Donna, 227, 230, 231, 233–34
Baudrillard, Jean, 15, 50
  on antiques, 183, 193, 195, 204
  Merleau-Ponty and, 183
  on resurrection, 174–75
  on semiotics, 187, 191–92
  on simulation, 134, 140, 147, 174
Baysa, Koan Jeff, 235
Bedient, Calvin, 25–26, 30, 35
Benjamin, Jessica, 25
Bennett, Jill, 233
Berger, John, 118
The Birth of the Clinic (Foucault), 20–22, 32, 76
Blais, Joann, 115, 133–34, 244nn12–16
blood donations, 230–31
Bloomer, Kent, 70, 72, 79, 122
The Body Artist (DeLillo), 15, 133–35, 153–73
body image, 7, 92
The Body in Pain (Scarry), 27, 42

259

Bond, Anthony, 185
Bordo, Susan, 3
Brandon, Joey, 56
Brewster, David, 44–46
Bronfen, Elisabeth, 24–25, 46, 50, 117–18, 222
Brooks, Peter, 29, 75, 238n4
Brophy, Sarah, 93, 94
Brown, Bill, 184, 187, 190, 191, 210
Brown, Megan Jewel Ashley, 203–4
Broyard, Anatole, 21–22, 28–30, 33, 38–39
Broyard, Sandy, 22–23

Camera Lucida (Barthes), 5, 14, 43–44, 54–56, 107–16, 127, 177
    Blais on, 133–34, 245n16
Cameron, Sharon, 101
Casey, Edward, 64, 71–75, 77, 167, 168
castration fear, 23–24
Cataldi, Suzanne, 90–92, 106
Caver, Christine, 244n8
Certeau, Michel de, 68–69
Chasin, Alex, xii
chiasm theory, 149, 181, 182, 205, 210
    of Merleau-Ponty, 87–92, 99, 135, 158, 166, 178–79, 183
cinema
    Lacanian theories of, 243n5
    masochism and, 34
    voyeurism and, 11, 19, 23
    World Trade Center attacks and, 223
Clark, Elsa Louise, 176–77
Clewell, Tammy, 244n6
Connerton, Paul, 183–84, 187–90, 192
Corrigan, Maureen, 155
Crane, Mary, xiii
Creekmur, Corey, 122
Crimp, Douglas, 239n1
cryptophore, 140, 201

Darton, Eric, 232–33
Davis, Lennard, 64, 76, 78, 80, 242n4
Dawes, James, 21, 42, 43, 55
A Death in the Family (Agee), 84–87, 89
death-watch, 11–12, 25–38, 238n3
DeLillo, Don
    The Body Artist, 15, 133–35, 153–73
    critics' reactions to, 155, 162
    on World Trade Center attacks, 234, 236
Descartes, René, 168, 191, 244n14

De Zengotita, Thomas, 174, 224, 236
Dickinson, Emily, 218, 238n3
disability theory, 6, 64, 66, 76, 80
Discipline and Punish (Foucault), 77, 78
Doane, Mary Ann, 34–36
The Dogs of Babel (Parkhurst), 14–15, 133, 134, 137–53
Doty, Mark, 60, 63, 237n1
    Heaven's Coast, 242n3
    Still Life with Oysters and Lemon, 188, 204
    "The Wings," 15–16, 185–201, 246n2
Douglas, Mary, 36

Eco, Umberto, 192, 201
Electra complex, 25
Elkins, James, 118–21, 124–25
Elsey, Judy, 201–2
embodied perception, 6–8, 13, 142
    Merleau-Ponty on, 8, 10, 87–88, 90, 124, 171
Emerson, Ralph Waldo, 111, 177, 178
"Experience," 101–2, 106, 181
Enforcing Normalcy (Davis), 64, 76
erotic gaze, 24–26, 39, 239n1

The Fate of Place (Casey), 71–72
The Father (Olds), 11–12, 20, 25–38
Featherstone, Mike, 3
fetishism
    Freud on, 46–47
    gaze and, 19–20
    photography and, 11, 46–47, 50, 53, 56
    Stallybrass on, 191
film. *See* cinema
Fleche, Anne, xiii, 247n1
Foucault, Michel, 20–22, 32, 76–78
Fowler, Paul, 55
Freud, Sigmund
    on daughter's death, 244n10
    eros and, 26
    on fetishism, 46–47
    Lacan and, 152–53
    on mourning, 13, 15, 92–95, 103–4, 107, 136, 177–78, 182

Gagnon, Monika, 240n7
Gannett, George, 61–63
gaze, 11–12, 19–20, 122
    distance of, 20, 23, 26, 35, 38, 78–79
    embodied, 127
    erotic, 24–26, 39, 239n1

gendered, 24–25, 34–35, 76, 240n12
healing, 29–30
medical, 21–22, 32–35, 68, 76
photographic, 5, 45–46, 117, 118
reciprocated, 124–25
semiotic, 191
sympathetic, 34–35, 38–39, 60–61
uncomfortable, 1, 11, 19, 51, 54, 238n1
gesture, 164, 168, 246n13
ghosts, 64, 121, 136, 155, 162, 167, 221, 226
Gilbert, Sandra M., 237n4, 244n7
Gilman, Sander, 23
globalization, 4
Gole, Nilufer, 233
Gonzalez, Jennifer, 206
Goodwin, Sarah, 50
Graver, Elizabeth, xii
Greenberg, Judith, 226, 227, 231–33
greeting cards, 16, 212–15, 218
grief
　Cataldi on, 92
　definitions of, 92, 96–97
　embodied, 92, 138, 149, 153–55, 174, 221, 222
　gender and, 244n7
　language of, 7, 15, 133–35, 138, 142, 213–15
　C. S. Lewis on, 121
　Merleau-Ponty on, 89–90
　mourning versus, 243n1
　objects of, 176–81
　phantom, 226, 227, 230, 233, 234, 236
　Marilynne Robinson on, 95–96
　See also loss
grief-work
　Barthes and, 114
　Bronfen on, 117–18
　Woodward on, 13, 93–94, 105, 107
Grosz, Elizabeth, 7, 84, 95, 124, 246n14
Grover, Jan Zita, 241n14
Grundberg, Andy, 45, 54

Hall, Donald, 118–21, 124–25
Hallam, Elizabeth, 178, 193, 194
Halli, Joseph, xii
hallucination, 46–47, 49, 78, 97, 113
Hamilton, Jane, 13, 67, 72–74
hands, 2, 83–87, 132, 166, 238n2, 246n14
Hardy, Thomas, 192

Harmon, Louise, 23–24, 238n2
Harrison, Kathryn, 209–10
Harrison, Robert Pogue, 16, 217, 225–26
Hatley, James, 88
Hawkins, Peter, 201
Hentz, Patricia, 131–32, 215
Herzlich, Claudine, 73, 75
HIV disease. *See* AIDS
Hockey, Jenny, 178, 193, 194
Holland, Sharon Patricia, 9
homosexuality, 94, 240n2, 240n12
hospices, 60, 238n3
Housekeeping (Robinson), 13–14, 87, 95–107, 114, 116, 132
Howard, Billy, xi, 12, 41–42, 44–54
How Societies Remember (Connerton), 183–84
Husserl, Edmund, 71
hysteria, 35

identity
　female, 95–96
　language and, 163–64
　loss of, 23
　mourner's, 90
　patient, 21–22, 66–68, 79–80
incorporation, psychoanalytic, 135–37, 149, 150, 184, 195
intercorporeality, 13, 88, 102, 124, 141, 151, 162, 164, 173
In the Unlikely Event of a Water Landing (Noel), 181–82
Irigaray, Luce, 38

Jones, R. S., 77–78

Kahane, Claire, 223
Kaplan, E. Ann, 223–24, 232, 236
Kaposi's sarcoma, 44, 46, 55
Kaviola, Karen, 244n9
Kenney, Susan, 13, 67, 71
King, Kristin, 95–96
Kirby, Kathleen, 92
Krasner, James, xiii, 226, 237n1, 243n2, 245n7
Kristeva, Julia, 23
　on abjection, 9, 24, 43, 65, 78
　on the corpse, 23
　on "extrication," 36–37
　on life-death boundary, 30, 65
　on visual apprehension, 20
Kybartas, Stashu, 239n1

Lacan, Jacques, 152–53, 223, 243n5
LaCapra, Dominick, 7
  on empathy, 239n7
  Ricciardi and, 237n7
  on trauma, 226–27, 232
Laderman, Gary, 211, 219, 221
language
  Connerton on, 183–84, 188–89
  cryptophore and, 140, 201
  de Certeau on, 69
  games, 144–45
  of grief, 7, 15, 133–35, 138, 142, 213–15
  identity and, 163–64
  psychoanalytic, 146
  See also semiotics
langue, 142
Lefebvre, Henri, 242n1
Lennon, John, 209
Levine, Claire, 22–23
Lewis, C. S., 121
Lingis, Alphonso, 127
loss, 11, 51, 209–10, 234
  castration fears and, 23–24
  Freud on, 178
  hermeneutics of, 152
  of identity, 23
  imagined, 83–84, 89, 236
  incorporation of, 135–36
  Lacan on, 223
  map of, 229
  Metz on, 46–47
  Sebold on, 216
  Toles on, 244n9
  Woodward on, 13
  See also mourning
The Lovely Bones (Sebold), 215–19, 223
Lubin, Orly, 228
Lupton, Deborah, 178, 205
Lyndenberg, Robin, xii

Maldiney, Henri, 182
A Map of the World (Hamilton), 72–74
masochism, 34
Mazis, Glen, 179
McElreavy, Timothy, 115
McFarland, Dennis, 180–82
memory
  consolation of, 212
  false, 236
  incorporation and, 136, 184, 192
  mourning and, 84, 89, 95–100, 103–5, 182
  of objects, 194–95
  sensory, 178
  tattoos and, 230
Merleau-Ponty, Maurice, 188, 202, 204–5, 241n1
  Baudrillard and, 183
  chiasm theory of, 87–92, 99, 135, 158, 166, 178–79, 183
  on consciousness, 157–59, 165, 246n13
  on embodied perception, 8, 10, 87–88, 90, 124, 171
  on gesture, 164, 168, 246n13
  on intercorporeality, 13, 88, 102, 124, 151, 162, 164, 173
  on mind/body problem, 2–3, 149, 170
  on negotiation of space, 73, 88
  on "thickness of the body," 1, 87, 113, 116, 130, 150, 183
Metz, Christian, 46–48, 50, 53
Mile, Sian, 96
Miller, Nancy K., 228–30
Mills, Randy Jon, 207
mimesis, 114
mind/body problem
  Merleau-Ponty on, 2–3, 149, 170
  Katharine Young on, 67–68
Mitchell, Erin C., 108, 117, 244n12
Moon, Michael, 93, 94
Moore, Charles, 70, 72, 79, 122
Moore, Lorrie, 13, 67, 74
Moran, Tom, 55–58
Moriarty, Michael, 110, 244n15
Morris, Mary, 67, 74–76
Mother, pre-Oedipal, 95–97
mourning
  Abraham and Torok on, 135–42, 152
  Bassin on, 230
  Freud on, 13, 15, 92–95, 103–4, 107, 136, 177
  grief versus, 243n1
  Hentz on, 131–32, 215
  memory and, 84, 89, 95–100, 103–5, 178, 182
  "normal," 92–93
  postmodern, 152–53, 223
  unsuccessful, 87, 104, 107, 135–37
  Woodward on, 92–97, 107
  See also grief
Mulvey, Laura, 19, 20, 23, 24

NAMES Project. *See* AIDS Quilt
navel scar, 24, 222
9/11. *See* World Trade Center attacks
Nixon, Bebe, 54
Nixon, Nicholas, xi, 12, 41–42, 53–63
Noel, Christopher, 181–82
Nussbaum, Martha, 4

Oedipus complex, 25, 95–97
Ogdon, Bethany, 241n16, 241n18
Oguibe, Olu, xii, 5, 16, 234–36
Ohi, Kevin, xii, 237n3
Olds, Sharon, 221
  critical reactions to, 25–26
  The Father, 11–12, 20, 25–38
  "The Glass," 26
  "Last Acts," 37–38
  "The Last Day," 35–38
  "The Lifting," 30–35
  "My Father's Eyes," 26, 28
  "The Waiting," 26–28, 30, 37, 38
The Optimist's Daughter (Welty), 70
organ transplants, 149–50
Ortiz, Brian, 207
Over Her Dead Body (Bronfen), 24–25, 117–18

The Painted Bed (Hall), 118–21, 124–25
Panopticon, 77, 78
Parkhurst, Carolyn, 14–15, 133, 134, 137–53
Parkinson's disease, 22
patient roles
  Foucault on, 21–22
  in waiting room, 66–68, 79–80
Pels, Peter, 188–89
Perham, Donald, 57–59
phantom grief, 226, 227, 230, 233, 234, 236
phantom limb, 158, 226, 233, 243n2
Phillips, Carl, 132
photography
  AIDS and, 12, 40–63, 239n1
  Barthes on, 5, 14, 43–44, 54–56, 107–16, 127, 177
  fetishism and, 11, 46–47, 50, 53, 56
  Hirsch on, 230
  Howard's, 12, 41–42, 44–54
  immobility of, 55–56, 117
  Metz on, 46–48
  Nixon's, 12, 41–42, 53–63

Sontag on, 111–12, 117
  Thurber on, 115–31
  Thurber's, 14, 115–31
  World Trade Center attacks and, 225, 228–30
Pierret, Janine, 73, 75
The Practice of Everyday Life (de Certeau), 68–69
pre-Oedipal Mother, 95–97
Presence in the Flesh (Young), 65
Presley, Elvis, 209

Quilt. *See* AIDS Memorial Quilt

Rand, Nicholas, 201
Red Cross, 230–31, 247n5
resurrection, 105–6, 174–75
Ricciardi, Alessia, 152–53, 223, 236, 237n7, 243n5
Richardson, Miles, 114
Riley, James Whitcomb, 212–14, 218
Robinson, Marilynne, 13–14, 87, 95–107, 114, 116, 132
Ruskin, Cindy, 202
Russo, Maria, 155, 217–18

Sacks, Oliver, 28–30
Sailing (Kenney), 70–71
Sanders, Scott Russell, 179–80
Sappenfield, Bob, 55
Sartre, Jean-Paul, 89–90, 99–102, 116, 117, 122, 129
Scarry, Elaine, 8, 27, 42–43, 45, 114, 192, 194
scopophilia. *See* voyeurism
Sebold, Alice, 215–19, 223
semiotics
  Baudrillard on, 187, 191–92
  Eco on, 192, 201
  sensory, 182–85
  Stallybrass on, 191
  See also language
Sennett, Richard, 242n1
September 11, 2001. *See* World Trade Center attacks
Shapiro, Michael J., 58–59, 240n4, 241n15
Silverman, Kaja, 5, 44, 238n1
  on "discursively implanted memories," 62
  on "productive" look, 239n6

Singing Boy (McFarland), 180–82
Six Feet Under (TV series), 219–23
Smith, Jennifer, 226, 228
Snyder, Laurie Sieverts, 184–85
Sontag, Susan, 111–12, 117, 240n5
space
   disembodied, 115–31
   negotiation of, 73, 88
   place and, 68–73
Stallybrass, Peter, 191, 246n1
Still Life with Oysters and Lemon (Doty), 188, 204
Storey, Helen, 203
Studlar, Gaylyn, 34
Su, Tsu-Chung, 244n11
sympathy
   defined, 34–35
   greeting cards and, 16, 212–15, 218
   LaCapra on, 239n7
   seeing and, 38–39, 60–61

Tanner, Donald, 1–2, 83, 212–13, 238n2
tattoos, 230
television, 16, 211, 219–23
Thomson, Rosemarie, 66, 76, 242n2
The Threshold of the Visible World (Silverman), 5, 44, 60–61
Thurber, Shellburne, xi, 14, 87, 115–31
Toles, George, 244n9
Torok, Maria
   on incorporation, 135–37, 149, 150, 195
   on mourning, 14, 135–42, 152
   on psychoanalytic listening, 146
Trachtenberg, Alan, 53
transplants, organ, 149–50
trauma, 222–23
   Bassin on, 233–34
   LaCapra on, 226–27, 232
   secondary, 226–27, 234, 236
   Yaeger on, 10, 226–227

virtuality
   in *The Body Artist*, 162
   of World Trade Center attacks, 223–24
voyeurism
   cinema and, 11, 19, 23
   waiting rooms and, 78–79
   World Trade Center attacks and, 225

The Waiting Room (Morris), 74–75
waiting rooms, 12–13, 64–80
Walking on Air (Jones), 77–78
Weaver, Darlene Fozard, 93–94
Weiss, Gail, 7, 88
Welty, Eudora, 13, 67, 70
Wenders, Wim, 246n2
White, Allon, 191
Williams, William Carlos, 184
Wilson, Chris, xii
"The Wings" (Doty), 15–16, 185–201, 246n2
Wiseman, Mary Bittner, 244n13
Wittgenstein, Ludwig, 145, 183
Wittmershaus, Eric, 155, 162
Wolterstorff, Nicholas, 215
Women's Army Corp Chaplain's Handbook, 214
Woodward, Kathleen, 13, 92–97, 105, 107, 244n6
World Trade Center attacks, 16, 222–36

Yaeger, Patricia, 10
Yingling, Thomas, 41
Young, Katharine, 65, 67–68

Žižek, Slavoj, 232
Zola, Irving Kenneth, 3–4, 241n19
Zweig, Paul, 242n5